A WOMAN'S WAR, TOO

A **WOMAN'S** *War, Too*

Women at Work During World War II

VIRGINIA M. WRIGHT-PETERSON

MINNESOTA
HISTORICAL
SOCIETY PRESS

CLEAN
WATER
LAND &
LEGACY
AMENDMENT

This activity is made possible by the voters of Minnesota through a grant from the Southeastern Minnesota Arts Council thanks to a legislative appropriation from the Arts & Cultural Heritage Fund.

mnhspress.org

The Minnesota Historical Society Press is a member of the Association of University Presses.

Manufactured in the United States of America

10 9 8 7 6 5 4 3 2 1

∞ The paper used in this publication meets the minimum requirements of the American National Standard for Information Sciences—Permanence for Printed Library Materials, ANSI Z39.48-1984.

International Standard Book Number
ISBN: 978-1-68134-151-4 (paper)
ISBN: 978-1-68134-152-1 (e-book)

Library of Congress Cataloging-in-Publication Data

Names: Wright-Peterson, Virginia M., author.
Title: A woman's war, too : women at work during World War II / Virginia M. Wright-Peterson.
Other titles: Women at work during World War II
Description: Saint Paul, MN : Minnesota Historical Society Press, [2020] | Includes bibliographical references and index. | Summary: "During World War II, women in Minnesota—like women across the country—made bold, unconventional, and important contributions to the war effort. They enlisted in all branches of the military and worked for the military as civilians. They labored in factories, mines, and shipyards. They were also tireless peace activists, and they worked to relocate interned Japanese American citizens and European refugees. They served as cryptologists, journalists, pilots, riveters, factory workers, nurses, entertainers, and spies. This rich chronological account relates dramatic stories of women discovering their own potential in a time of national need, surprising themselves and others—and setting the roots of second-wave feminism."— Provided by publisher.
Identifiers: LCCN 2019055252 | ISBN 9781681341514 (paperback) | ISBN 9781681341521 (ebook)
Subjects: LCSH: World War, 1939–1945—Women—Minnesota. | World War, 1939–1945—War work—Minnesota. | Women—Employment—Minnesota—History—20th century. | World War, 1939–1945—Minnesota. | United States—Armed Forces—Biography. | Women—Minnesota—Biography.
Classification: LCC D810.W7 W75 2020 | DDC 940.3/77609252—dc23
LC record available at https://lccn.loc.gov/2019055252

. . . . .

Dedicated to my husband, Ralph (1922–1995),
who served with the US Army Twenty-Seventh Infantry Division (1943–1946),
including in Okinawa, Japan,
and as a
civil education officer in Niigata, Japan (1946–1949)

and to

all of the women, men, and children worldwide
who made contributions and sacrifices during World War II

. . . . .

CONTENTS

THE PACIFIC THEATER AND END OF THE WAR

A WOMAN'S WAR, TOO

PREFACE

This book could have been thousands of pages long, filled with the stories of contributions and sacrifices made by women from every walk of life in every city, town, farm, and forest of Minnesota during World War II. I first became aware of the stories of a few women when I was writing *Women of Mayo Clinic: The Founding Generation*. As that book came to a close with the events of 1943, I learned about Julia F. Herrick, a biophysicist at Mayo Clinic in Rochester, Minnesota, who was recruited by the US Army Signal Corps during the war to conduct radar research at Fort Monmouth in New Jersey. Next, I found the harrowing and brave narrative of Ruth Erickson, a navy corps nurse from Virginia, Minnesota, who valiantly saved lives during the attack on Pearl Harbor.

Once I started collecting stories, there seemed to be no end. One story led to a dozen more, much beyond Rosie the Riveter or the dates, descriptions of battles, and stories of generals I learned about in school, a history almost entirely devoid of women. How could half of the population be left out of the history of such a critical period?

The women of Minnesota, like women throughout the United States, strove for peace and freedom during the World War II years in vital and varied ways. They built ships in the Duluth-Superior Harbor, replaced men in the mines of the Iron Range, and worked in factories throughout the state. Minnesota women were present in every branch of the military. At home and abroad, women served as cryptologists, journalists, pilots, riveters, mechanics, nurses, entertainers, and spies.

Nearly all of the women included in this book were born in Minnesota or were living in the state during the war. I also included a French woman who worked for the US Army before becoming a "war bride" and moving to Minnesota and a German Jewish woman whose involvement in the resistance movement resulted in her incarceration in concentration camps; her connection to Minnesota came after the war when she became an internationally respected faculty member at the University of Minnesota. These women, as immigrants, brought with them important stories of courage, resilience, and dedication that should be recognized as an important part of Minnesota's heritage.

Perhaps most surprising is that in addition to important contributions at home, women from Minnesota directly witnessed and participated in many important milestones of the war overseas: the Battle of Britain, the fall and liberation of France, Operation Torch in North Africa, the reoccupation of the Aleutian Islands, D-Day, the Battle of the Bulge, the liberation of Dachau concentration camp, the reclamation of the Philippines and New Guinea, the Manhattan Project, and the dropping of the atomic bombs in Japan.

I found many more stories than I could include in this book. And yet, I am certain there are many stories of bravery and sacrifice that I did not find. Please consider these narratives to be a sample of what actually occurred. I was committed to including stories from women of all races, classes, and areas of the state, which was challenging. According to the US Census, Minnesota was 99.2 percent white in 1940. My research is also somewhat biased because white, educated, and economically privileged people are more likely to leave behind written records of their lives, and those records are more likely to be preserved in historical societies and libraries than those of women of color, women with less formal schooling, and women of less economic means. In addition, white, formally educated, middle-class women were more likely to be accepted into the military and employed by businesses during the war. Native American women are also an important part of the World War II story. I included one powerful story of an Ojibwe woman from White Earth and her community in Minneapolis; I suspect there are many more stories that could accompany hers.

Incidents and attitudes of racism, sexism, anti-Semitism, and homophobia that these women experienced or witnessed are included. I did not try to hide or erase these injustices. Please do not think that I am endorsing such acts or beliefs in any way; we should own and learn from these parts of our complex history.

This narrative of World War II is told primarily in chronological order to provide a retelling of the war as it transpired from the attack on Pearl Harbor to dropping the atomic bomb on Japan. Some of the prewar period is also included because women were a part of the story from its earliest developments. Some of the narratives are organized by topics rather than chronology when it seemed more readable to do so. For example, many of the women's stories on the home front, including in mines, shipyards, and factories, are told together, rather than interspersing them throughout to avoid jumping back and forth between locations and industries. A chronology of the war is included at the end of the book for reference.

Occasionally, I deviated to include stories of injustices and costs of the war that have not been well known when these details intersected with the women's experiences. The unjust internment of Japanese people on the West Coast and the involuntary and devastating relocation of the Aleut people in Alaska by the US government, as well as the detrimental impact of munition plants on the environment in Minnesota are examples of issues I felt compelled to include because they are also often omitted from published and taught histories of World War II.

The stories of women from Minnesota illuminate a perspective of World War II that has been missing. I hope that this volume, alongside the plethora of male-dominated books, will provide a more comprehensive perspective of the war and the acknowledgment that the Axis forces would not have been deterred without millions of women who assured that vital supplies of food, ammunition, ships, and planes were produced and that military and service organizations were sufficiently staffed.

In so many ways, women successfully stepped up to the challenge and replaced men in new and demanding vocations. They excelled at what they did. After the war, many women chose to return to their homes, but many also wanted to stay in the workforce as pilots, journalists, and shipbuilders. Practically, there were not enough jobs for everyone once the servicemen returned, but there was also a vein of sexism that was not expelled by the women's proven competence. Indeed, sexism might have been exacerbated by the women's success. Many employers, like the airlines, would not offer jobs to women. Seasoned flyers, for example, were offered jobs as airline stewardesses, but they could not be pilots despite their stellar records during their war service. Even today few women pilot commercial aircraft even though women more than proved their competence seventy-five years ago.

Whenever possible I included the women's motivations for their decisions and their reactions to their experiences. Some women explained why they joined the military and were explicit about the impact their experiences had on them; others were not. If they only reported what happened, that is all I included. I did not speculate or editorialize about their motivations or how they felt about their experiences. I did include relevant historical context while trying to remain as true as possible to the women's words.

In addition to providing a more inclusive view of World War II, I hope these stories inspire readers with ancestors in Minnesota at the time of the war to wonder, "What did my grandmother, great-grandmother, or great-aunt do during World War II?" igniting a resurgence of discovery, preservation, and sharing of women's stories locally, statewide, and nationally. I hope more oral tales can be preserved and teachers will expand courses to include the stories of women for students starting in kindergarten. All children regardless of their gender identity deserve to know about challenges overcome and barriers shattered by women who went before them. Sharing powerful stories helps us reflect on the spirit of innovation, strength, and courage of a past time that is relevant and important for addressing the challenges we face today.

The Beginning

1

A LONG WAY FROM HOME

Ruth Erickson was four thousand miles from her hometown of Virginia, Minnesota, when fighter planes began bombing the naval base where she was stationed. That Sunday morning, still in her housecoat and curlers, she was having a quiet breakfast in the dining room with three other nurses. Ruth had plans to picnic with friends later in the day on the other side of the island. While she and the nurses were talking, they heard the deep hum of planes coming in close and assumed pilots were doing extra reserve flying. When they started to hear noise that sounded like shooting, Ruth went into the corridor to look out a window. She saw a plane with a large rising sun insignia fly by low, so low that if Ruth had known the pilot, she could have recognized him through his goggles and called him by name. Fortunately, he passed by, presumably looking for a more significant target. A few moments later, shortly before 8:00 AM on December 7, 1941, the attack on Pearl Harbor began.

View of Pearl Harbor taken by an Imperial Japanese pilot in the first minutes of the attack on December 7, 1941. *US Navy NH 50930, courtesy of the Naval History and Heritage Command*

Ruth ran to her room, pulling out her pin curls along the way. Phones began ringing, and the chief nurse yelled, "Girls, get in your uniforms at once! This is the real thing!" After quickly dressing, Ruth dashed across the street through a shower of shrapnel. Her sense of purpose carried her as far as the lanai, a screened porch outside the administrative section of the navy hospital. Once she stopped, she froze, unable to move until an inner voice told her to *get going!* She ran to the orthopedic dressing room but found it locked. She shouted to a corpsman to get the keys. It seemed to take him forever to return and open the door. By then, several nurses had arrived, and they began to prepare for possible casualties. Little did they know 2,403 servicemen would die and 1,143 would be injured that day. The first casualty arrived at 8:25 AM.

· · · · ·

Ruth Erickson, the oldest of five children, was born in 1913 in the town of Virginia in northern Minnesota to Swedish and Norwegian American parents. Her hometown, in a region once inhabited by the Ojibwe, rests on an ancient mountain range, the Mesabi, which was leveled by two massive glaciers in prehistoric times, exposing mineral ore and paving a path for vast, fertile pine forests. Mining and lumbering industries boomed during Ruth's childhood. Iron ore and timber were transported by train to Lake Superior, only sixty miles away, for export around the world. Ruth's father was a deputy sheriff and her mother was a homemaker.

At Roosevelt High School, Ruth played flute in orchestra and band, and she was chair of the senior sewing club. In her high school yearbook, she was described as "a blue-eyed optimist viewing life through rose-colored glasses—Pipes of Pan smiling through good fortune or bad." By the time of Ruth's graduation in 1931, the lumber industry had started moving west, where the trees were larger and closer together, and many of the mines had been exhausted. The impact of the Great Depression further squelched opportunity in Virginia. Economic growth stopped, and the population of the once-booming town dropped 15 percent between 1920 and 1930. Jobs were scarce. Ruth decided it was a good time to see more of the world, so she entered the Kahler School of Nursing in Rochester, Minnesota, affiliated with the renowned Mayo Clinic medical practice. After three years of nursing school, she worked in hospitals, caring for Mayo Clinic patients with a wide range of conditions: goiters, hernias, diabetes, and epilepsy.

As the world came to Ruth through the international clientele of the Mayo practice, she realized she "had adventure in her soul" and wanted to see more. Ruth decided to follow friends of hers who had joined the Veterans Administration. During the physical examination that was part of the application process, a Mayo Clinic physician asked her, "What do you want to be interested in the Veterans Administration for? That's a political setup." He encouraged her to consider nursing in the military instead, and put her in touch with a navy physician who happened to be

Ruth Erickson, Kahler School of Nursing, 1934. *Used with permission of Mayo Foundation for Medical Education and Research. All rights reserved.*

at Mayo Clinic working in aviation medicine. Dr. Joe White told Ruth she could see the Philippines, Hawaii, and the Caribbean with the navy, which sounded pretty good to a restless twenty-three-year-old woman in Minnesota.

Ruth applied to the Navy Nurse Corps, and after being accepted and going home to visit her parents and siblings, on July 27, 1936, she found herself on her way to US Naval Base San Diego, watching through the train window as palm trees and a desert landscape passed by. Her first assignment was on the USS *Relief*, a 550-bed hospital vessel. Aboard this ship for the next three years, Ruth traveled to the Mediterranean, Jamaica, and Haiti.

In 1939, after finishing five days of R & R on the beaches of Charlotte Amalie in the Virgin Islands, the crew of the USS *Relief* headed for their next assignment, helping set up for the World's Fair in New York City, slated to open in April. But threats from Japan were mounting, and all navy ships were ordered back to the West Coast. The USS *Relief* conducted routine maneuvers along the coast and into the Pacific Ocean along the Honolulu chain of islands.

In May 1940, Ruth was sent to US Naval Hospital Pearl Harbor. She and seven other nurses assigned there enjoyed a posh, tropical lifestyle. The nursing quarters were comfortable, and they felt almost spoiled by the regular supply of iced tea and fresh pineapple. Most of the servicemen on the base were young and healthy and avoided the hospital, so the workload was light. The sailors occasionally came down with "cat fever," or catarrhal fever, a viral respiratory infection. Some servicemen required minor surgeries—appendectomies, hernia repairs, and tonsillectomies. In their off-hours, the nurses enjoyed playing tennis, swimming at the beach, and picnicking throughout the island. They dated aviators attached to the base and found themselves dancing under starlit skies at the Royal Hawaiian Hotel in Waikiki. It was a pretty good assignment until December 7, 1941.

• • • • •

The first serviceman brought into the unit was bleeding profusely from an abdominal gunshot wound. The medical team, shaking in fear, managed to start an IV on him. By 8:10, the USS *Arizona* was hit by an armor-piercing shell and began sinking, taking with it eleven hundred lives. As the USS *Arizona* was sinking, the USS *Nevada* attempted to pull out of the channel when it was hit and went aground near the hospital. The men were ordered to dive off and swim to shore, but the thick oil on the water ignited, and they found themselves swimming through fire. Their tropical uniforms, t-shirts and shorts, provided little protection, and their exposed skin burned as they swam through the flames; they arrived on the shores badly injured.

Just as the first patient, who had been bleeding badly, died, burn victims began streaming in. The hospital staff had to be innovative. In a storage unit, they found small hand pumps intended for spraying insecticide. They filled the pumps with tannic acid and sprayed the burned sailors. They hoped the tannic acid, with its strong antimicrobial impact, would reduce mortality rates.

The air was thick with smoke, and the medical team worked with flashlights as evening came. Anyone who could manage a hammer was helping to cover windows with black drapes or paper to prevent light from seeping out. Around 10 or 11 o'clock that evening, they heard planes heading toward them again. Ruth's knees were knocking and patients were calling out in fear. The priest went from bed to bed trying to comfort the injured and frightened sailors. When the noise ended, they realized the sounds had come from US, not enemy, planes.

When it was her turn to take a break, Ruth went to the basement of the hospital, where the staff and some of their families were brought that night. No one got much sleep.

For a week and a half, Ruth and the medical team took care of patients as best they could. On the evening of December 17, the chief nurse told Ruth to pack a bag and be ready to leave at noon the next day. When Ruth asked where she was being sent, the chief nurse said she had no idea. The commanding officer asked for three nurses to be ready to leave in uniform. So Ruth and two others, dressed in their white uniforms, blue capes, and felt hats, were picked up by a car and taken to get their orders. They learned they were going aboard the SS *President Coolidge*, a steamship, to escort 125 wounded sailors back to a base on the mainland. Patients needing more than three months to recover were being relocated.

The journey was trying. The waters were rough and tensions were high. The steamship was part of a caravan carrying navy patients, missionaries, and countless others who were evacuating the area now considered a war zone. The vessels traveled without exterior lights. At one point, a rumor circulated that they were being followed by an enemy submarine. They arrived in San Francisco Christmas morning. Ruth and her colleagues were cheered to see the Red Cross serving donuts and coffee. They transferred their patients to ambulances that took them to the naval hospital at Mare Island and several nearby civilian hospitals.

By December 27, Ruth and the other nurses had settled all of the patients in their new hospitals, and they were ordered to return to Pearl Harbor on the USS

Henderson, part of a huge influx of ten thousand troops into the Pacific theater. Ruth remained at Pearl Harbor working in the naval hospital until July 1942, when she was transferred to the base at Corona, California. By then she was six years into what would become a twenty-six-year career in the navy, which would take her around the world. Eventually she would be known as Captain Ruth Erickson, director of the US Naval Nurse Corps, a position that was later given admiral rank.

· · · · ·

Ruth was not the only woman from the Virginia, Minnesota, area, often called the Iron Range, to serve in the military during World War II. More than three hundred women from this region alone and many more from throughout Minnesota left their hometowns to join the Navy and Army Nurse Corps, Marine Reserves, Women's Army Auxiliary Corps (WAAC), Women's Army Corps (WAC), Women Accepted for Volunteer Emergency Service in the Navy (WAVES), women's Coast Guard reserve *Semper Paratus*, Always Ready (SPAR), Women Airforce Service Pilots (WASP), and various state and local reserve units. They also entered the workforce in a wide range of industries in addition to making significant contributions in communities and at home during the ominous and crucial years of World War II. They demonstrated abilities to work as well as, if not better than, men in some fields, a realization that would have long-reaching implications for how women were viewed in the decades following the war.

2

INTERNMENT, RESETTLEMENT, AND ADVOCATING FOR PEACE

On February 19, 1942, ten weeks after the bombing of Pearl Harbor, President Franklin D. Roosevelt signed Executive Order 9066, authorizing the removal of people from military areas "as deemed necessary or desirable." The entire West Coast, home to almost all people of Japanese ancestry in the United States, was deemed to be a military area, and all Japanese people, including American-born citizens of one-eighth or more Japanese descent, were ordered to leave. With short notice, they had to abandon, sell, or find caretakers for their homes, belongings, and businesses.

Within four months, more than one hundred ten thousand Japanese people, including eighty thousand who were US born, were involuntarily relocated from the West Coast to fourteen internment camps quickly built by the US military in remote locations around the country. Several governors fought to avoid having camps in their states because of the widespread fear of Japanese people after the Pearl Harbor attack. Centers for individuals and families who were not considered imminently dangerous were built in arid, intensely hot or cold, and swampy areas of California, Arizona, Wyoming, Utah, Colorado, Idaho, and Arkansas.

Before placement in the relocation camps, these residents, now considered prisoners, were processed through regional assembly centers, often on county fairgrounds. A hundred Japanese orphans were included in the relocation. For the next two and a half years, the Japanese American occupants of these camps endured extremely difficult living conditions and humiliating treatment by their military guards. Even President Roosevelt referred to the camps as concentration camps.

When Eleanor Roosevelt heard the news of her husband's proclamation, she was shaken and ardently lobbied him not to intern Japanese people living in the United States, but he refused to discuss the matter with her. On April 23, 1943, the first lady visited the Gila River Camp, which held fourteen thousand people. In a newspaper column a few days later, Mrs. Roosevelt described what she saw: "barracks had been set down in a field of sand and hard baked ground. When the wind blows everything is covered in sand." Despite the sparse facilities and minimal resources, she found that "Everything is spotlessly clean. . . . The community mess halls have nearly all been decorated with paper streamers, paper flowers and paintings." Mrs. Roosevelt passionately addressed the nation after her tour:

I can well understand the bitterness of people who have lost loved ones at the hands of the Japanese military authorities, and we know that the totalitarian philosophy, whether it is in Nazi Germany or Fascist Italy or in Japan, is one of cruelty and brutality. It is not hard to understand why people living here in hourly anxiety for those they love have difficulty in viewing this problem objectively, but for the honor of our country the rest of us must do so. These understandable feelings are aggravated by the old time economic fear on the West Coast and the unreasoning racial feeling which certain people, through ignorance, have always had wherever they came in contact with people who are different from themselves.

She encouraged the War Relocation Authority to allow the camp prisoners to leave as soon as possible so they could begin "independent and productive lives again." She implored communities throughout the country to welcome Japanese people and give them a fair chance to prove themselves. She argued that "Every citizen in this country has a right to our basic freedoms, to justice and to equality of opportunity. We retain the right to lead our individual lives as we please, but we can only do so if we grant to others the freedoms that we wish for ourselves."

· · · · ·

Resettlement began shortly after the first lady's address. Those wishing to leave the camps were screened. Those not deemed a security risk were permitted to leave the camps if they could prove they had a job and housing away from the West Coast. Communities, especially in the Midwest, welcomed Japanese people. Resettlement opportunities arose across the nation, including in Minnesota. Two hospital-based nursing programs affiliated with Mayo Clinic in Rochester invited fifty-three Japanese women to enroll in their nursing schools, providing them with an opportunity to leave internment camps. Sister Antonia Rostomily, originally from the small town of Fulda in southwestern Minnesota, was the director of the Saint Marys Nursing School during the war years. Her leadership and the support of the hospital administrator, Sister Domitilla DuRocher, elevated the proposal to accept Japanese women into their school.

After receiving approval from the War Relocation Authority, the army, the navy, the Federal Bureau of Investigation (FBI), and the National Student Relocation Council, on October 5, 1942, Saint Marys School of Nursing admitted its first Japanese transfer student. Earlier in the year, they had hired five Japanese women from Seattle, Washington, who were already nurses, helping them avoid internment. A Mayo-trained physician on the West Coast in 1941 had encouraged several Japanese women, including five nurses, one dietitian, and one secretary, to contact Sister Domitilla because she was willing to hire them.

The efforts of Sister Domitilla and Sister Antonia to reach out to these Japanese women was an expression of their values. The Franciscan congregation in Rochester was founded in 1871 by Mother Alfred Moes, who later convinced Dr. William Worrall Mayo that he and his sons needed a hospital for their medical practice. Dr. Mayo was hesitant, but Mother Alfred persevered and raised the money to open Saint Marys Hospital in 1889 with twenty-seven beds. Her successor, Sister Joseph Dempsey, an organizational and management genius as well as a compassionate woman, expanded the hospital to six hundred beds during her forty-seven-year tenure, making it the largest and finest privately owned hospital in the country, welcoming patients from throughout the world. Saint Marys Hospital was a cornerstone of the Mayo Clinic practice. By integrating Japanese students into their school, Sister Domitilla and Sister Antonia were continuing the legacy established by their predecessors: "All are welcome regardless of race, religion, ethnicity, or socioeconomic status."

· · · · ·

Bringing Japanese women to Rochester was a bold move. According to the 1940 census, there were no people of Japanese descent living in Rochester and only fifty-one in the entire state of Minnesota. Immigrants of Asian descent were viewed with elevated suspicion nationally because of the Pearl Harbor attack, but Asian immigrants had never been welcomed into the United States and were not eligible for naturalized citizenship until Congress passed the Immigration and Nationality Act in 1952. Until then only American-born Asians were granted citizenship. Although schools throughout the United States admitted Japanese students, the nursing programs at Saint Marys Hospital School of Nursing admitted more Japanese students than any other educational facility in the nation. Kahler Hospital, also affiliated with Mayo Clinic, also admitted Japanese students. Between the two schools, more than fifty women were accepted from internment camps. Nursing programs throughout the nation may have been apprehensive, fearing patients would resist treatment from Japanese women.

· · · · ·

The war precipitated a nationwide shortage of nurses. The nursing schools in Rochester were able to expand their programs when the cadet nursing corps was implemented. In early 1943, Frances Bolton, congresswoman from Ohio, introduced a bill in Congress intended to increase the number of nursing students quickly. The proposed legislation would provide funding for tuition, books, and a stipend for students. A companion bill introduced in the Senate prohibited discrimination based on race, creed, or color. In exchange, graduates were required to provide service in a military hospital, public health agency, or anywhere else a nurse shortage existed for the duration of the war. The Nurse Training Act passed unanimously and was signed by President Roosevelt in June. With this funding,

Japanese cadet nurses Grace Obata and Fumiye Yoshida, Saint Marys Hospital School of Nursing. *W. Bruce Fye Center for the History of Medicine at Mayo Clinic*

the US Cadet Nursing Corps program was established, and between 1943 and 1948, one hundred twenty-four thousand nurses graduated from nursing schools across the country.

Sister Antonia brought the proposal to admit more Japanese women into the St. Marys program to an all-school meeting. Students were in favor of the proposal, seeing no reason that Japanese American students should not be admitted. Saint Marys Hospital School of Nursing quickly became an approved school under this new program, and three hundred women enrolled as cadet nurses from 1943 to 1945, including Japanese women from internment camps.

In addition to the welcoming attitude at Saint Marys and Kahler Hospitals, a community group organized to assist Japanese people desiring to move to town despite its small population of 28,312. The Rochester Japanese-American Resettlement Committee was established with membership made up of representatives from Olmsted County Welfare, the Methodist church, the Rotary Club, the Mayo Clinic, the YWCA, the Unitarian church, the chamber of commerce, the US Employment Service, the Jewish synagogue, and Saint Marys Hospital.

· · · · ·

In August 1942, Aiko "Grace" Obata and her family were interned at the Gila River War Relocation Camp from their home in the San Francisco Bay area of California. Grace knew from the time she was eight years old that she wanted to be a nurse, a desire that was strengthened after her father died of a heart attack when she was ten. Her mother, who had been a home economics teacher in Japan, began teaching Japanese language classes after her husband died. Grace focused on her studies and became the valedictorian of her San Francisco high school. She enrolled in the University of Berkeley's pre-nursing program in 1938 and transferred to the University of California School of Nursing in 1941 to fulfill her dream. But her education was interrupted within a year when she and her family were sent to the assembly center in Turlock, California, and then to the Gila River installation in Arizona, located on a corner of the Gila River Indian reservation, fifty miles south of Phoenix. This location was considered one of the hottest places in the United States. One of Grace's brothers, who was already in the US military, had relocated to Michigan. Eventually he was assigned to Unit 442, entirely comprised of Japanese men. The four thousand soldiers in Unit 442 had to be replaced almost twice during the war due to heavy casualties, and it became the most decorated unit in the war. Another brother joined the military while Grace and her family were in the camp.

Grace became a nurse aid at the camp hospital, where she saw so many of the patients, especially the older Issei, suffer. These Japanese-born immigrants became especially distressed, and some threatened suicide. Grace and another student from nursing school were determined to continue their studies. Although they were assigned to different camps, they both obtained permission to work as a cook and housekeeper in Illinois until they could be accepted in a nursing program. They applied to many schools but received letters back saying that the quota of "your kind is full," until they were accepted by Saint Marys in 1943.

Grace completed her nursing studies in Rochester in March 1946, and as a member of the cadets she spent her obligatory six months of service at Schick Army Hospital in Clinton, Iowa. This hospital primarily cared for soldiers with injuries incurred on the front during the war. They also admitted soldiers who had been prisoners of war. Grace's supervising nurse was concerned that some of the soldiers might react negatively to a Japanese nurse. She told Grace to report any incidents. Grace and another Nisei (American-born Japanese) cadet nurse were escorted to and from their housing quarters and the ward. Grace did not experience prejudice from the soldiers; they expressed gratitude for her care and that the war was over. Grace said the nurses were also grateful for their contact with the soldiers, which gave them a better understanding of the devastating impact the war had on soldiers and their loved ones.

·····

Fumiye Yoshida was admitted to Saint Marys School of Nursing in February 1943, and in July 1943 she became one of the first students to transfer into the cadet nursing program at the school. She and her family were living at the Minidoka Relocation Camp in Idaho. The Yoshida family had been farming near Tacoma, Washington. Fumiye's life changed on December 7, 1941, when she heard a special news bulletin about the Pearl Harbor attack while she was at a bowling alley with friends. Within hours, the FBI swept through communities on the West Coast and rounded up many Issei and some Nisei community leaders. A curfew was immediately imposed on all people of Japanese ancestry, which was upsetting for obvious reasons but especially since the curfew did not apply to Germans or Italians.

The Yoshida family and others detected animosity from the Associated Farmers Association in California, which they felt was behind demanding the evacuation of Japanese people, so those who remained could take over their successful farms. They felt the greed of this organization fueled the president's Executive Order 9006 because many Japanese immigrants had become successful farmers on the West Coast.

Fumiye and her two brothers, sister, and parents were tagged by the War Relocation Authority, "herded" onto military trucks on May 14, 1943, and taken to the fairgrounds at Puyallup, Washington, which was an assembly area ironically named Camp Harmony. Her sister and brother-in-law were among those sheltered in horse stalls; others were assigned to hastily built barracks. They could take only what they could carry and were given only a folding cot, canvas ticking to fill with straw, and an army blanket. Barbed wire was strung along the perimeter, and armed soldiers stood guard from sentry towers.

After three months in this rustic facility, the Yoshida family was placed on a train and transported to Minidoka internment camp, in south-central Idaho near Jerome. They found it to be "hot, desolate sagebrush country," where the dust was so thick that at times Fumiye could not see her hand in front of her. When it rained, the dust and dirt turned into thick mud. Their toilets were made of a long plank along one wall of the restroom with holes spaced equidistantly and a trough of water running underneath. The facility was unsanitary and allowed for no privacy. After they protested for a more decent bathroom, partitions were added. Again, at this facility, barbed wire kept them in, and they were guarded by armed soldiers. Although it was called a "relocation center," many saw it as a concentration camp.

The prisoners lived in barracks and had the option of working for wages of twelve to nineteen dollars per month. Japanese nurses and doctors staffed a hospital on-site, and others worked as teachers in a school with classes for first through twelfth grades or became cooks in the mess hall. Several members of Fumiye's family went out to work at nearby Idaho farms. Fumiye worked as an athletic director until she was accepted into the nursing program at Saint Marys in January 1943. She had originally sent her application to the University of Minnesota, but it had adopted a policy of not admitting any Japanese students. However, her application was forwarded to Saint Marys Hospital. Later in 1943, the University of Minnesota reversed its policy and began admitting Japanese students.

Fumiye's nursing class at Saint Marys included thirteen Nisei students. Fumiye was excited about the opportunity to get out of the camp and study at a well-known institution, but she was also nervous about her family's reaction and expectations. Many Japanese families did not want their daughters to become nurses. They considered nursing a menial profession and discouraged pursuing it because of the contact with death. On January 21, 1943, when the camp "gates clanged behind [her] . . . [she] left with mixed feelings . . . elated on one hand to be rid of the morbid situation, disheartened at leaving [her] family behind, and then apprehensive, after all the negative propaganda, about what kind of reception awaited [her]."

Fumiye arrived in Rochester by train and found her experience to be a silver lining in the dark cloud that had descended on her and her family. Rochester could be bitter cold in the winter, but the accommodations were good and the Japanese students were accepted by the staff, fellow students, and even patients from the Midwest, who were unused to seeing Asian people. Once as Fumiye cared for a patient, she felt the woman's eyes following her around the room. In response, Fumiye slowed down and gave the woman time to get used to how she looked. Over the two weeks that the patient was hospitalized, Fumiye won her over with patience and by providing excellent care. At the time of her discharge, the woman extended an invitation to Fumiye to visit her in Iowa. Fumiye hoped this patient would tell others of her positive experience and help change attitudes toward Japanese Americans. Fumiye had to be tolerant. While she was helping organize newspapers spread across another woman's bed, the patient asked her, "My dear, can you read?" Fumiye responded to the woman's racist comment by explaining that she would not be a nursing student if she could not read.

Fumiye joined the US Nurse Cadet program when it became available at Saint Marys, but not because of the financial benefits. At first, she was skeptical of a government program because of how the US government had treated Japanese people. Ultimately, she decided to join to help "offset the prejudice aroused by the anti-Japanese propaganda." From their internment, many Japanese people, like Fumiye, strove to prove their loyalty to the United States. She also felt she had "to excel for my folks, for myself, for all Americans of Japanese ancestry." After three years of nursing training at Saint Marys, she graduated in May 1946 and returned to Tacoma, Washington, as a surgical nurse. Eleven other women from Minidoka Camp also became students at Saint Marys School of Nursing.

· · · · ·

In addition to the nursing schools in Rochester, other communities in Minnesota opened their doors, but sometimes not without controversy. St. Paul was among only twenty-four communities nationwide that reached out to assist Japanese Americans wanting to leave the relocation camps. Although Minnesota was not in the military zone requiring internment of Japanese people, two Japanese families were put under house arrest in St. Paul by the evening of December 7, 1941. Initiated by treasury department officials in St. Paul, under the order of secretary Henry Morgenthau Jr., the financial records of Dr. Kano Ikeda, a well-respected pathologist at Miller Hospital, and Mr. Jiro Akamatsu, the owner of a successful gift shop, were investigated to assure they were not financing the Japanese war efforts. Coworkers and fellow church members of the two men and their families petitioned and complained until officials released them.

The *St. Paul Pioneer Press and Dispatch* and many citizens were supportive of Japanese immigrants who had lived and worked among them, demonstrating as much loyalty as members of any other ethnic group. The St. Paul chief of police attempted to get a city ordinance passed that would prohibit the relocation of Japanese people to St. Paul. In a unified cause to resist passage of this ordinance, a group of residents already part of the International Institute of St. Paul formed the St. Paul Resettlement Committee in the fall of 1942. Alice Sickels was a leader within the International Institute, an organization originally founded by the YWCA in 1911 with a long history of welcoming immigrants and helping to

restore a normal way of life to transplanted people and to blend the best elements in the cultures of their homelands into a truly American culture. Toward this end, the Institute staffs of well-trained specialists provide a host of vitally necessary services for the foreign-born and their children. They teach the immigrant English and civics; they help him apply for his citizenship papers and secure the necessary witnesses and documents; they stand by his side in the court proceedings and welcome him into the ranks of American citizens at receptions in his honor. They guide him through the intricacies of the immigration laws to bring his scattered family together, and by explanation and advice help him to understand the ways of people of other origins and of his American-born children. In countless ways they give him counsel and assurance, very often in his mother tongue. . . . Why all this is necessary, what it involves, and what it means— not only for the immigrant but for the city and the nation as well.

· · · · ·

Ruth Numura Tanbara and her husband, Earl, were the first Japanese couple to arrive in St. Paul in August 1942 and be welcomed by the International Institute. They had come to Minnesota when "war, politics, and war hysteria had swept them from their home and their jobs in Berkeley, California." Alice Sickels quickly helped Ruth find a secretarial job with the YWCA.

Ruth and Earl were followed by the wives and family members of Japanese men training with the Military Intelligence Service Language School (MISLS), part of the US Army at Camp Savage, Minnesota. The school moved to Minnesota from San Francisco after the Pearl Harbor attack because the army "pinpointed Minnesota as the geographic area with the best record of racial amity" and Governor Harold Stassen assured the military that Minnesota would provide a "friendly and accepting atmosphere." As the school, which began with two hundred students in June 1942, grew to eleven hundred and moved to Fort Snelling in 1944, many Japanese families and friends followed the MISLS students to St. Paul.

Members of the International Institute sought jobs for Japanese people in the internment camps who wanted to relocate to Minnesota. Within a month, they had one hundred fifty offers from Minnesota residents to hire household help: cooks, housekeepers, butlers. It was easiest to place people who were willing to work as household help because room and board typically came with these positions. While many people were open to Japanese moving to Minnesota, many were not willing to rent apartments or sell houses to them.

Ruth and Earl Tanbara had trouble buying a house. They made an offer that was accepted, but when the neighbors found out and objected, the seller reneged. Eventually, they were able to purchase a two-bedroom house. They temporarily boarded others moving to the state as well as some of their own family and friends. At one point, eleven people were living in their five-room house. As they were able to stabilize their lives within the community, Ruth and Earl became active in assisting other Japanese people to move to Minnesota.

Alice Sickels recounted the story of trying to help a seamstress and a young

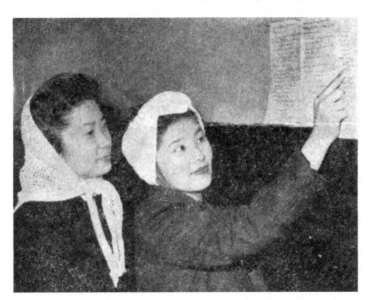

Alice Tokuno (left) and Kate Iwasaki checking work assignments at the St. Paul Resettlement Hostel. *St. Paul Resettlement Committee records, 1942–1953, MNHS Collections*

secretary, who had secured a job at a local hospital, find housing. Every time they answered an ad for an open apartment, it was apparently rented when they arrived. Alice spent an evening making calls with no success. She personally went to the address of one of the first apartments the women had tried to rent and found that it indeed had not been rented. She pleaded a case to the landlady, who seemed sympathetic and agreed to talk with her husband. When Alice returned a day later, one of the neighbors snapped, "We won't have any Japs living around us." Instead of bristling or walking away, Alice stayed and told the neighbors about the girls, including explaining that they each had a brother in the service. The neighbors changed their minds, but the landlord did not. Alice and the women ended up trying thirty-six places before they found a converted garage.

To help address the need for housing, the St. Paul Resettlement Committee bought a hostel in 1945. Although the war was ending and the internment camps were closed on January 2, 1945, only thirty-five thousand of the one hundred ten thousand inhabitants had relocated. The rest were given a train ticket and twenty-five dollars upon departure. Many did not want to return to California, where they had been treated with such hostility. Other members of the St. Paul community served on the board, including Warren Burger, who would later become a Supreme Court justice. In the two years it operated, the hostel served one hundred sixty people.

.....

In addition to challenges finding housing, securing work was also difficult. Two women who were especially committed helped a thousand Japanese people find jobs in the three peak years of relocation, 1942–45. Ruth Gage Colby, a peace activist, became a volunteer placement officer for the St. Paul Resettlement Committee, and Genevieve Steefel volunteered for the US Employment Services office in Minneapolis. Ruth was born in the small town of Olivia, in southwest Minnesota. Her father was an attorney and judge, and her mother encouraged her education. After graduation in 1915, Ruth attended Stanley College, a private women's college in Minneapolis, but after one year, she and her younger sister were diagnosed with polio. Ruth survived, but Lucille died. Ruth and her mother moved to Minneapolis after her recovery so she could attend the University of Minnesota. In 1919, she graduated with a degree in political science and married Woodard Colby, a physician she met while she was hospitalized with polio.

Ruth and her husband spent the first two years of their marriage in Venice, Italy, where Woodard studied pediatric medicine and Ruth studied voice and, as a volunteer, helped distribute food to children through the American Friends Service Committee. Through this work, Ruth became involved with the Women's International League for Peace and Freedom, which led her to the St. Paul Resettlement Committee.

Ruth Gage Colby traveling to New York, 1940s. *Ruth Gage Colby papers, MNHS Collections*

Through all of these initiatives, primarily led by women, fourteen hundred Japanese people relocated to Minnesota from the internment camps.

·····

While Ruth Gage Colby, Alice Sickels, Ruth Numura Tanbara, and others were dedicated to assisting Japanese Americans, Fanny Figelman Brin was advocating for peace and leading a statewide initiative to bring European refugees to Minnesota. In 1932, Fanny became president of the National Council of Jewish Women (NCJW), an organization founded in 1893. Fanny saw the organization as a way to unite Jewish women and create a means for them to work side by side with non-Jewish groups on issues of common welfare. She was personally dedicated to promoting women's rights, world peace, Jewish heritage, and democracy through her work with the NCJW.

Born in Berlad, Romania, Fanny came to the United States in 1884 with her parents when she was three months old. They settled in a Romanian Jewish community in Minneapolis, where her father made a living repairing watches and jewelry and her mother cared for the family and strongly encouraged her children to become educated. Fanny enjoyed participating in the debate league at South High School and went on to become the first woman to place in the Pillsbury oratorical contest at the University of Minnesota. She took second prize, and Theodore Christianson, who would later serve as governor of Minnesota, won first place.

Fanny became passionate about women's rights while she was a student at the University of Minnesota. She was influenced by her mother as well as by Frances Quire Potter, an English professor at the university, and by other women in Minnesota who were deeply involved in the suffrage movement. In 1907, Fanny graduated from the university with honors and began teaching Latin, civics, literature, and English, first in Northfield and later at West High School in Minneapolis. In 1913, she married Arthur Brin, an immigrant who began as an office boy in a glass company that he later owned. Arthur was supportive of Fanny's activism and only asked that she not picket. She divided her time between volunteerism and caring for their three children.

After the women's suffrage movement was finally successful in 1920 with the ratification of the Nineteenth Amendment to the US Constitution, many women's organizations and clubs shifted their focus to issues of community and global well-being. Fanny became the president of the Minneapolis Women's Committee for World Disarmament and expanded her involvement in the NCJW. Members of these groups protested the mandatory military readiness drills and course content provided by officers detailed by the War Department in Minneapolis high schools and the University of Minnesota after World War I. They supported the formation of and involvement in the League of Nations and the passage of the Kellogg-Briand Pact in 1928, legislation renouncing war as a tool of national policy and endorsing a commitment to resolve international disputes peacefully.

By 1932, when Fanny became president of NCJW, aspirations of world peace began evaporating. Japan's invasion of Manchuria in 1931 was the first in a chain of military aggressions: Italy attacked Ethiopia in 1935 and Spain became embroiled in civil war in 1936. In 1938, Adolf Hitler invaded Austria. Shortly thereafter, Great Britain, France, and Italy permitted his annexation of the German-speaking portion of Czechoslovakia. By that time, even most of the women's groups were abandoning hopes for peaceful resolutions.

Fanny and a local attorney began collaborating with a chapter of the National Emergency Committee in Aid of Displaced Foreign Scholars at the University of Minnesota. They coordinated the placement of refugee scholars, mostly Jewish individuals and families beginning in the mid-1930s, when Hitler's personal hatred of Jewish people became evident.

In 1940, Fanny represented several women's groups at the centennial congress of the National American Woman Suffrage Association, which recognized that in 1840 "there was no woman college graduate in the entire world and no married woman could collect her own wages." The gathering in New York City celebrated progress and committed to a "Declaration of Intentions" focused on protecting "married women in their right to work, to obtain equal pay for equal work in industry and the professions, equal opportunity in politics, to raise the moral and ethical standing of our nation, and, more than all else to find the quickest way to end war." Fanny called together the Minnesota state presidents of nine organizations to discuss the issues and send delegates to the meeting in New York. The organizations included:

American Association of University Women
General Federation of Women's Clubs
National Board YWCA
National Committee of Church Women
National Council of Jewish Women (NCJW)
National Federation of Business and Professional Women's Club
National League of Women Voters
National Woman's Christian Temperance Union
National Women's Trade Union League

These organizations, many of them with roots in the suffrage movement, now focused their energies on world peace and furthering opportunities and equity for women.

During this same period, Fanny was chair of the Minnesota Refugee Service Committee, which coordinated the relocation of individuals and families throughout the state. In 1940, its first year, the committee assisted in the relocation of four hundred forty-seven people, mostly Jewish, to Minnesota. The committee members celebrated their success but also mourned that there were many times they could not fulfill all of the requests to immigrate from the war-ravaged countries in Europe. In addition to facilitating opportunities for refugees, Fanny and others in the NCJW began advocating for open immigration for Jewish people into Palestine. They did not specifically call for a new state, but they did not preclude the idea.

Following the attack on Pearl Harbor, Fanny wrote "We are at war. . . . We must never forget the lessons we have learned, that isolation does not protect us, that it breaks down [and] ends in intervention . . . that we can only avoid intervention by setting up agencies which make possible collective action. We must learn and teach the lesson of cooperation. . . . We must build up now safeguards against an upsurge in isolationist thinking after the war. Unless we can, we shall go through the same cycle of isolation and intervention."

Fanny and other women continued to meet and urge their elected officials to make plans for the postwar period. In response to the women and others advocating for peace, in March 1943 Senator Joseph H. Ball, a Republican from Minnesota, joined with three other senators in drafting a bipartisan bill to express

Fanny Brin with the Women's International League for Peace and Freedom greeted by Minneapolis mayor William A. Anderson, 1931. *MNHS Collections*

congressional support for US participation in an international organization to be formed after the war to resolve international conflicts without aggression, an organization that would later be known as the United Nations.

As an effective public speaker from her days as a high school and college debater, and throughout all of her work during World War II, Fanny remained firmly committed to education as the key to women's rights and peace. Much of this work she accomplished at a time when anti-Semitism was prevalent in Minnesota. Although a few people found her approach pushy and elitist, she was considered by most to be a warm and modest woman. While the women's organizations made progress during the war years, even in 1948 Fanny recognized that "Today's world is a difficult one for women to find their place. But someday there will be a truer integration of women's abilities and contributions . . . and it will be a better world."

· · · · ·

On December 8, 1941, the day after the attack on Pearl Harbor, another Minnesota woman advocating for peace, as well as worker's rights, was sentenced to sixteen months in prison. A federal grand jury found Grace Holmes Carlson and twelve other defendants guilty under the Smith Act of attempting to overthrow the US government. They were members of the Socialist Workers Party (SWP), which had supported the Minneapolis Truckers' Strike in 1934. J. Edgar Hoover, director of the FBI, claimed the SWP's antiwar position and its ability to organize protestors was a threat to national security.

Grace was raised in St. Paul in the Rice Street neighborhood of working-class families. Her father was a boilermaker for the Great Northern Railroad. Her mother, afflicted with Parkinson's disease, encouraged Grace and her sister to read and pursue education, which they did. Grace spent much of her childhood walking to the library to get books for her mother and herself. She later earned her doctorate in psychology with a minor in educational psychology from the University of Minnesota, and her sister completed degrees in political science. They both became involved in the Teamsters Union and SWP during the 1930s, seeking decent working conditions and wages for workers in the midst of the Great Depression.

Grace had first connected with SWP during its national convention in 1936. She became increasingly committed, volunteering at the state level. Her enthusiasm for the party's goals grew to the point that, in 1940, she left her full-time job as a vocational rehabilitation counselor with the Minnesota Department of Education to work for SWP. In addition to polling and office work, Grace became part of the forefront of the party, an effective public speaker on its behalf.

As tensions in Europe grew and fears of immigrants rose in the United States, in June 1940 Congress passed the Alien Registration Act, better known as the Smith Act. This legislation required aliens over the age of fourteen to register and be fingerprinted, it allowed criminals and subversives to be deported, and it criminalized advocating the overthrow of the US government by force.

The Socialist Workers Party's primary focus was advocating for rights for truckers, gas station workers, and warehouse employees, including the right to unionize. Its position on the war arose when Hitler broke his alliance with Joseph Stalin in 1941 and invaded the Soviet Union. In response to this action, the US Communist Party switched from its antiwar position to ardently advocating for war. The SWP wanted to support the Marxists in the Soviet Union without endorsing Stalin or the Communist Party. As strong supporters of Leon Trotsky, the SWP took an antiwar stand.

These threads converged: the SWP's antiwar stance, Grace's growing commitment to the party, and rising fears of Soviet and other foreign influence within the United States. The American Federation of Labor (AFL) and the Congress of Industrial Organizations (CIO) became increasingly concerned about the socialist agenda and their loss of membership to SWP. They appealed to President Roosevelt to help them purge this influence from their ranks. They argued that if the United States went to war, the truckers would be critical to transporting supplies. On June 27, 1941, the Department of Justice raided the SWP offices, seizing books

Grace Carlson at a Socialist Workers Party meeting, 1940s. *MNHS Collections*

and pamphlets, resulting in the indictment of twenty-seven SWP members, including Grace, who was in the office that day.

Grace and the other defendants argued they were not advocating for overthrowing the government but rather predicting violence and insurrection if conditions did not improve for masses of workers. Despite support from the American Civil Liberties Union, the Workers Defense League, and the National Association for the Advancement of Colored People, thirteen of the twenty-eight defendants were convicted. One defendant committed suicide before the trial. Grace was the only woman. After the Supreme Court refused to hear their appeal, on December 31, 1943, Grace was taken into custody at the Hennepin County jail and transferred to Alderson Women's Prison in West Virginia, where she served thirteen months of her sixteen-month sentence.

At Alderson Prison, Grace found herself incarcerated with poor white women from the area who had been arrested for prostitution. With military installations nearby, they resorted to prostitution as a way to survive their desperate poverty. Although Grace was sympathetic to their situation, many of them were racist, and Grace found it difficult to endure hearing their antiblack sentiments. The only other political prisoners had assisted German spies, actions Grace did not support. Eventually, the warden utilized Grace's skills as a vocational counselor and her PhD in providing psychological testing and treatment in the prison. Grace appreciated the opportunity to work with these inmates and challenge their embedded attitudes about race and subordinated roles of women in society.

After her release, Grace continued her involvement with SWP and began working at St. Mary's Hospital in Minneapolis. Eventually she taught at St. Mary's Junior College. Her activism and conviction made her a celebrity. She toured the country as a speaker and ran for public office. She was a candidate for US Senate in 1946, for vice president on the Socialist Workers Party ticket with Farrell Dobbs in 1948, and for US Congress in 1950.

3

WITNESSING THE WAR EMERGE

In late September 1938, Mary Welsh, originally from Walker, Minnesota, was the only woman attached to the British Armed Forces. A correspondent for the *London Daily Times*, she was sitting in the office at a long wood table resembling a quick-lunch counter with her typewriter and pencils, working late on a story, when she "heard the heels" of her editor approaching on the bare wood floor.

"Mary, how about flying to Munich?" he asked.

British prime minister Neville Chamberlain was making a sudden trip to meet directly with Hitler in Munich. Mary chartered a plane and was soon on her way to Germany with the European head of the Associated Press and a couple of other men who begged to fly with her when they discovered she had the only available plane. The German consulate in London had closed for the evening, so, taking a chance, she left without a visa. Fortunately, when they landed in Frankfurt to refuel, the Associated Press executive convinced the German immigration officer that she was "harmless," and she was allowed into the country.

Once in Munich, Mary and her fellow journalists obtained a suite at the Grand Regina Palast Hotel, where they frequently stayed when on assignment. She immediately initiated the "classic ploy of keeping a [phone] line to London constantly occupied" by having a local boy read the Bible in English to *Express* telephone operators for hours until the journalists broke in on him to dictate a story. Mary then left for the train station, where she saw Benito Mussolini arrive, greeted by a band and a crowd waving red flags with black swastikas. Édouard Daladier, the French prime minister, arrived next, looking glum.

When she returned to the hotel, Mary talked her way into Prime Minister Chamberlain's suite, which was a smaller unit than hers since he did not have a standing relationship with the hotel like the press did. The bedroom was covered in blue wallpaper, the toilet paper was pink, and a battered suitcase sat in the corner among "girl" secretaries. Nothing was happening there, so Mary left for Braun Haus in time to see Hitler arrive in his car, waving to acknowledge the crowd's calls of "Heil, heil." There at Braun Haus, Hitler, Chamberlain, Mussolini, and Daladier met until after midnight, discussing Hitler's threat to invade the German-speaking regions of Czechoslovakia, a country not represented at the meeting. The leaders left Braun Haus looking noncommittal.

The next morning, Mary watched as Prime Minister Chamberlain in his "stiff collar and scraggly mustache" acknowledged the crowds through a light rain from his third-floor window of the Regina Palast Hotel. The European leaders and their staffs met further, and eventually Chamberlain held a press conference in his hotel suite and announced that Great Britain and France had agreed to Germany's annexation of Czechoslovakia's Sudetenland, which included three million people and important factories. Mary quickly wrote and dictated her story for publication in the *London Daily Express.*

Chamberlain returned to London and at the airport claimed that the agreement with Hitler was successful, as it represented "the desire of our two peoples never to go to war with one another again." Shortly thereafter he made the speech on Downing Street known for its erroneous prophecy of "peace for our time." King George VI honored him at Buckingham Palace, and Londoners were greatly relieved that Britain was not going to war; however, within months, Czechoslovakia surrendered completely to Germany, and by September 1939 Germany invaded Poland. In response, Chamberlain, in collaboration with France, gave Germany an ultimatum to leave Poland. Hitler remained resolute, and Britain and France declared war on Germany on September 3, 1939. Chamberlain's proclamation of "peace for our time" was shattered and his acquiescence to Hitler was greatly resented by many British citizens and politicians, leading eight months later to his resignation, followed by King George VI naming Winston Churchill prime minister.

· · · · ·

Mary Welsh, who had witnessed these crucial moments in Europe, had been born in 1908 in the town of Walker in northern Minnesota, near Leech Lake, part of the vast area historically home to the Ojibwe. She was raised by a father of Irish descent, who started a logging business, and a mother of German descent, who was an avid reader committed to education. While both parents had an impact on her childhood, Mary wrote more about the time spent with her father in the north woods, where she "explored, dawdled, and daydreamed." He often took her with him on trips to check on his logging interests. All summer, whether by canoe or riverboat, Mary was usually at his side outdoors, observing nesting habits of birds and discussing reasons bogs grow. He pointed out the constellations while they discussed Bible passages and aphorisms from *Hamlet.* Her father, a graduate of Valparaiso University, enjoyed literature and music.

The Northland, their Mississippi-type riverboat, was one hundred twenty feet long and three decks high. Mary and her father rode the boat to check on his logging holdings. Along the way they listened to Chopin études and Mozart sonatas on a scratchy phonograph. They read state history and talked with Ojibwe men and women. Mary developed a deep respect for Native Americans as she watched her father do business with them. She admired their sugar camps for making maple syrup and their conscientious methods of harvesting wild rice. When the boat docked, Mary was encouraged to explore the shore, which allowed her to develop a sense of personal freedom.

Mary learned lessons during this time with her father that would guide her later in life as she encountered barriers and obstacles. When she was eight or nine years old, he advised her to "never be a sheep. Never follow a leader only because he is ahead of you. Take time to look around and see for yourself if you are going in the right direction." She also remembered him telling her not to worry: "If it is something that can be fixed, fix it. If it is something impossible to fix, all your worrying won't help it." On one of the many nights they camped under balsam pines during a canoe trip downriver looking for missing logs, Mary tried to account for night noises while she wanted to fall asleep. Hearing twigs snap and footsteps near their campsite, she asked her father if he heard a bear. He told her nothing would harm them and that whatever it was just came to see the campfire. Mary thought of all the bears, timber wolves, foxes, coyotes, and lynx, with "their eerie, terrifying screams," that lived in that part of the country, but she reminded herself that her father had slept in the wilderness hundreds of times. She remembered all the advice she had received that "being frightened was a waste of time."

Mary and her father encountered challenging passages on the trip. As they paddled into midstream to avoid the rocks along the shore at Dead Man Rapids, the almost silent waterway became louder as the current accelerated, and they could see boulders scattered across their path. Mary's father sat tall in the canoe and paddled forcefully, attempting to steer away from the most dangerous obstacles. The "river roared, creaming and frothing white and splashing onto" them. They brushed over the top of a big stone as her father called, "Pull deep," so they could slip off of the rock. They covered two miles in this manner, bouncing along the rushing water. Finally, they saw calm water ahead. These experiences were part of Mary Welsh's education, a primer in observation, courage, and persistence.

Having been inspired by the editor of the Bemidji, Minnesota, *Pioneer* and his wife, Mary wanted to pursue a career in journalism. After graduating from high school in Bemidji, she enrolled at Northwestern University because it was in Chicago. She had read Carl Sandburg's poem "Chicago" and felt herself drawn to the city with "Big Shoulders . . . with lifted head singing so proud to be alive and coarse and strong and cunning." However, Northwestern, "with its snobbery and pretensions did not seem the best fit" for Mary. She began spending her free time at the Chicago Art Institute, and in less than two years, she left school and took a job editing *The American Florist*. She soon joined the staff writing the society page of the *Chicago Daily News*. She worked for Leola Allard, who for five years "wore down to a skeleton" what she called Mary's "boon companion, sloth." Leola "also . . . forged among the four girls on the society page a chain of mutual esteem and affection . . . much like that of fellow soldiers who have survived a long and bitter siege."

After a few years, a political writer for *Paris-Soir* stopped by the office, and his visit ignited a desire in Mary to see Paris, which she did within a few months. While there she visited the offices of *Paris-Soir* and was invited to dinner with the staff. After a rousing discussion about world events, including Hitler's rise, a fair amount of wine, dancing, and a bowl of onion soup, one of the men suggested, "If you're so keen about the news in Europe, why don't you quit that paper in Chicago and stay on here?" In response to her concern that her French was not good enough to work in France, they suggested she try the *London Daily Express* and gave her the owner's phone number.

Before she left Europe, Mary managed a brief visit with Lord Beaverbrook, owner of the *London Daily Express*. She boldly proposed he hire her to help cover the war in Europe. He did not think there was going to be a war, but put her in contact with the Fleet Street editor, who—when Mary called—claimed he already had one American and a good woman reporter, too, so he "couldn't possibly use" another. She returned to Chicago and begged to be assigned in Europe, but her requests were not granted.

A short time later, Beaverbrook rang from the Waldorf Astoria Hotel in New York and suggested she come to see him. She clarified that they would talk about a potential job, otherwise she was too busy to leave her post. After assurances, she went to New York, where Beaverbrook asked Mary to accompany him on a voyage up the Nile as a reader. She told him she was a reporter, not a reader. His attempts to persuade her to accompany him on the Nile trip included a "short dry kiss" on her head while she was trying to explain her interest in working in London. He told her that if she wished to be a woman of the world she needed patronage by an "important and influential man." He said that romantic love was a "waste of time" and that she should learn to "please men in every aspect of physical living." Mary replied that her father had told her to never mix business with pleasure and asserted that her talents were in reporting, not pleasing a man. He gave up on trying to convince her to go on the Nile trip and said the *Daily News* still did not have any openings, but if she came to London, he would see what he could do about getting her a position.

In earnest and quickly, Mary gave up her job at the *Chicago Daily News* and sold her furniture to raise enough money to cross the Atlantic, but not enough for return fare. She worried that she was being foolish, and she had second thoughts about her decision until she received advice from the managing partner at the *Daily News* that she remembered the rest of her life: "Never reverse a decision because of fear." Shortly after her arrival in London, Mary became a reporter for the *London Daily Express*, the newspaper with the largest circulation in Great Britain. Amelia Earhart's plane went missing on Mary's first day of work, July 2, 1937, and that incident became her first story in Europe.

Mary began covering stories for the *Daily Express* and became acquainted with reporters from other papers in London, including Noel Monks, an Australian working for the *London Daily Mail*. On December 31, 1939, months after Prime Minister Chamberlain announced Great Britain was at war with Germany, Mary married Noel and they moved into a small house in the Chelsea area of London. Throughout most of 1939, little was happening in Great Britain related to the war. Mary convinced her editor to let her move closer to the action in France. In 1940, the war escalated as Germany invaded Denmark, Norway, Belgium, Holland, and Luxembourg. By spring, Mary and Noel were living in Paris and covering the war from there. To her amusement, many of Mary's stories during this period "filled in around the edges" of the war, descriptions of the latest fashions by Jeanne Lanvin and Edith Piaf "in her scraggy black dress moaning her Paris waif songs."

On a particularly warm day in May, Mary and Noel were with friends playing tennis, followed by eating lunch at the Ritz Hotel and swimming. Later that lazy Sunday afternoon, Mary developed a high fever, which a local physician diagnosed as sunstroke. She went to bed and listened to the happy sounds of children playing outside. By evening, Noel left, intending to return to Royal Air Force (RAF) headquarters near Reims, but when he missed his train, he went to the office instead, where he heard that the Germans had crossed the French border and were headed for Paris.

Although Mary was weak and blurry from the fever, she and Noel hurriedly packed and took a taxi to the train station. As they attempted to escape before the Germans arrived, Mary looked out the taxi windows and thought Paris in the twilight looked "like a dream city. A slim slice of moon was mirrored in the satin of the river and silhouetted the shapes of ancient stones." She heard only "the peace and gentle sounds of a summer evening" until they arrived at the train station, "where the whole world was clamoring at ticket windows . . . [and] the doors of the jammed trains." Mary and Noel ran blocks down a platform, trying all of the doors, but they were closed tight, packed with people. Finally, they pulled one open and Mary found herself, still with a fever, stuffed between a spaniel dog and the "knees of a sad, haggard, old man who mentioned . . . he was one of the curators of the Louvre." They got off the train in Blois, where they heard the French government had moved.

Lucky to find a room in a small inn, Mary and Noel witnessed a chaotic, crowded situation. Mary was still suffering from heatstroke, and her hair had begun to fall out. Noel tried to find news of the RAF and French government, but the following day Mary decided Blois was too crowded to get access to a telegraph office or phone, so she made her way to Biarritz with her minimal luggage: a few changes of clothes, a tweed coat, a little money, and her portable typewriter, which she set up and used to start writing.

While Mary worked out of this small town at the very southern border of France, the War Department and Churchill were planning the Dunkirk evacuation in northern France. Between May 26 and June 4, 1940, a miraculous escape of more than three hundred thousand British, French, and Belgian troops took place just before German troops cut them off. The rescue was possible because of the bravery of everyday citizens piloting fishing boats, ferries, and pleasure cruisers in combination with British military fleets.

Eventually, Noel caught up with Mary in Biarritz after piecing together whatever transportation he could find, including a hearse for part of the trip. Soon they were evacuated by a cargo ship that took five days to make its way up the Atlantic Ocean, zigzagging constantly to avoid being torpedoed.

By this point, American newspapers had become interested in the war since Britain was involved. Mary was hired by the London bureau of *Time* and *Life* magazines. The first day of her new assignment, July 10, 1940, was also the first day of the Battle of Britain, intense daytime battles between the British and German air forces, which, by fall of that year, evolved into the night bombings referred to as the Blitz. In addition to sending stories back to her editors in the United States, Mary began broadcasting short, thirteen-and-a-half-minute reports back to the United States for the British Broadcasting Corporation (BBC) two or three times a week. Her time slot was scheduled between the well-known novelist J. B. Priestley and Leslie Howard, one of the stars in the film *Gone with the Wind*.

The five-note warning sirens regularly filled the London airspace, causing the newspaper staff to drop their work at the office and clamor down to the basements while the air-raid wardens were out in the streets with "only tin hats for protection." Eventually, the news staff began ignoring the warnings and worked at their desks amid the bombing, praying "for a miracle which would instantly transform [them] into experienced fighter pilots" as they pounded away on their typewriters.

Mary met women who were supporting the war effort in various ways. One pretended to deliver eggs in France but had guns and ammunition hidden underneath the egg crates. This same woman offered to introduce Mary to a wounded RAF officer. She delivered him to Mary at tea one day, a man in uniform "surmounted by a protrusion of hair and flesh, hardly to be described as a head. Aluminum hooks extended from the coat sleeves." A fire in his cockpit had ravaged him when he was shot down in France, and some local partisans had rescued him. A country doctor tended to his extensive burns until he was well enough for the egg lady to sneak him back into Britain.

Many of the bombs dropped on London in the fall of 1940 were incendiaries, firebombs, tubes "hissing white-hot fire from one end." The bombing went on for months. Some days were worse than others. On October 15, the Germans dropped seventy thousand incendiary bombs on London. During this long siege, a bomb dropped on Mary and Noel's building one evening while they were having dinner. The building's operator called them and told them to go outside: "We have a fire bomb." They helped put out flames on the grass and trees while the fire brigade worked. They could "see tin-hatted figures silhouetted against the flames, pushing open trap doors, swinging sandbags and quickly disappearing."

One morning when Mary arrived at an incident near Paddington Square where personal belongings and papers were scattered among the rubble, a little boy four or five years old ran to her and clutched her knees, sobbing, "My mum's down there, my mum's down there." He was wearing his pajamas and a large sweater. Mary asked him, "Where's your dad, ducks?" He replied, "In the army. My mum's down there." She sat on a pile of bricks and rubble and held him, saying something she couldn't really promise: "It's going to be all right, buddy, don't you fret. It's going to be all right." He seemed to relax. In a bit, the air warden led him away, assuring Mary they had found his mother and "She's not in too bad shape," which Mary thought "could mean anything short of dead."

Mary relentlessly worked to cover the war and send stories back to the Time-Life offices in New York. In one article published in the April 1941 issue of *Life*, Mary described her heart pounding, her knees "wobbling," and her "hands shaking aimlessly" one night in her seventh-floor apartment during a bombing raid. Ironically, the next morning, London appeared beautiful to her, "the tender blue of a spring morning sky and drifting toward it from the perimeter of London, soft cumulous clouds of pink, orange, lavender and gray, all glowing from the fires. They counted 16 of them, including one three doors away." On her way to the office, she saw "more gay new spring hats" than she had seen in a week. The only grim people were those picking through piles of rubble looking for survivors. She saw an ambulance drive by with two flat rear tires, and she felt bad for the injured inside enduring a painful ride until she saw the vehicle stop and unload "not injured, but shapeless dead."

· · · · ·

Later, in August, Mary's article "British Women at War" was the cover story in *Life*. She described the women's units in three branches of government and the Women's Land Army, a unit with thirteen thousand women that kept the farms operating during the war: "Under the brand of 'semi-skilled females' they hold snorting pneumatic riveters to the spars of Spitfire skeletons. Walking on rubber soles and wearing rubber gloves, they weave and wind and cut long gelatinous strands of raw, but dangerous, explosive that look like giant macaroni. In camouflaged hangars they punch bullets into machine-gun ammunition belts. They plot the courses of His Majesty's warships. They milk cows and pitch hay. They build boats and fight fires. They fly planes and shoot anti-aircraft guns and drive ambulances."

In total, two million British women joined the military and industry to allow for the release of men to combat positions. Mary described the stories of two young women who were widowed when their husbands were deployed. One woman became an industrial engineer and the other mapped military movements at RAF

Mary Welsh observing troops in England. *Photo by Cecil Beaton, published in* How It Was *by Mary Welsh Hemingway (New York: Ballantine Books, 1967)*

headquarters. Most women, like these two, voluntarily entered the workforce. Other women were invited to work through a mandatory registration with the British government under the Labor Minister based on their ages.

When she was not writing, Mary spent some of her downtime reading. She came across a copy of *For Whom the Bell Tolls,* a recently published novel by Ernest Hemingway. After reading it one weekend, she wrote in her diary, "excellent book," not knowing that within months she would meet the author.

· · · · ·

As Ruth Erickson was working to save lives in the naval hospital at Pearl Harbor, Mary and her husband heard the news of the attack while having dinner at a restaurant in London. They hurried to a radio to hear the BBC's report. At first there were very few details. Most people did not know where Pearl Harbor was. They listened to President Roosevelt address Congress the following day by radio, stating that December 7, 1941, would be a day that would "live in infamy."

The president detailed the attacks the Japanese government deployed in the hours following its invasion on Pearl Harbor: Malaya, Hong Kong, Guam, the Philippine Islands, Wake Island, and Midway Island. Roosevelt said with authority, "No matter how long it may take us to overcome this premeditated invasion, the American people in their righteous might, will win through to absolute victory . . . we will not only defend ourselves to the uttermost but will make very certain that this form of treachery shall never endanger us again." He called on Congress to declare war on Japan, which it did with only one dissenting vote. Jeannette Rankin, the first woman elected to Congress, a representative from Montana and a pacifist, cast the only vote against going to war.

As Christmas approached, Mary reflected on the losses. From the first bombings in July 1940 to the end of 1941, thirty thousand British people, mostly civilians, had died and more than three and a half million homes were bombed, leaving more than a million people homeless.

· · · · ·

Mary Welsh was not the only American woman journalist to cover World War II. Women journalists and correspondents emerged during World War I, paving the way for others to follow. Like in many other industries, such as shipbuilding and mining, women filled positions in journalism and publishing left open by men when they joined the military. In addition, Eleanor Roosevelt gave women new access and additional credibility when she began holding press conferences for women only, forcing newspapers to assign women to their staff. The first lady also wrote a regular newspaper column herself. Women went from having a small representation as journalists, often being limited to the family and society pages, to making up 50 percent of the staff at many newspapers during the war.

At the national level, Anne O'Hare McCormick, who began writing for the *New York Times* in 1921, became a well-respected columnist and foreign correspondent. In 1936, she was the first woman appointed to the *Times* editorial board, and in 1937, she won the Pulitzer Prize for distinguished foreign correspondence. Her coverage of World War II earned her a medal from the US War Department in 1946.

Probably best known was Dorothy Thompson from Lancaster, New York. Dorothy, a strong activist in the women's suffrage movement, moved to Europe to pursue a career in journalism after women were granted the right to vote in the United States. She was assigned to the Berlin office of the *New York Post* in 1925. There she met the well-known author Sinclair Lewis, from Sauk Centre, Minnesota, and they married in 1928. Lewis became the first writer from the United States to be awarded the Nobel Prize in Literature, in 1930. Dorothy had their child and lived in the United States for a while, but returned to Germany and interviewed Hitler in 1931. She warned the world about "the future dictator of Germany . . . the very prototype of the 'Little Man,'" a reference that led her to be the first journalist expelled from Germany.

· · · · ·

In Minnesota, women also increased their presence as reporters and editors. Virginia Taylor became the first managing editor of a daily paper when she assumed the position at the *New Ulm Daily Journal,* where a third of the newspaper staff were women. Carol Max became editor of the *Owatonna Photo News.* In Austin, Minnesota, Louise Flynn was named assistant sportswriter and photographer for the *Daily Herald* after three of the sports writers left for military assignments. Gwenyth Jones and her mother, who had been a longtime newspaper journalist and publisher, both worked at the *Northfield Independent.* Toward the end of the war, Harriet Sitz replaced a man at the *Grand Rapids Herald Review* who wrote a column titled "Thoughts While Shaving." She renamed the column "Meditations While Putting in Bobby Pins."

While some single women might have independently had aspirations to go into journalism, married women occasionally replaced their husbands. The *Fairmont Daily Sentinel* reported that "Mister Guckeen," an employee with eighteen years of experience, was headed to basic training at the Great Lakes Naval Training station in Pensacola, Florida. He was entering the navy as a photographer's mate. He spent several weeks before his departure teaching "Mrs. Guckeen" what he had learned over the years "the hard way." She would take over his responsibilities as news photographer and electrotype maker. The headline announcing this assignment read, "Wife of Man Employed by Sentinel More Than 18 Years to 'Carry on' as Husband Goes to War."

Women held positions in the production areas of newspapers and also as

Linotype machine operators and printer's devils (errand persons and apprentices). The University of Minnesota School of Journalism developed a six-quarter training course, half of the usual time, to help women learn their new roles. Circulation was up, as newspapers provided vital information on the war and home front updates on rationing plans, war bond drives, scrap collection, and other important issues. Newspapers also played a vital role fueling patriotism. But these were not easy times for newspapers. Despite the increase in circulation, advertising revenues were down, newsprint and chemicals became scarcer, and gasoline and tire shortages created challenges in delivery. Many newspapers reduced circulation, and forty-seven papers in Minnesota suspended publication for a period during the war.

In 1941, women journalists formed a new association, Minnesota Press Women, to elevate their standing in the field and support each other. Margaret Towey Evans of Minneapolis wrote a column that was published in the September 1944 issue of *Gopher Tidings*, the association's newsletter. The column, titled "Women's Part in the War," noted: "The part women are playing in the war should not be discounted but it can be badly mis-directed. Just as long as there are men and unmarried women available, wives and mothers should not be selected for military service. After all, we are fighting to preserve our country. What will it behoove us if we save our country and by doing so, we sacrifice the home?" The column goes on to explain the economics of working outside of the home and the cost for childcare in comparison to pay for such work. Further, Evans writes,

There is no greater responsibility, no cause more patriotic than the part women alone can do—and that is to preserve the homes which is the bulwark upon which our country rests. We have just to examine the police records of the average city to prove that this statement is not an imagination. We would invite you to stand outside one of the school buildings of an average city where children of war workers are cared for during the day. See them led out by tired and impatient mothers who have spent their working hours in some defense plant. These children have been well fed but on their faces is written a hunger that is more poignant than lack of food. It is a hunger for mother love. Nothing can ever take its place, and years cannot efface its effect on children. . . . We do not refer to women who have to work to maintain the home. They are in an unfortunate class by themselves. But, before the services of any wife or mother are accepted by the government, there should be a complete check-up and it should be proven beyond a reasonable doubt that there is not a man or single woman who could take her place in the workplace, so she can maintain her position in the home, and after all, there is no nobler cause.

This statement reveals the varying perspectives that women held about their roles during the war. Millions of women joined the workforce outside of the home and enlisted in the military, while others volunteered for community organizations and assorted initiatives. They seemed united in their commitment to participate in some way—advocating for peace, collecting grease in their kitchens, and cooking within the rations—but their expectations about their innate and ultimate roles in the home, workplace, and military varied widely.

4

WITHIN THE GERMAN RESISTANCE MOVEMENT

Early one morning in the spring of 1941, under the gaze of the Statue of Liberty, thirty-one-year-old Gisela Peiper stepped off a crowded boat of refugees in New York Harbor. She was surprised to see so many green trees among the skyscrapers and was "filled with a jubilant joy" she had not felt for a long time. They had been at sea for fourteen days, having left Lisbon, Portugal, to escape the Nazis, who had imprisoned Gisela twice, once in a concentration camp near her home in Hamburg, Germany. Her journey was not over; eventually Minnesota would be her home.

Early Years in Berlin (1910–28)

Gisela was born in Berlin in 1910. Her parents, Jewish immigrants of Austrian and Polish descent, struggled financially. They owned a small grocery store, and as a young girl Gisela delivered orders to wealthy people in the neighborhood. She resented being required to use the ugly back stairs intended for beggars, servants, and all "inferior" people instead of the beautiful carpeted stairs in front. Her parents spoke only German; Polish was forbidden in their home. Even as a child, Gisela was aware that her immigrant family was not highly respected in society.

Gisela enjoyed school and reading, especially after vision problems were identified and resolved. She felt self-conscious wearing glasses that she thought made her look uglier than she already believed herself to be in contrast to her older and younger sisters. A highlight of her younger years was her involvement in a youth movement group. Youth movements were strong in the years following World War I as young people sought reform. There were groups for almost every political party and religion. Members gathered to talk about philosophy and politics, read poetry, and sing. They also spent time outdoors, hiking and camping. Gisela enjoyed the companionship and the intellectual stimulation.

University Years in Hamburg and the Rise of Nazism (1929–33)

When she finished school, Gisela decided not to go on to university immediately. She wanted to be independent of her family and learn more about the world, so she moved to Hamburg in 1929 to work in a factory. Her youth movement group helped her get settled. Work was hard to find, but eventually she got a job in a bottle factory. The dirty, smelly basement facility was filled with women working on long, rough, wooden tables. They linked two pieces of metal together to make the closing of the bottle. Their hands were filthy and torn by the metal. They were paid by the piece, and the pay was unfair. Gisela joined the Metal Workers' Union, hoping to get relief on their behalf. She was able to organize some of the women, but they were quickly fired, and because there were not enough of them, the union did not help them. Gisela worked in another factory, where she observed that women were given tedious and dirty work while men walked around supervising. The noise was deafening. Gisela became increasingly involved in labor union and youth movement work.

After a year of factory and union work, friends convinced Gisela to go to the university, arguing that with an education, she could better help their causes. She entered the University of Hamburg in 1930 and completed a degree with study in education, history, philosophy, and psychology in 1933, just months after Hitler was appointed chancellor of Germany. Gisela was relieved to get her diploma, worried that her status as a Jew would prevent her from completing her studies.

The Nazi influence and presence were readily apparent. Storm troopers with brown shirts had begun marching in 1932, sometimes passing her apartment. Their songs included bold and violent anti-Semitic lyrics: "Wenn das Judenblut vom Messer spritzt (When the blood of the Jews is on our knives)." Unemployment was high; people could easily be convinced to become brown shirts because of the benefits. New storm troopers were given the uniform, two marks, and a heightened sense of importance. The recruits believed their country would be better when they drove out the Jews, who had taken all of the good jobs; the intellectuals, who belittled the working man; and the socialists, who were international and not committed to Germany's success.

Involvement with the Resistance Movement (1933–35)

A few artists and scientists united with the labor unions and began to resist the Nazi takeover. Gisela and others handed out leaflets in the last months of her studies at the university. A few weeks after Hitler was appointed chancellor, a policeman came to Gisela and her friend Paul's apartment. When the policeman finished questioning her, he told her he would not arrest her then, although that had been his intention. He warned her to stop her activism. Paul, a factory worker, was not Jewish and not a university student. He was not questioned. Quickly the swastika appeared on the lapels and armbands of people they knew. Some wore them out of fear; others for advantages for jobs.

One day, Gisela's neighbor invited her to her apartment. When Gisela arrived, she and a few others who had been quietly included listened to a union organizer from Switzerland. They discussed the possibility of acting against the regime.

They knew that anti-Nazi activity would be punished with incarceration in concentration camps, torture, and death. They agreed the best course of action was to covertly let people know that not everyone supported Nazism and to "keep an anti-Nazi spirit alive among all decent people regardless of religion or party affiliation." They also planned to develop an underground escape route for people in imminent danger.

The group began producing a small newspaper that carried information about anti-Nazi activities in other parts of Germany and international resistance to the Nazis. They distributed the newspaper through a network of sympathizers. From experience, members of the movement learned to carry the leaflets in the front of their bikes so that if the papers flew off they would know and could retrieve them quickly. The newsletters included information about phony elections and other false news stories. They reported the use of storm troopers dressed like workers in a shipyard when Hitler visited. The real workers were known to hate Hitler and were given the day off with pay so they would not be at the shipyard for his visit.

One winter day in 1935, Gisela received notification from the police in Berlin, where she had been born, that her German citizenship was being rescinded because she had received it by naturalization. Gisela had never lived anywhere but in Germany. The document stated that withdrawal of her citizenship could not be contested by any means. She was ordered to finalize the documents with a clerk at the police office. The man processing the papers suggested that with her education she should "shake the dust of this 'beautiful country'" off her shoes. She pointed out that only people with money could emigrate, and without citizenship or a passport, emigration was even less likely for her.

Gisela remained in Hamburg and continued resistance activities. Members of the group placed small stickers in places for others to know they were not alone in their disdain for the Nazis. She made her living by tutoring and working in a bookstore. In the winter of 1936, the activists became suspicious that poisonous gas was being produced in factories around Hamburg. The resistance workers went for casual bike rides and "accidentally" encountered fences of barbed wire with signs warning people to stay out. Once an explosion occurred in one of these facilities, confirming their fears. They made maps of the factory locations and smuggled the information out to the Allied forces.

Arrest in 1936

The Nazi Gestapo came to Gisela's apartment at 2 AM in December 1936. She had just enough time to swallow a thin piece of paper with names and addresses related to the resistance members before they came into her room. They told her to get dressed in front of them. They questioned her about her contacts. She gave her remaining money to the landlady and asked that she send it to Gisela's mother in

Berlin. The officers picked up another member of the underground on the way to the police station.

The SS officer who questioned Gisela hurled insults at her, calling her a whore and a Jewish pig. She found herself intrigued, wondering why someone would want to treat another person this way. She felt detached, and as he yelled at her, she thought, "How strange. I feel as though I'm wearing a raincoat. The flood is just sliding off of me. This kind of person cannot really insult me."

Several women, including Gisela, were taken into the basement and put into wooden containers that resembled standing coffins. They could not sit down or turn around. There was no window or outlet. It was dark and locked. At first, Gisela felt as if she were choking and all of her muscles ached. Her feet hurt and her mind began to swirl, as she worried about her mother, Paul, and fellow resistance members. She knew she needed to relax and sleep to avoid breaking down. She closed her eyes and told herself she "was lying on a comfortable bed, that there was soft music in the air" and she was "in a sun filled meadow." She did relax and was able to sleep lightly. The man next to her began screaming to be let out. He could not take it anymore, and he agreed to confess.

After an indeterminate amount of time, Gisela heard the key turn. When the door opened, she fell into the arms of an older guard, who muttered, "I won't keep her in here any longer. This is inhuman. This is terrible." He lined up the prisoners, and soon huge pots of soup were brought in. The women were grateful to the guard for his kindness. Gisela decided sometimes angels wear beards and faded blue prison guard uniforms. After the meal, the SS guards came and handcuffed two prisoners together and marched all of the women, many of them older, to a patrol wagon as if they were dangerous criminals. The women were mostly Jews and Jehovah's Witnesses, who refused to say "Heil Hitler." The wagon took them to Fuhlsbüttel concentration camp.

Gisela was put into solitary confinement. Her small cell contained a sharp knife often given to prisoners the Nazis hoped would commit suicide. Some did. Gisela pledged to herself she would only use the knife if she felt after torture she might give in and reveal names of other underground members. The guards kept her alone without anything to read, write, or do, hoping she would become desperate to talk. She was given coffee and dry bread in the morning and soup in the evening. Soon she found herself pacing in the cell like an animal in a cage at the zoo. She became hungry and lonely. One evening the young woman who handed her the soup whispered, "Chin up," a small but powerful gesture of encouragement.

Gisela knew she had to organize and fill her day. She began with a long walk in place before breakfast. She sang songs from her youth movement days. After breakfast, she began to repeat her Latin and French vocabulary and work arithmetic problems in her head since she did not have paper. In the afternoons, she developed elaborate daydreams of climbing mountains and visiting with friends, including Paul, storylines that were painful. She missed her friends and family terribly and was worried about them feeling anxious about her imprisonment. She also found a way to slowly make patterns on a handkerchief by pulling threads out of it with a bobby pin. She recited poetry she could remember.

Intermittently Gisela was interrogated by the Gestapo. They showed her examples of the underground leaflets they had confiscated. They showed her lists of resistance members' names. Paul's name was on one of the lists. Had they imprisoned him, too? After these sessions, the calm Gisela had created faded, leaving her anxious, fearful, and eventually hateful. And yet, more acts of kindness motivated her to remain committed to humanity. Once the morning guard, a woman, entered her cell and quickly said, "If you prefer it, I don't have to turn on the electric light. The sun is coming up so beautifully and you can see a little of it if I don't turn on the light." Another time an officer gave a coat to a woman who was shivering and crying in the cold. A guard tended to Gisela's finger when it got infected, and another guard smuggled two magazines into her cell during her shift. One morning, deflected light revealed a message from a woman who had been held in the cell before Gisela. The message, written with a fine needle in the paint on the wall, encouraged those who followed not to despair. Gisela was grateful and inspired to leave a message of her own: "In spite of everything, humanity will live."

Release and Escape to France (1937–39)

In early 1937, about a year after her arrest, Gisela was suddenly released. She was shocked. During her most recent interrogation the Gestapo officer had screamed that she "was the most stubborn person he had ever talked to." He told her she could plan on being with them for the rest of her life, but surprisingly, they returned her clothes to her and released her. Her landlady looked as though Gisela had "arisen from the grave" when she returned to her apartment. She surmised that she had been released as bait, to allow the Gestapo to follow her and capture others. She secretly contacted people through her landlady's daughter and shared everything she had learned during her incarceration. She also learned that her mother had displayed previously unknown reserves of courage: she had written to the Gestapo and had repeatedly gone to their offices and pleaded for her daughter's release. Gisela cried for the first time since her arrest. She cried as she told the other resistance members about the beatings she witnessed and her guilt at being free while others were still in the concentration camp.

Now a danger to her family, her friends, and the other members of the underground, Gisela had to leave Hamburg. Her first goal was to get her mother out of Germany. Her sister, Hanna, had emigrated to Israel (then Palestine) and obtained the paperwork for their mother to join her in Tel Aviv. Gisela helped her mother pack and escorted her to Leipzig, where they were to meet a couple also emigrating to Israel by car and then boat. Gisela's other sister, a nurse, had emigrated to England and occasionally cryptically wrote that Paul was there, too.

All that remained was for Gisela to leave, but she was committed to finding a legal way to emigrate, which would not be easy without a passport. She heard the Gestapo had been asking about her in Hamburg, so she could not return there. A courageous cousin was willing to hide her in Berlin. Her sister in England tried to get permission for her to enter, but in an attempt to keep on good terms with Hitler, England had reduced the number of visas it issued. France let some people in illegally, but those refugees could not work. Gisela asked at embassy after embassy while hearing that the Gestapo was continuing to pursue her.

Gisela learned of a doctor at the Czechoslovakian embassy who would certify stateless people in need of medical care for a visa to one of the country's health spas. Gisela went to the embassy and was seen by the kind, older Czech doctor. He gave her the certificate she needed for a visa to go to Czechoslovakia. She was able to take only a small amount of money, so she ate very little when she arrived in 1937. Soon she received news from underground workers in Karlsbad that she should go to Bratislava. A lawyer there could help her get into Austria, where the resistance was hoping to stop the spread of Nazism.

· · · · ·

Vienna was a beautiful city. Gisela rented an apartment with another underground member. They began writing and distributing leaflets, encouraging the Austrians to resist Nazi control. Their group enjoyed wonderful evenings meeting along the banks of the Danube River. Shortly after New Year's 1938, the Austrian police knocked on their door. After interrogating them, much more gently than the Gestapo had, the police decided to arrest the women even though they found no evidence in the rooms. The women were taken to a dirty local jail. After three days, Gisela heard their landlady angrily yelling at the police that they should not keep a young woman in such a filthy place. She brought clean clothes, soap, and a loaf of fresh bread.

This time Gisela was taken to a concentration camp in the middle of Vienna. Upon her arrival, the camp commander seemed bewildered, not sure what to do with one woman in a camp made up entirely of male prisoners. In this prison, she again experienced hardships and unexpected kindness. Another prisoner managed to get a newspaper for her to read, and he inscribed words of encouragement in the margins: "Don't despair. All of us will get out of this someday. . . . Keep up your courage, we are all standing for what humanity needs." Eventually she was released, but just as the Nazis took over Austria.

Once again, the underground movement found a way out of a Nazi-controlled country. Gisela followed their instructions and secretly arrived in Paris. No one was there to greet her because no one knew when she would arrive. She found

Paul, and they pursued life as refugees in France, which was difficult and degrading. Paul was arrested at one point when his visa expired and the officials arbitrarily refused to renew it. Gisela worked in Lyon for a family as a housekeeper.

Life in France and Escaping Again (1939–41)

Months later, in 1939, gas masks were distributed in Paris in anticipation of a German attack. Paul was attached to the French Army poised to resist the Germans. As a refugee, he could not bear arms, but he worked with the military. Gisela got what work she could, caring for children or older people. On May 10, 1940, the Germans invaded Belgium. Belgian refugees poured into France, and air raids pummeled Paris. Gisela was caring for a family in a village outside the city. Sporadic bombs hit power lines and trees. She witnessed horrible losses: a man left home with his wife and five children; a bomb hit them and he was the only survivor. Humor surfaced as well. When a bomb destroyed a family's greenhouse, the little girl of the household said, "Oh, what will Dad say, I promised to take care of his plants!"

Gisela's only regular news during this period was from her sister Ruth in England. She had received permission to remain there indefinitely working as a nurse, and she had fallen in love. Then, suddenly, Gisela received a telegram saying Ruth was dead, killed in a car accident. This was a devasting loss for Gisela at a time when she already felt deeply isolated.

The Germans kept pressing forward until they occupied Paris. And then France surrendered. At first, Gisela and Paul went into hiding because all anti-Nazi people were being hunted. A mayor of a small rural village agreed to let them stay if they pretended to be Belgian. They were allowed to live in an abandoned house and work odd jobs. They were resigned to waiting out the war by hiding in the French countryside—until an underground worker appeared and announced that Gisela's visa for the United States had arrived. At first, she did not want to leave Paul. The villagers promised to take care of him. They showed her the food they had secretly stored away. There would be plenty for everyone, and they had a room ready to hide Paul. They insisted that she must go if she had the opportunity. She agreed and boarded the train in Montauban for the American consul in Marseille.

· · · · ·

Gisela missed her first appointment with the American consul because of an unusually violent snowstorm along the train route to Marseille. The consul had been issuing visitor visas that would have allowed her to stay in the United States for a limited time, but she would not have been able to work. The morning Gisela arrived, a day after her scheduled appointment, the office received a telegram allowing them to issue immigration visas. If she had arrived on the day of her original appointment, she would have been given only a visitor visa.

Gisela was deeply grateful to the trade unions and the American Unitarian Service Committee that made her escape from the Nazis possible. Just before she left Marseille, a local leader of the American Unitarian Service Committee asked her to take one last risk and carry a list of people. The Nazis had recently issued a list of the people they considered the most dangerous anti-Nazis. They were hunting those people. If Gisela could get the list to the United States, the Americans could help save them. She agreed. Carrying the information helped alleviate her feeling of guilt about leaving.

Arrival in the United States (1941)

Once Gisela arrived in New York, the trade unions and American Unitarian Service Committee found work for her as a housekeeper until her longtime soul mate, Paul Konopka, also arrived in the United States. They were married and settled in Pennsylvania, where Gisela received a scholarship to study social work at the University of Pittsburgh. Paul worked in a factory for several months until the United States declared war on Japan and Germany. He was drafted in August 1942. Once while Paul was stationed near Washington, DC, Gisela took the train to visit him. They searched listings in a newspaper for a resort where they could stay in Virginia. Many of the resorts were "restricted," which meant that Blacks and Jews were prohibited from staying there. Gisela and Paul were disappointed to learn that discriminatory practices existed in a country fighting the Nazis.

Gisela Peiper Konopka, 1953. *Courtesy of University of Minnesota Archives, University of Minnesota–Twin Cities*

Gisela continued her studies in social work while Paul was deployed to England in 1944. While he was away, Gisela fell down a stairway on her way to give a talk. The next day, she experienced a problem with her vision. The eye doctor called an ambulance to take her to the hospital for emergency surgery to correct a detached retina. Her recovery required her to lie still for weeks with bandages covering her eyes and her head immobilized. She felt deep despair and began having night-mares that she was back imprisoned by the Nazis. Nurses tried to comfort her, but the dreams caused her to scream. Friends also helped during her hospitalization and cared for her at home. The situation became so difficult that one of her friends contacted the American Red Cross to request Paul's release from the military. Gise-la's condition might be known later as post-traumatic stress disorder (PTSD). Paul was granted a leave. He expected to return to London, but because the end of the war was near, he was discharged. During his military service, Paul became a US citizen, and Gisela became a naturalized citizen in December 1944.

Gisela completed a doctorate degree in social welfare from Columbia Univer-sity. She worked and taught courses in social work and adolescent development. Eventually, she joined the faculty of the University of Minnesota, where she be-came a renowned expert and teacher in her field. The US State Department re-quested Gisela's assistance in helping Germany in the postwar years. She was awarded the Highest Meritorious Medal from the Federal Republic of Germany for her work rebuilding German social services. She wrote three hundred scholarly articles and eleven books during her career. She established the Konopka Insti-tute for Adolescent Health, one of the earliest collaborations among the schools of medicine, nursing, and public health at the University of Minnesota. Gisela Peiper Konopka is also recognized in the hall of fame at Columbia's School of Social Work. Although she was not born in Minnesota, her story as an immigrant is relevant to this narrative and she contributed much during her long career in the state.

War Production, North Africa, and the Aleutian Islands

5

CAROL THE RIVETER, MILLIE THE MINER, AND THE WOWS

Producing SPAM

It was not long after Gisela Peiper escaped from France to the United States that Japanese planes bombed Pearl Harbor. Within days of the attack, a steel security fence and bright lights were installed at the Hormel meatpacking plant in Austin, Minnesota. Hormel employees were fingerprinted and photo IDs issued. All public tours were canceled. Security increased because the facility had been designated a war production plant. According to the company newsletter, pounds of meat were "as important in the prosecution of the war, as bullets from a bullet factory or airplanes from an airplane factory." The troops needed to be fed.

Despite Jay C. Hormel's initial resistance to entering World War II, he had been convinced to produce food, including SPAM, the company's popular canned spiced ham, for Britain and Russia under the Lend-Lease Act passed in March 1941. By fall, Hormel had doubled its lines and hours and was producing fifteen million cans of meat products weekly. After the attack on Pearl Harbor, the need for SPAM and other canned meat increased dramatically, and men from the plant were enlisting and being drafted.

The draft of ten million men into military service began on October 29, 1940, part of the US plans for readiness even before the country declared war on Japan, Germany, and Italy. By the end of the war, 1,965 men and women from Hormel served in the military and an additional 1,400 women were among the workforce hired to meet production quotas. In 1944, Hormel reached an all-time record, processing 646.5 million pounds of food, 90 percent of which went to the government. At that point, the 1,922 women working in the plant represented over 30 percent of the Hormel workforce.

Female employees were not new for Hormel: 482 women, representing 17 percent of the workforce, were working in the plant before the United States entered the war. Their presence, especially in the earliest years, might have reflected the highly seasonal nature of hog processing before refrigeration was available. From the company's beginning in 1891, Hormel needed to hire enough staff from a relatively sparsely populated area to handle the fall harvesting of livestock.

In these early years at Hormel, women were primarily employed in office work and segregated production areas, such as sausage casing and sliced bacon packing rooms, where all workers were women except for the foremen. After 1941, women were employed in just about every department, including in the hog cut and sheep dressing areas, which had been entirely staffed by men in the past. The company newsletter noted that the women were doing well and in "instance after instance, they've surprised everyone with their competence."

Single women were assigned to areas within Hormel where they were needed most, but many married women assumed their husbands' jobs when the men were deployed. Inez Bailey Miller distilled ammonia as a test for protein in the chemical laboratory, a job her husband did before he was deployed and a position previously held exclusively by men.

Hormel sales representatives had been entirely men until Peggy O'Neill "stepped into her husband's civilian shoes," covering Cincinnati, Springfield, Portsmouth, Dayton, Covington, and other Ohio river towns when her husband joined the army. At about the same time, Wanda Clayworth Powers began covering the St. Louis territory for her husband. The company newsletter congratulated these women but warned them "not to do so well that your customers will insist upon you staying on the road and your husband doing the housework after the war."

All indications are that women were paid the same amount as men for the work they did at Hormel; however, they did not become supervisors or foremen in areas where men worked until years later. While working conditions for the women were primarily positive, a woman in the dry sausage department convinced another woman to get the casings out of the barrel because she did not like the gang whistling at her, and there were hints that even when women with children picked up full-time work, they were still expected to maintain the household. In one company newsletter, Mrs. Lorenz Torke was photographed in her new home and celebrated for becoming a new employee in the flavor-sealed department while keeping "her kitchen spic and span, too."

Expanding production capacity during the war years was not without challenges. Japanese forces controlled the primary sources of tin in southeast Asia, which had been used to make the cans. Legislation was passed to limit the use of tin cans so that adequate materials would be available to Hormel and other food manufacturers supplying the troops, and tin was restricted from use for domestic products. Sugar was also rationed, but Hormel could get extra sugar allocations for military orders. Limits on gasoline and rubber used to make tires caused problems for people getting to work and for the sales force. The fluctuations in supply and demand for hogs and price ceilings implemented by the government to protect consumers from skyrocketing food prices also created challenges for the Hormel management and leadership.

It was a difficult time, but the ability to hire enough staff was likely the biggest problem for a company in a rural area. Despite the fact that a high proportion of the employees, men and women, were relatively new, they were highly motivated and became productive quickly. A note in the company newsletter pointed to the critical relationship between Hormel employees producing food and the need to "sustain the life of the fighters for freedom." The employees celebrated producing K-1 rations that blended pork, carrots, and an apple nugget. The ingredients were subjected to strict regulatory standards. Every carrot was scrupulously cleaned. Then, and only then, came the signal to blend the ingredients, which provided an abundance of calories for energy and vitamins A, B1, C, and riboflavin (G) for vigorous health. Cutting and blending were done at many thousands of revolutions in a machine designed for speed and accuracy: "Each tick of the second hand on the clock reckons four cans of this product." Wilma Helle is shown in a company newsletter photograph blending the pork while Arleen Hagen loads the tins into the machine and Marjorie Lawson guides the machinery in rapidly filling the cans with a "quarter pound of Fighting food."

Women employees and wives were highly encouraged to support the war effort by gardening, canning food, and keeping the house and family. The company newsletter encouraged all of these activities with informative articles highlighting women who were leading the efforts. The newsletter also encouraged the collection of cooking grease, a nationwide program. Glycerin in the fat could be processed into nitroglycerin for use in double-base propellant powders. The War Production Board collaborated with Walt Disney Corporation to create a cartoon with Minnie and Pluto urging women to save kitchen fat, claiming that bacon grease is a "little munitions factory." Although this campaign was possibly somewhat useful for ammunition production, it was probably more important as a way to continue to engage the country in the war effort. Households were already saving grease, but for reuse in their own cooking. This practice became essential in 1943 when lard and butter were rationed. About 50 percent of households nationwide turned in cooking grease.

Hormel employees and their families were also expected to support the war by buying war bonds. The hog dressing floor employees were among the departments that reached their bond-buying quotas. A hundred percent of the employees in each department were expected to allocate ten percent of their wages to buying bonds. Those that reached the goal were featured in the company newsletter.

· · · · ·

In addition to their contributions working the production lines, 1,965 Hormel employees served in the military, including more than a hundred women. Most of the women enlisted in the Women's Army Corps (WAC), which was called the Women's Army Auxiliary Corps (WAAC) until 1943, when the name was changed and women were given full military benefits. Harriet Hinckley from the Hormel baking department was one of the first women from the company to join the army and take military leave. After basic training at Fort Des Moines, Iowa,

Harriet was assigned to the motor pool, where she drove "anything from a jeep to a five-ton semi," including an amphibious vehicle called a seep, a seagoing version of a jeep.

Barbara Hadley from the fresh sausage packing department was also one of the first from the Austin area to enlist with the army. She hoped to be assigned to the air branch. She was mechanically inclined and had experience plowing with her father on their farm. Her hobby of building model airplanes spurred her interest in aviation, and she took flying lessons in Austin every time she had an extra four dollars. Upon graduation from officers' training and as a second lieutenant, she became a company commander at Fort Des Moines, where she was a basic training instructor. Through her officers' training, she learned about company administration, chemical warfare, and air attacks. Later she was promoted to first lieutenant and then captain. Barbara was ultimately assigned to be the quartermaster corps sales officer in charge of the food supply to Fort Belvoir, Virginia.

The women at Hormel were not the only women in the Austin area to enlist. Elizabeth Dahlgren of Grand Meadow joined the WAC in 1943 and was a member of the first unit of WACs assigned to Eglin Field, Florida, after basic training at Fort Des Moines. Before enlisting, she completed teachers' training at Aberdeen, South Dakota, and taught in Grand Meadow before managing a hunting and fishing lodge near Wabasha. She also had been employed as chief stewardess on the *North Star*, a yacht on the Mississippi River owned by William and Hattie Mayo of Rochester, founders of Mayo Clinic.

Elizabeth enlisted in the WAC because it was hard to make a living in the hunting and fishing business with gas rationing and many fishermen and hunters away in the armed forces. She anticipated being assigned to food service when she enlisted. She was surprised to be trained in weather observation and assigned to the air forces at Eglin Field as part of the 118th WAC Post Headquarters Company from April through December 1943. The women from Elizabeth's unit were "scattered" to Hawaii, the South Pacific, England, Africa, India, and France for various assignments.

Registering for the Draft

Reika Mary Drake Schwanke made national news in November 1940 when she registered for the Selective Service. After hearing on the radio that registration had begun in Austin, Minnesota, she signed up because she "had been trying to get into some form of service, rolling bandages, driving an ambulance," or anything else in which she might help. Reika and the local registration board member were unaware that only men could register; she was given serial number 14. Once the local draft board realized that a woman had registered, Governor Harold Stassen and the Minnesota Selective Service were consulted. It was not possible to void the registration, so Reika's paperwork was processed, but when her number was drawn, she was immediately classified as 4F, "physically unfit for service," because she was a woman.

Reika was waiting tables at Dunsmore's Café in Austin when she registered for the draft. She was considered courageous when she registered, but people in the surrounding area knew how brave she really was. Ten years earlier, Reika, her mother, and her fourteen-year-old brother were shot outside their home by a man who wanted to date her twin sister. Her brother died from a bullet wound to his head. Her mother was shot in the wrist and suffered a broken ankle. Reika was shot in the abdomen and crawled half a mile to a neighbor's home. A local doctor drove both mother and daughter to Mayo Clinic in Rochester, where Reika's recovery was doubtful because her intestines had been perforated in fifteen locations. She survived, but only after several operations.

After the nationwide news coverage of her attempt to join the armed forces, Reika received hundreds of letters from people commending her for her desire to serve. One of those letters offered an opportunity to become part of an ambulance corps, which was "the one thing she want[ed] above all." The ambulance service was being organized in Chicago and planned to sail to Europe the first of January 1941.

Ultimately, Reika did not go with the ambulance service. Instead, she went to the Twin Cities, where she was employed in one of the new large munitions factories. There she joined tens of thousands of women and men in producing supplies and equipment vital to the war effort.

Keep 'em Shooting

On August 28, 1941, a crowd of thousands of people gathered in New Brighton, Minnesota, as ground was broken for the Twin Cities Ordnance Plant (TCOP), a government-owned, contractor-operated facility built to provide thirty- and fifty-caliber shells for the US Army. After choosing the location, the US government condemned 2,425 acres in the small farming community just north of downtown Minneapolis and ordered all forty-five families living on the site to relocate, including the Christensens. Dr. Jonas Christensen, a University of Minnesota assistant professor and plant pathologist, his wife, Hildur, and their family had to abandon their forty-acre arboretum, which included more than three hundred species of trees, shrubs, and vines. They had to move or lose five thousand full-grown trees and eighteen thousand evergreen seedlings. They had two thousand gladiolus flowers in addition to rare plants including the South African Hottentot bread plant.

The US Army chose the site because its distance from the coasts made it less vulnerable to enemy attack and the location provided good access to the railroad, abundant water, and ample labor. By early December, eleven thousand construction workers descended on New Brighton, which had a population of 658 in 1940. They worked seven days a week, living in campers and commuting, which caused traffic jams. The first phase of construction was complete by January 1942, and the plant included 323 buildings, twenty-two miles of roads, sixteen miles of rail, and a million-gallon water reservoir. The company had its own fire department, police force, radio station, and hospital.

TCOP recruited a diverse workforce. The first issue of the company newsletter, published in May 1942, included a photo of eight employees—women, Filipino, African American, and Asian workers—walking arm in arm under the headline "Sure We'll Keep 'em Shooting!" The private company owner, Charles Horn, was personally committed to an integrated facility. He announced that if a white person did not want to work side by side with an African American, they should not apply for work there. Also, President Roosevelt had issued an executive order on June 25, 1941, directing that federal government contractors could not discriminate based on race. To help with African American recruitment, TCOP hired well-known African American leader and newspaper publisher Cecil Newman. The company ultimately hired twelve hundred African American men and women, about 20 percent of the working-age population in the state at that time.

By 1943, 60 percent of the TCOP workforce was made up of women. They were called WOWs (Women Ordnance Workers). The women worked side by side with men and held many positions previously staffed only by men, including as guards. They ran machines and worked in the drafting room. When President Roosevelt visited the plant in September 1942 on his eight-thousand-mile, two-week tour of twenty-one defense plants, he was amazed at the number of women and African Americans working there. One of the women, Peggy Jolst, presented him with a golden cartridge. The plant earned four awards for excellence, the coveted "E" awards from the army and navy for quality and production rates. More than twenty thousand employees and their guests gathered to be recognized and celebrate the company's success.

Company management boosted workers' motivation by adopting the "Keep 'em Shooting" campaign. Many workers had sons, husbands, and brothers in the military. They had a vested interest in producing the supplies the military needed. Management also solicited and implemented suggestions from employees to improve conditions and production. The plant operated six days a week, with three shifts, and filled six railroad cars of ammunition every day. To help employees rest and relax, the company invested in a recreation department that provided archery, softball, bowling, golf, chorus, and band activities. It also supported several clubs, including trap shooting, photography, horseback riding, and dancing. It helped employees carpool to mitigate the problems with gas and tire (rubber) rationing, shared letters from servicemen who appreciated the cartridges, and brought

TWIN CITIES ORDNANCE NEWS

VOLUME 1 NUMBER 1   Wednesday, May 20, 1942

SURE WE'LL KEEP 'EM SHOOTING!

10% Bond Buying Is New Goal

TCOP Employees Set Pace for Nation in 20-Hour Drive

Flushed with success over their first War Bond buying drive, Twin Cities Ordnance employees and officials are now preparing a new drive. Goal of this drive is to have each employee subscribe for war bonds in amounts not less than 10% of his income.

TCOP employees set an example for the ENTIRE NATION in subscribing during the initial drive 100 per cent—to exactly 20 hours to the payroll savings plan.

So far as is known, no other ordnance plant in the United States can equal nor even closely approach this.
(Continued on Page 7)

Take This Paper Home for the Family to Read

Here's your first issue of the new newspaper edited in the interests of employees of Federal Cartridge Corporation, operators of the Twin Cities Ordnance Plant.

Take this issue, and every other one, home with you. Show it to your wife. She's interested in hearing about happenings in the plant.

F ILIPINO .... nurse .... army man .... Negro factory worker .... guard .... youth .... age .... Chinese .... we're all part of TCOP .... we're all part of AMERICA. .... and it's our job to "Keep 'Em Shooting!"

The smile which lights our face is not one of levity. It reflects the Spirit, Faith, and Courage glowing within our hearts. It is the trademark of a democratic people— a ray of hope for the conquered and oppressed.

To our boys at the Front, we say, "SURE, WE'LL KEEP 'EM SHOOTING!"

HORN, EHLEN AND HINRICHS GIVE FIRST ISSUE OF NEWSPAPER A HEARTY SEND-OFF

CHARLES L. HORN
President of Federal Cartridge Corporation

This is the first issue of the Twin Cities Ordnance Plant paper which will be followed by regular issues, carrying news about the employees. This is your paper and its success will depend upon the news items supplied by the reporters.
(Continued on Page 7)

R. B. EHLEN
General Manager of Federal Cartridge Corporation

This paper is published for news concerning information of activities and items of interest to you as employees of the Twin Cities Ordnance Plant. We invite everyone to join in to assist in making this publication of great interest
(Continued on Page 7)

LT. COL. HINRICHS
Commanding Officer of Twin Cities Ordnance Plant

I wish to congratulate the Federal Cartridge Corporation on establishing this paper. I feel that it will contribute in a very substantial way to making our organization the closely knit unit which is so necessary to obtain the maximum
(Continued on Page 7)

Production Army Has a New War Cry

Workers Will Pledge Full Co-operation In Drive

"Keep 'Em Shooting!" That's the new war cry you'll hear on every worker's lips these days!

It's the slogan of the Production Army ... the men and women who are making vital munitions for the Armies actually fighting the war throughout the world.

It's the workers' response to a message to every employee of Twin Cities Ordnance Plant from Major General C. M. Wesson, Chief of Ordnance, U. S. Army. Here are General Wesson's own words:

"Enough—and on Time!

"Let that be our answer to those who have thrown at the Democracies the charge: 'too little and too late!'

"Enough—and on Time!

"That means that heavy responsibilities rest upon all of us engaged in Ordnance Production:

".... the responsibility to make every minute count.

".... the responsibility to do our work with thoroughness and care, to cut down rejected material, to eliminate waste, to avoid accidents, to work together as a team.
(Continued on Page 6)

Front page of *Twin Cities Ordnance News,* May 20, 1942

Ordnance plant workers. *Minneapolis Newspaper Photograph Collection, Hennepin County Library*

celebrities, including Patty Berg, a well-known professional golfer from Minnesota, on-site to encourage morale.

Because more than half of the employees were women, the company offered them special services, including counselors and welfare workers, and made connections with community childcare resources. A woman inspector from Chicago claimed, "No plant in the country approaches the work being done at Twin Cities Ordnance Plant in behalf of women." While many services were provided, Horn, the company president, noted that all women with young children had to "provide satisfactory proof" that their children "will be adequately cared for before they can obtain work."

Women who came to work at TCOP had a wide range of backgrounds. Three deaf women were hired through a collaboration with the school for the deaf in Faribault. Evelyn Krause from Mound paused her house moving business to come work for TCOP. After getting herself in shape at Mound High School by going out for football practice with boys who went on to play on the University of Minnesota Gophers football team, she became a house mover, possibly the country's first woman to take up this work. She could jack up a house and relocate it to a new site as quickly as a man could. She also dug basements and carried pianos and refrigerators on her back before joining the TCOP workforce.

By the time war production wound down and TCOP closed in September 1945, the company had produced four and a half billion cartridges and thirty-seven thousand people had worked there at an average pay rate of forty-five dollars per month.

Shipping and Mining

Women were not only in factories. After the United States declared war on Japan and Germany, there was a sudden and extreme need for more military ships, planes, and tanks. Women in Minnesota stepped up and went to work in shipping yards and mines for the first time. In early 1942, Mary Johnson of Cloquet took a welding class at the Superior, Wisconsin, vocational school and became the first student to complete the course in three days, passing all tests on her welds on the fourth day. Most students took three to four weeks to complete the course. In early 1943, when the local shipyards obtained government contracts to build ships, she applied for work as an arc welder. Mary was among the first group, a total of seventeen women, to be hired in the Duluth-Superior shipyards.

In the fall of 1943, Mary Johnson's daughter, Carol, set off for school at the Chicago Institute of Art after graduating from Cloquet High School. Her time at the school was cut short when, after a few weeks, her father suffered a severe stroke and she had to return to Cloquet to help at home. She decided to follow her mother's example and go to welding school. She could not match her mother's record of completing the course in three days, but she finished within two weeks and was hired at Globe Shipyard in Superior. Carol's brother, Gene, joined the same shipyard as a painter. He was deferred from the service because he had two small children and his wife was chronically ill due to issues with her gallbladder.

Upon completion of the course, Carol was able to "stitch" two pieces of iron together with a metal rod. When the tip of the rod is scraped against the metal plate, "a bright electric 'arc' is created" and the immense heat melts the tip of the rod and the surfaces of the two butted plates. A welder then "paddles" the molten iron from the rod in small quarter- to half-inch waves in a careful rhythm. The process takes stamina and a sensitive touch. As Carol worked her way along the pieces, she had to endure bright light, heat, smoke, sparks, and droplets of molten metal. Carol sang to herself while she welded to help get the pattern just right. When the weld was finished, she had to knock off the crusty surface with a dull ax and a metal brush.

Although welders wore protective gear, Carol developed scars around her wrists and collarbone, where small gaps in her clothes left some of her skin exposed. Once one of her shoelaces caught fire, and she could smell the burning fabric, but she didn't want to stop. By the time a fellow welder began frantically beating out the flames, four inches of Carol's jeans had burned off. After that, she switched to leather shoelaces.

Overhead welding was the most frightening for Carol: "When all of those sizzling sparks are raining directly down on you and bouncing off the face of your mask. . . . I was so very much afraid of this crackling, electrical rain of fire and metal that it took every bit of my willpower and determination. . . . I would grit my teeth and weld a few inches before tears filled my eyes. I'd stop a moment, crying quietly. Then I would wipe my eyes, pull my mask down again, and weld some more." Despite her fear of overhead welding, she sought out difficult welds so she would improve. Soon she became a first-class welder and was picked to become part of a special team that made corrections on various pieces throughout the shipyard.

The work was sometimes dangerous, especially on the special assignment team that Carol joined. They were responsible for quickly fixing mistakes or problems that inspectors found. Sometimes they skipped standard safety guidelines to get the job done fast. Once Carol was asked to put more welds along a beam that extended out of the engine room three feet, with a twenty-foot drop to the engines below. Normally workers built a platform for the welder to stand on, but they were in a hurry, so her coworker just grabbed onto her jacket and, with her feet braced against the wall, Carol leaned out backward far enough to do the welding. Another time she crawled through the cube-like structure of the bilge in the very bottom of the ship. The circular opening was only twenty inches wide. Team members dropped her stinger, cable, and rods to the bottom, and then she crawled on her back with her equipment through to the prow of the ship so she could fix the problem.

> It was a very claustrophobic experience. Not only was there the usual danger of setting my hair on fire or shirt on fire, but in that cramped space, there was no way I could get out of there quickly, even with Joe's help. . . . Only my stubbornness, to prove that there was nothing that I couldn't weld, kept me there. I had no trouble with the fire, but because the ventilation hoses were not installed, the smoke was really bad. . . . I managed to complete the welding. . . . By the time I got up on deck to the welcome fresh air, I found myself panting in short labored breaths. I leaned on the ship's rail . . . gasping and feeling pretty weak. . . I was sick at home for a couple of days. . . . It was not wise to be without air down there. But I doubt if there was room enough for me to crawl through the cubes if those thick air hoses had made the openings any smaller.

Once a repair needed to be made on the ship's mast on the crow's nest, about seventy feet above the water. Carol's coworker Joe volunteered her, saying, "Carol can do it. She can do anything." Carol was not so confident, but she was never going to show fear. She took pride in her work and in being a part of the special daredevil crew. She climbed up and looked down only once, just before getting to the platform, a move she regretted, but she made the repair and climbed down, later hearing that her brother, Gene, had been on the ground waving and yelling, "That's my kid sister up there!"

The shipyards worked year-round to produce the vessels needed for the war, and workers welded in the winter as long as the temperature was ten degrees Fahrenheit or warmer. Ten degrees along the North Shore with the wind can be very chilling. Carol wore a wool stocking cap under a quilted cap, a thick leather jacket, thick wool men's pants under a pair of blue jeans, two-piece long underwear, a wool sweater, and a flannel shirt. She wore cotton socks and as many pairs of wool socks as she could fit into her high-topped leather work boots, usually two or three pair. She put on heavy wool gloves underneath her heavy leather welding gloves. Yet all of these clothes "never felt like enough when [she] crawled around on [an] icy-cold slab" of iron plates lying on platforms.

One winter day, Carol and two other members of their special team were outside welding plates onto the side of the ship. A winter storm came up with some snow and a bitterly cold wind that was hitting them head-on. They worked through it to finish the job before dark. Carol called in sick for the next three days with a fever and congested lungs. When she got back to work, she heard that one of the men on the team had died of pneumonia.

· · · · ·

The Duluth-Superior shipyards produced several types of vessels for the US Navy. Carol's mother, Mary, enjoyed working on the Coast Guard cutters. Carol's favorite was the frigate, one of the larger destroyers often used as an escort for convoys. One time she had an opportunity to stow away on a test run of one of the frigates. Welders and other workers were not allowed on test runs. She admired the way the ship cut through the large Lake Superior waves.

During her second summer welding, the shipyards switched to making cargo ships for the Merchant Marines, vessels that were large, bulky, and less interesting to build, so Carol decided to work the night shifts so she could take flying lessons during the day. Government contracts slowed as orders were filled, and the shipyards began to lay off workers. Carol wanted to find more work to "be of value to the war effort." Not only was she patriotic; she wanted to support the troops because of her connection to several servicemen who had died, including three high school classmates who had enlisted the day after the Pearl Harbor attack, her sister-in-law's only brother, and a cousin.

Carol admitted that the timing of her decision to leave the shipyards in late summer 1945 was influenced by grotesque beetles she encountered on the night shift. The light from the welder's torch attracted all sorts of bugs, but she hated these two-inch-long, heavily plated insects that looked like they were panting when they walked. She just could not keep welding when she saw them. They could be killed with the slag hammer, which looked like a small, dull ax, but regardless if they were crushed or burned in the arc flame, it was a disgusting sight and sound. Carol knew she wanted to leave before she was laid off; putting in her notice in the early summer ended her contact with the ugly beetles.

Carol joined the "Purple Heart Corps" of the Women's Army Corps as a medic in an army air force hospital. The day she left Minneapolis for basic training at Fort Des Moines in Iowa, Germany surrendered. The WAC recruits continued to help

WOMEN, HAVING PROVED THEIR WORTH AT ZENITH DREDGE SHIPYARD OF DULUTH, WERE SOON HIRED BY THE OTHER SHIPYARDS.

The women welders of Globe SHipbuilding Co.

(ME) Miss CAROL JOHNSON OF Cloquet, MN. FRONT ROW, SIXTH FROM THE RIGHT.
(ME)

Carol Johnson (Fistler) with a crew of women welders at Globe Shipyard, Superior, Wisconsin. *Douglas County Historical Society, Superior, Wisconsin*

with postwar work. Carol subsequently met Captain Raymond Fistler, a veterinarian serving in the army in Italy, and they married.

· · · · ·

Carol was one of two hundred twenty-nine women at the time of peak employment in Globe Company shipyards. These women were among the two thousand workers employed from 1942 to 1945. As Globe Shipyard closed after the government contracts ended, the company posted a notice to other employers stating that it was

> releasing for your employment one of the most able and dependable groups of men and women workers in America. This group includes carpenters, electricians, pipefitters, painters, welders, sheet metal workers, machinists, boiler makers . . . bookkeepers, stenographers. . . . **These men and women have done an outstanding job for Globe and their country during the war.** It is conceded that they have built as good or better ships than were built in any other shipyard in America. It is a matter of record that most of the ships were built in less man-hours at Globe than any other shipyard in America. . . . These men and women have proven individually and collectively that they are able and willing to co-operate with management and each other to expedite the completion of any job assigned to them.

The posting encouraged other employers to hire these workers, including the women. In addition to their strong work ethic, Globe workers also set a US record for buying war bonds. Globe employees topped their goal of $200,000 of war bonds purchased, the first shipyard in the nation to do so. Globe had two thousand employees at the time.

· · · · ·

Northern Minnesota not only built a significant number of the vessels needed for the war effort; it also provided 70 percent of the national ore production during the peak war years. The Iron Range, made up of many mines running across the northeastern region of the state, boomed around the turn of the twentieth century and then declined as the quality of the remaining ore diminished. The region was particularly hard hit economically during the Great Depression in the 1930s. Once the United States was engaged in the war and planes, ships, and tanks needed to be built, mine activity increased. Similar to the shipyards, the mines were willing to hire women to fill jobs, including as miners. According to the St. Louis County inspector of mines, one hundred sixty-three women worked in the mines in 1945 alongside eight thousand men. Although the numbers were not high, the mines reported they could not have done it without the women. Mostly in open-pit mines above ground, women worked on the conveyor belts that crushed the ore, laid railroad track, sampled ore, drove trucks, and performed other jobs.

Mildred "Millie" Mandich, who had four young children, was encouraged by her husband, who worked in the mine, to get a job there when the company started hiring women. She took a job working with the crusher to get better wages, more than double what she was making as a cook at the Cozy Café in Coleraine, a mining town outside of Grand Rapids. Steam shovels dug out the ore, which was loaded into railroad cars that took it to a washhouse four stories high. Conveyor belts carried the rock to crushers and then to railroad cars that would take it to the harbor for transport to steel mills in Cleveland and Pittsburgh. Millie worked the night shift, took care of her children during the day, slept for a few hours, and then went back in to work. Her sister-in-law lived with them and helped with the kids and household work while her husband was in the service.

Childcare was a challenge for many of the women trying to work outside of the home. In most cases, like Millie's, a family member was recruited to help. Another miner, Ann Lendacky, worked in the Scranton mine in 1944, motivated by the good pay. She earned fifty dollars a week, double what most factory workers were paid. She had to quit after a couple of months because her mother was unable to care for her one-year-old daughter. To resolve the day care problem, Ann moved in with her in-laws near Calumet in Itasca County, where she found a job in the washhouse at the Cleveland-Cliffs mine.

At the Scranton mine, Dorothy Ban worked on the track gang, spiking ties with a sledgehammer: "We tamped the ties, we spiked the ties, we did just what the men did ... swung the sledge hammer ... did the job." The women wore men's work clothes and steel-toed shoes. Dorothy ended most days covered with dust from the ore. Zoery Rukavina worked at the Danube mine in Bovey, cleaning up the rocky gravel pieces of ore that fell off the conveyor belt. "You cleaned it all, then you turned around twice and it was full again. You heaved it on the belt, that's all you did, all eight hours."

Most women felt appreciated and respected by the men. Some of the men grumbled, and some of them played tricks on the women such as nailing their lunch pails to a bench. A few of the men seriously pestered the women and lost their jobs because of it. Eleanor "Peggy" Travica worked at the Canisteo mine near Coleraine, where her husband also worked as a heavy machine operator, digging ore out of the pit. The women working on the conveyor belt with her made sure everything was cleaned up at the end of their shifts, all of the ore swept off the floor. They also started cleaning the windows of the washing plant, something the men had not done before. Their supervisor said, "first thing I know, you'll be wanting to put curtains up." But they did not. They had plenty of curtains to take care of at home.

Women track gang workers, Oliver Mining Company. *Lorraine Novak World War Two photographic collection, Minnesota Discovery Center, Chisholm*

In most jobs, the women carried their coffee thermoses and lunch pails with them to the jobsite. They didn't have breaks; they just ate while they worked. Some of the women had coffeepots and hot plates in their work areas. In what little time off they had, the women without children would get together and play cards or go to a local bar and dance to the nickelodeon, often with each other due to the shortage of men.

As the war ended, the women were no longer needed in the mines. According to their own statements in interviews given years later, most of them were happy to return home and glad to have their husbands and boyfriends back from the service. On their last day at the Canisteo mine, their supervisor said, "I'm sorry to lose you. We couldn't have done it without you."

6

ACCOMPANYING GENERAL EISENHOWER AND THE TROOPS INTO AFRICA

The American Red Cross (ARC) commitment to supporting troops during times of war evolved out of Clara Barton's courageous and relentless service to the sick, wounded, and imprisoned during the Civil War, and the organization has provided support in every war the United States has been involved in ever since. In 1882, her persistent advocacy resulted in the establishment of the American organization, chartered by the international Red Cross and adopted, along with the Geneva Convention, by Presidents James A. Garfield and Chester A. Arthur in conjunction with the US Senate committee on foreign relations. As a quasi-government agency commissioned by Congress, the ARC was authorized to administer relief to the sick and wounded in times of war and national disaster, including epidemics, pestilence, and famine.

During World War II, the ARC provided services at home and abroad. More than thirty-six million people supported the ARC with money, blood donations, supplies, and time during the war years. The number of local chapters grew to 3,757 across the county, and chapters in Minnesota were an important part of this national effort. Overseas services included field representatives embedded in army and navy units, blood collection and distribution, hospital work, support for prisoners of war held by the German and Italian forces, and service clubs and canteens.

Throughout the war, ARC workers distributed 1.6 billion donuts, 39 million packages of gum and hard candy, 1.8 billion cigarettes, 12 million pocket-size books of popular titles, as well as razors, decks of playing cards, and harmonicas. They gave these items away through one hundred canteens, three hundred club mobiles, and eight hundred clubs. The canteens were opened on military installations, and club mobiles, sometimes called *rangers*, were two-and-a-half-ton trucks that Red Cross workers, mostly women, drove out to forward camps and other units that could not leave their posts. The clubs were often hotels that the Red Cross converted into places of respite for soldiers to use when on leave. These clubs provided a place to stay, laundry, dining, and recreation including pianos, phonographs, writing tables, sports equipment, and small libraries. Red Cross staff also arranged for tours to see local sights and planned dances and other entertainment.

· · · · ·

Mildred Louise Boie, from Plainview, Minnesota, was one of the Red Cross service club workers who followed the troops in November 1942 when General Dwight D. Eisenhower led Operation Torch into the North African countries of Morocco, Algeria, Tunisia, and Egypt, then under German and Italian control. Like many women who served with the ARC, Louise's path to service overseas was a diversion from her intended career. She and her twin sister, Maurine, were born in 1907 to a bank cashier and homemaker in Plainview, a small farming community in southeastern Minnesota. They both completed bachelor's degrees in education from the University of Minnesota in Mankato and studied English at the graduate level at the University of Minnesota in Minneapolis, but subsequently their lives diverged. Maurine finished master's degrees in social work at the University of Minnesota and Bryn Mawr. Her career followed a more traditional path in education, publication, and counseling. She married and was a homemaker during World War II.

Louise, after graduating with her bachelor's degree, worked for an advertising agency in Minneapolis. The co-owner of the firm, Mr. M. E. Harrison, noted that she had the "natural equipment, the energy, the honesty, and the all-round ability to make a success of any work [she] seriously attempted." After two years, she left that position and, led by her adventurous nature, traveled to Newnham College at Cambridge University to study English literature. She thrived during this experience and wrote for the London *Morning Post* and the *Spectator*. She continued graduate studies at the University of Minnesota, completing her master's degree in English in 1934, and subsequently accepted a fellowship to study creative writing at Radcliffe College. In 1935, she began teaching English at Smith College as an assistant professor, and in 1937, she became the first woman on the editorial staff of the *Atlantic Magazine* as the associate editor for poetry. Her own poetry was being widely published by that time in esteemed periodicals including the *North American Review, Harpers*, and the *Atlantic.* In 1940, she became the editor of the *Christian Register*, the prestigious religious journal published by the Unitarian Church. Her life as a writer and educator was developing nicely, and yet she had her share of challenges, too.

Louise suffered with depression throughout her life. During her years in the Boston area, she began psychoanalysis. She sought to continue her creative work and eventually marry and have a family. She struggled to meet the right man and endured several failed relationships. As the United States became involved in the war, Louise became anxious about the situation and wanted to help. She was interested in pursuing work that would extend beyond the end of the war into the inevitable reconstruction efforts. The Unitarian Church had war relief opportunities, but she preferred a nonreligious organization and considered the Women's Army Auxiliary Corps (WAAC), the United Service Organization (USO), and the Red Cross.

She wrote to her sister that she had "managed to work steadily all week . . . although I still feel coiled in depression as in an octopus' fangs. . . . It's astonishing how Lady in the Dark keeps coming back to me . . . perhaps I am too impatient, and I know I must remember that anyone would feel depressed by death, and by the war." She was grieving the death of her fiancé. Hearing the details of his death made her "recall so vividly the months of [their] engagement, and all the hope and promise that went into them, and then the agonizing months of one disaster and disappointment after another. I wonder if I shall ever succeed in a happy, normal love relation; I think I would ask so little now, if only it could be secure and normal."

By July 1942, Louise wanted to do something adventurous again, recalling her positive experiences overseas at Newnham College. She wanted something more than another office job this time. In a letter to her sister, she admitted that she had "impulses to 'serve' abroad before, and always had to suspect [herself] of a hero, martyr, or adventurous streak," but she had thought seriously about it and sincerely wanted to travel again. Alaska, Africa, and Australia sounded fun to her. She decided against applying to the USO because it was unlikely to continue after the war. The Red Cross pay was good, so she began the application process. In the meantime, she flattened cans for recycling into the war effort and gave blood, which offered her some satisfaction.

Louise Boie (Saunders) helping soldiers arrange sight-seeing tours of Cairo at the American Red Cross serviceman's club in Cairo, Egypt. *Mildred Louise Boie Saunders Papers, Sophia Smith Collection, Smith College, Northampton, Massachusetts*

By fall, Louise was headed to the Red Cross Club in Cairo, one of the most glamorous outposts in the system. The Red Cross Club was established in the Grand Hotel, opening just before Christmas 1942. Louise was involved in arranging for tours to local sites, planning dances, and the logistics of procuring supplies to keep the dining room, laundry facilities, and rooms operating. She found that she was a capable administrator and was soon appointed director of the club in Alexandria. She was gratified to learn that the staff "likes their lady boss very much." She tried to provide "steadiness and trust and appreciation and friendliness." This success was important to her after getting stern feedback from her boss at the *Christian Register*, who once, after a staff meeting, told her she was authoritative and dictatorial. She had these same difficulties when she worked at the *Atlantic*. The Red Cross work gave her the opportunity to develop her management skills.

"How happy I am here," she wrote to her sister, noting that she would probably never find anyplace as comfortable or beautiful as Alexandria. Her enthusiasm might have been fed by the attention she was receiving from men on leave. She noted that she would "miss these good friends and their teasing and friendship. In war it does not pay to get attached—too attached to anyone or any place or anything," but loving someone even for a short time gave "clarity and direction . . . to [her] life, relations with people, [her] work, everything!"

• • • • •

The American Red Cross experienced some criticism for hosting clubs. The Red Cross "girls" were accused of being impudent or snobs if they did not socialize sufficiently with the servicemen. At the same time, they needed to guard against being labeled as whores or broadly considered lesbians, accusations that were also made of women in the branches of the military. Some of the clubs were designated by the military to be only for officers. This was not a Red Cross decision. Also, the Red Cross women were bound by military rules, which considered them at an equivalent rank to commissioned officers, which limited their socializing to officers. Some of this attitude was attributed to men being uncomfortable with women in untraditional roles. Despite these issues, the clubs were quickly seen as valuable. In many areas, especially those that experienced the ravages of war, there were few places for servicemen on leave to relax. Many local venues were considered dives that took advantage of patrons. The Red Cross clubs provided a homelike atmosphere. The army noted that the rate of sexually transmitted infections declined measurably in regions with a Red Cross program.

• • • • •

Louise used her talents as a writer to describe her experiences at the Alexandria club in an article published in the *Ladies' Home Journal* in August 1944. The club had capacity for three hundred servicemen, which could seem like a lot, but Louise saw them as individuals, and many left an indelible impression. One man, Oldanni, arrived at the club after two violent months in Tunisia. He had crushed a finger while trying to keep a soldier from falling off a stretcher during a rough ambulance ride. He talked with Louise about poetry and peace. He described how soldiers could keep clean on one helmet of water a day for drinking, shaving, brushing teeth, washing clothes, and bathing. And mostly, he told her how it was possible to keep love in one's heart despite "mixed rations of violence and destruction, the vast impersonal cruelty of war—your side's as well as the other's."

Most provocatively, the soldier asked, "Louise, what do you think about most of the time?" She was struck with the directness of his question, coming from the "essential, noble human spirit." She felt that the often "unspoken desire of the heart to know another heart, to be reassured, in war, of what is valid and enduring—that comes out." She marveled at how remarkable, "how decent and clean, how hungry for affection and interest, how home-loving and brave and sensitive and how full of mistake—how *human*" the servicemen were. She didn't expect them to stay decent in the indecent business of war. She expected them to drink, swear, fight. She did not expect them to "shave every day, to open the door for a girl, to be concerned for spots on their best uniforms . . . but they do." She found that they revealed their real selves "with startling clarity through the dust and heat and bugs and terror . . . [they hung] on to the things that made" them themselves.

Despite the bravado the men sometimes displayed, they also admitted to Louise that they were scared. They talked about the flying missions, the gunner doing his best, but they also admitted to fears as they fought in a foreign desert and lived in tents five thousand miles from home. And yet, they were courageous and proud: "They are full of pride in their own hard bodies, their fists, themselves." Louise found that while the soldiers liked to drink and act out, they wanted a place like home more, "a clean, attractive place to stay, good food, that will give them pleasure and strength instead of gyppy tummy; girls to talk to, books to read, dances and tours, swimming and sailing parties, table-tennis tournaments; someone to sew on buttons, someone to be folks—home."

The servicemen were not perfect. Some complained about being in Africa for eight months when others had been there for four years. They did not know what it was like to be fighting like the British and French forces, whose families and homes had been bombed. What Louise worried about the most, though, was that their experience would fuel a wave of isolationism. She sensed that the war was making great home lovers of the Americans overseas and that they wanted to go home and "settle down with a wife and kids and a nice little business of [their] own, and never leave the U.S.A." She knew that they would "have to work harder on peace than on war," anticipating the challenges they would face when they returned home.

The Prisoner of War (POW) Program

Blanche Shoquist Erickson's husband, Bernard, landed in North Africa in December 1942, the same time Louise Boie did, as part of Operation Torch. Blanche and Bernard were married the day after Christmas 1941 by a Lutheran minister in the Iron Range town of Eveleth. Bernard was a private with the First Armored Division, Sixteenth Engineer Battalion, an armored tank unit. In February 1943, he was taken prisoner by the Germans in Tunisia and held prisoner at Stalag III-B in Furstenberg, Prussia, a camp that received support from the American Red Cross's Prisoner of War (POW) service.

The POW program may have been one of the lesser-known services despite the important impact it had for the 1.3 million Allied troops held prisoner in Europe and Asia during the war. The American Red Cross employed four hundred people to assist with the collection of funding and the distribution of two hundred tons of food and medical supplies to one hundred fifteen thousand US servicemen. They also facilitated correspondence between the prisoners and their families and assisted with tours of the camps to assure they were in compliance with the Geneva Convention. The food packages contained eleven pounds of carefully planned provisions: corned beef, dried milk, canned salmon, coffee, cheese, tuna, chocolate bars, cigarettes, and soap. The ARC also forwarded Christmas packages, medical supplies, and gardening kits so the prisoners could grow some of their own food.

To keep families apprised of the conditions in prison camps holding a loved one, the ARC started a prisoner of war newsletter sent free of charge to the next of kin of US soldiers held in a camp. Stalag III-B, where Blanche's husband was being held, was described in one of the newsletters. The troops captured during the Tunisian campaign arrived at the camp in need of clothing, which the ARC provided, and the YMCA sent sporting equipment. The camp, located in a pine forest near Berlin, was well organized, and the men formed a choral group and orchestra. They were allowed to send two letters and three postcards a month. The camp was relatively clean, experiencing only a minor outbreak of scarlet fever as of the time the newsletter was published. It also noted the weekly food rations that the prisoners were given, which included five pounds of bread and five pounds of vegetables but only ten ounces of meat. The Red Cross food packages supplemented these German provisions.

With Bernard's encouragement by letter before he was captured, Blanche entered the Women's Army Corps (WAC) in Duluth on December 23, 1943. A graduate of the Virginia, Minnesota, high school, she took some bookkeeping courses at the local community college. She and Bernard began dating in the late 1930s, but due to the Depression, jobs and money were scarce. Bernard worked for the Civilian Conservation Corps, one of President Roosevelt's New Deal work relief programs, which provided jobs clearing trails and building shelters in parks. Blanche worked at Montgomery Ward, a department store, in Virginia. In 1939, she was paid $4.96 for two days of work. Her rent was $4.75 a week. She had enough money to take the streetcar to work, but she walked home in the evenings. In March 1941, Bernard joined the army and was sent to Fort Knox, Kentucky, for training. He was assigned to an armored tank unit in an engineering battalion. Blanche looked for better-paying work in Grand Rapids and Hibbing. Some of the time she cleaned house for her grandmother and for her aunt. They paid her in cigarettes and a little money. At one point, she washed dishes at Canelake's Candy Shop in Hibbing.

Bernard was given a leave in December 1941, before his unit was deployed overseas. He and Blanche were married on December 26, 1941. After he left, Blanche became the air warden in Virginia, Minnesota. She received training and twenty-one dollars a month to lead and participate in air raid drills. Bernard wrote from Northern Ireland in June 1942. Shortly after that, Blanche moved to Tacoma, Washington, and stayed with her mother's relatives. She found work at North Star Glove Manufacturing. By the end of the year, she was working at a Boeing plant; then she and a friend relocated to Twentynine Palms, California, where she worked for Glider Academy, run by the army. Bernard encouraged her to join the WACs so she would have a steady paycheck and not have to move around as often.

On March 12, 1943, Blanche received a telegram that Bernard was "missing." She knew his unit had been in North Africa for several months. She returned to Virginia, Minnesota, and by December, she had a physical at Fort Snelling and was inducted into the WAC in Duluth.

She trained at Fort Des Moines, Iowa, and was transferred to Brooklyn Field, Birmingham Army Air Field, and Wright Field. She volunteered to go overseas, but her request was denied because her husband was a prisoner of war. She and Bernard wrote regularly, and she checked the Red Cross updates.

Unfortunately, despite the Geneva Convention guidelines and Red Cross involvement, the last letter the family received from Bernard was dated January 14, 1945. He was presumed dead a year later. Blanche remained in the WAC until the end of that year.

Hospital Services

In addition to the service clubs and prisoner of war support, the ARC was present in twenty-five hundred hospitals stateside and overseas; its employees provided nursing care, surgical dressings, dietary expertise, and recreational activities. They also offered four thousand personnel in the early years of the war before the military was able to recruit sufficient lab techs, pharmacists, nurses, dietitians, and occupational and physical therapists. Over the seven-year period of the war, chapters across the country collected, processed, and distributed more than 5,000 lifesaving pints of blood a day, totaling 13.3 million donated by 6.6 million donors.

The largest ARC chapters in Minnesota, Hennepin County and St. Paul, collected 407,000 pints of blood.

Numerous leaders in the army and navy, including General Eisenhower, expressed profound appreciation to the Red Cross and to the American people, acknowledging that US casualties would have been considerably higher without this support.

· · · · ·

Prudence Burns was one of the army nurses who administered blood during the war. Originally from Kansas City, Missouri, she came to the University of Minnesota to obtain her bachelor's degree and a certificate in public health. In 1942, the military was scrambling to hire enough nurses. During the expanded recruitment program, Eleanor Roosevelt put pressure on the army to hire African American nurses. As a part of this initiative, Prudence was asked to help recruit nurses for the army, and she soon put her studies on hold and recruited herself.

Prudence was initially assigned to Fort Huachuca in Arizona and then became a part of Hospital Station 268 in New Guinea. She worked there for fourteen months, but as a black nurse, she could only care for black soldiers. Once, however, a white soldier who was hemorrhaging badly was brought to her. She told him there was only "A" labeled blood, which meant it was African American blood. Type A blood was only supposed to be administered to African Americans. The soldier said, "I don't give a damn; don't let me die."

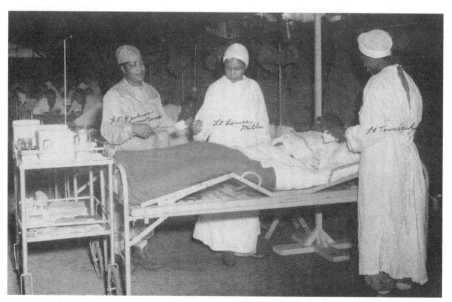

Prudence Burns (Burrell) (left) at Milne Bay, New Guinea, 1943. *From* Hathaway *by Prudence Burns Burrell (Detroit, MI: Harlo Press, 1997)*

The American Red Cross felt caught in this racial controversy about the blood it collected and distributed. Initially, the Red Cross and the military only collected blood from white donors. They politely thanked black people offering to donate blood but did not accept it until various organizations complained, the Quakers being among the most vocal. The policy was changed to accept blood from black donors but to only give it to black patients. The Quakers and others still protested. The Red Cross president responded by claiming the organization was not in the job of trying to "settle racial controversies or to take side in such controversies." He stated that the "Red Cross has no 'social theories,'" implied that the organization was trying to fulfill the service asked of it by the army, and he suggested that in a democracy it needed to follow what the majority wanted for a policy on the collection and distribution of blood, even if doing so meant discrimination against black citizens.

The army units were segregated as well. Hospital 268, where Prudence was assigned, was all black, staff and patients. The army infantry units in New Guinea were also segregated: the Ninety-Second Unit was white and the Ninety-Third was black. As Prudence continued her service as a first lieutenant with Hospital 268 in New Guinea, the unit was relocated to the Philippines as troops prepared to invade Japan under General Douglas MacArthur. President Harry S. Truman's decision to drop the atomic bomb on Japan changed that plan. It also changed an order already submitted to promote Prudence and others to the rank of captain. For some reason, President Truman rescinded the promotion order.

In October 1945, as she was preparing to return home after the war, Prudence married Lieutenant Lowell Burrell, whom she met while they were both stationed in New Guinea. A Red Cross nurse in Prudence's unit designed a dress for her, and a local woman made it out of a parachute. Prudence and her new husband both sent money home to his mother in Detroit so she could buy a house for them. A few years later, Prudence resumed her studies at the University of Minnesota, where in 1951 she became the first black person to graduate with a bachelor's degree in public health. She returned to Detroit, where she worked in the public schools and for the State of Michigan.

7

FIGHTER PLANES: WOMEN WHO FLEW THEM AND BUILT THEM

Flying Planes

"The use of women pilots serves no military purpose in a country" that has sufficient "manpower," according to General H. H. Arnold in 1941. He was also doubtful
that "a slip of a young girl could fight the controls of a B-17 in the heavy weather
they would naturally encounter." Further, housing and feeding women pilots
presented a "difficult situation." General Arnold was responding to Jacqueline
Cochran's proposal to establish an army organization of women pilots who could
ferry planes to where they were needed. At the time, two thousand women were
licensed pilots in the United States, and women in England and the Soviet Union
were already flying successfully to support the war effort.

· · · · ·

In 1937 when Amelia Earhart disappeared during her attempt to fly around the
world, Jacqueline Cochran was breaking multiple flying speed records. After a successful career as a beautician at Saks Fifth Avenue in New York, Jacqueline decided
to get her pilot's license and take the equivalent of the US Navy flight instructor
course. Even after marrying a wealthy businessman and starting her own cosmetic
company, Jacqueline, who spent most of her childhood in foster homes in Florida
and Georgia, never forgot the poverty of her childhood. She bought a building in
a low-income neighborhood and started a model orphanage. But flying was her
passion, and she began competing, often at events with Earhart.

Jacqueline did not give up when General Arnold initially rejected her proposal
to include women pilots in the war effort. Other women were also advocating,
including Eleanor Roosevelt. Finally, in 1942, when the military branches realized
they would not have enough staff without the women, the Women's Army Auxiliary Corps (WAAC) was formed and the Women's Auxiliary Ferrying Squadron
(WAFS) and Women's Flying Training Detachment (WFTD) were separately organized. On September 15, 1942, Eleanor Roosevelt wrote in her "My Day" newspaper
column that "women pilots were a weapon waiting to be used." The women would
ferry planes and serve as instructors for male pilots. In 1943, they were reorganized
into one unit, Women Airforce Service Pilots (WASP). Jacqueline was appointed
director of women pilots.

Training had been taking place at multiple airfields but began to concentrate at Howard Hughes Field in Houston. Competition for runways and other resources became challenging. Ultimately, Avenger Field in Sweetwater, Texas, became the training base for the WASPs and the only all-women air base. More than twenty-five thousand women applied to become a pilot in the army; 1,830 were accepted into the training program, and 1,074 graduated. Fifteen of those women were from Minnesota.

The WASP six-month training included not only rigorous flight instruction but also four hundred hours of aeronautics coursework: physics, aerodynamics, electronics and instruments, engine operations and maintenance, meteorology, navigation, military and civilian air regulations, and mathematics. During training, the women adjusted to wearing hand-me-down uniforms from the men that did not fit well. Sometimes they needed to wear extra socks in their boots to snug them up and had pillows on the seats in the planes so they could reach the pedals. They fondly called their overalls "zoot suits," after the wide-legged pants and long coats that were popular in the 1940s. Their base bus was another ill-fitting aspect of their training: a cattle truck was provided for transportation into town.

The women chose Fifinella, a female gremlin with blue wings wearing a red dress and red boots, gold tights, a gold helmet, and blue goggles, as their mascot, based on a character from Roald Dahl's book *Gremlins*, a fairy tale about the hazards of combat flying. Walt Disney Company gave the WASPs permission to use the design it had created for a potential film based on the book. They proudly wore Fifinella on a patch, and she adorned the front gate of Avenger Field.

After receiving their silver wings, the WASPs "flew nearly every type of airplane used by the AAF [army air force], from the small primary trainer to the Superfortress (B-29), including the Mustang, Thunderbolt, B-17, B-26, and C-54." They ferried planes, towed targets for combat practice, taught male pilots basics and instruments, and test-flew new and repaired planes, among other flying assignments.

· · · · ·

When Betty Wall from Faribault, Minnesota, finished her training at Avenger and earned her silver wings, she and seven other WASPs were sent to Las Vegas Army Airfield in February 1944. One of Betty's first assignments was flying B-26 bombers towing long muslin sleeves to give gunners on the ground and in the air practice with live ammunition. She also dived in at the bombers, and the crew would shoot at her with camera guns. She found it unnerving to participate when crew members reviewed the film to see if they had hit her; she imagined that they "shot her out of the air." Just flying the B-26 was an accomplishment given that its nickname was "The Widow Maker" because of its short wing span, which resulted in a high accident rate. Once Betty flew an AT-6 and dove in on gunners on the ground only fifty feet overhead, causing them to hit the deck. She had misread the instructions calling for her to stay five hundred feet above, not fifty.

After a few months, Betty took some additional training and became an instructor. If a male pilot seemed reluctant to fly with her, she would take him up to three thousand feet and then put the plane through every maneuver she knew, testing its limits. When they landed, the pilots tended to be convinced they could learn from her.

Betty Wall was born in 1919, the fifth of six children. By the time of her birth, her father had sold the family's farmland and moved into the town of Faribault. The family lost their savings in the 1929 stock market crash. The proceeds from the farm bought their house in town, but it did not pay for much more. They lived off of their "glorious" vegetable garden, which filled their root cellar, and they kept some chickens. Betty remembered her mother's home-baked bread and donuts. She did not realize until later, as an adult, that her family might have been considered poor.

After graduating from Faribault High School in 1937, Betty went to work in the deeds office at the Rice County Courthouse. She had a bicycle for transportation and was making good money to help her family. A member of the local flying club came into the courthouse regularly and once offered Betty a ride in his sixty-five-horsepower Piper Cub plane. They went to three thousand feet and then the pilot intentionally cut the engine, went into a spin, and spiraled down until he leveled out the plane.

From that ride on, Betty was hooked on flying. When the war began, opportunities to fly were reduced due to gasoline rationing, but Betty and three of her sisters joined the local Civil Air Patrol (CAP) so they could continue to ride. When one of the CAP members enlisted in the Army Air Corps, there was an opening in the local sky club. He offered it to Betty, but it cost one hundred dollars, which she did not have. Not to be dissuaded, Betty rode her bike to the bank and asked the president for a loan. He told her women do not fly. Betty said, "Well, this one is going to." He explained that she would need collateral for a loan. Betty eagerly offered her bike, which the bank president accepted without smiling. Later, Betty learned that the bank president had actually cosigned the loan so she would qualify.

Shortly after she joined the sky club, Betty saw a notice on the bulletin board announcing that the military was recruiting women who had either a pilot's license or thirty-five hours of flight time. Betty quickly put in her thirty-five hours and, along with her sister Mary and another friend, headed to Avenger Field in Sweetwater, Texas, to begin WASP training and service.

Another Betty, Betty Jane (B. J.) Hanson, fell in love with flying when she watched the barnstormer Rufus Rand fly into her hometown, Monticello, Minnesota, when she was a child. She was too shy to ask for a ride, but after the pilot had shut down for the day, B. J. climbed up into the old "War Jenny." When she looked

Betty Wall, Women Airforce Service Pilot (WASP), ca. 1940s. *Courtesy National WASP WWII Museum*

inside the plane, she told herself she was going to fly a plane like that someday. After high school, she asked her father if she could take a flying lesson. He said, "sure," but her mother said, "I got a big investment in you and I didn't bring you up just so you could go out and kill yourself in an airplane." Her father prevailed, and B. J. took one flying lesson in nearby Benson, which solidified her desire "to be a pilot and a doctor."

B. J. learned that the quickest way to become a pilot was through the newly formed Civil Aeronautics Administration (CAA), later known as the Federal Aviation Administration. The university in North Dakota at Grand Forks would not allow first-year students into the civilian pilot training program, so she transferred to the West Central Branch of the University of Minnesota, later known as the Morris campus. She was the only woman in her class in the ground school and only the second woman to enter the program. B. J. did well enough to earn a scholarship for flying school. She began flight school in June 1941, with the plan to return to Grand Forks when she was done so she could be a part of defending the United States through the CAA and continue her premed coursework. Her first solo flight was in a Piper Cub going from the Morris airport to Willmar, then Willmar to Marshall, and then back to Morris. Although she made a perfect landing, two cars quickly drove out onto the runway and several men "grabbed a hold of the wings to hold them down." A windstorm was moving into the area, and just before she landed, one plane had "cracked up" before they could get it to the hangar. When they found out B. J. was a student pilot just completing her first solo, she was invited to join the 99s, a group of ninety-nine women pilots in the area.

B. J. entered WASP in 1943 with her private pilot license, and after completing the training at Avenger Field and obtaining her commercial license, she was assigned to the ferrying division of the air transport command at New Castle Army Air Base, Wilmington, Delaware. She ferried planes from factory to embarkation points and sometimes retired planes to the aircraft graveyard in Brownsville, Texas. She flew BT-13s, L4–4s, PT-17s, AT-6s, AT-10s, and UC-78s. Toward the end of the war, she was transferred into the engineering test-flying unit. When a plane was damaged, a wing cracked, for example, and the plane was rebuilt, B. J. would take it for a test flight to assure it was sound.

Once, when B. J. picked up an AT-6 at Hensley Field in Texas, she found that she did not have any brakes when she landed. She went down the runway with no way to stop. The tower kept calling to her on the radio, but she could not pick up because she was too busy with the stick. She found that the wrong fluid was in the lining and the wobble pump was put in backward. She had noticed fluid leaking before takeoff, and the male mechanic had "fixed" it. The tampering was considered harassment, and B. J. was not the only woman whose equipment mysteriously malfunctioned. The incidents were investigated but not resolved. The WASPs were warned to "watch for any suspicious items" and to check their planes carefully themselves. Tolerating the actions of a few men who resented their presence was probably the best strategy for the WASPs. Raising the issues further might have backfired and resulted in more problems.

In late 1944, three weeks after D-Day, General Arnold ended the WASP training program. Congress had voted against bringing WASP into the army air force. The program at Avenger Field closed in December. The WASPs had civilian status, rather than military, which meant they were not compensated at military rates, they were not awarded veterans benefits, and their next of kin received no benefit for the thirty-eight who died in service. The WASPs, who flew sixty million miles during their tenure, maintained records for safety and endurance that were comparable to, if not better than, those of their male counterparts.

· · · · ·

One of the highest-rated WASPs was Virginia "Ginny" Mae Hope, the only child of Robert and Addaline Hope, farmers in the small town of Winnebago in south-central Minnesota. She loved helping with the harvest and life on the farm, but the Depression meant it was a tough place to make a living. After graduating from high school in the nearby town of Faribault, she became a student at Northwestern

University, where she enrolled in the civilian pilot training program. After getting her private and commercial pilot licenses in 1941, she went to work as an assistant airway traffic controller with the Civil Aeronautics Administration at a Minneapolis airport when she was twenty years old.

After graduating with a degree in commerce, Ginny joined the WASPs in May 1943 and completed her training at Avenger Field. She received "excellent" ratings in all categories: mechanical skill, accuracy of judgment, ability to organize "his" work, physical fitness, and cooperativeness. Her flying ratings were equally excellent. After a year of ferrying army air force weather service personnel on military missions across the country, Ginny received notice that the WASPs would be decommissioned. Based on her exemplary record, Major Eugene C. Parkerson, operations officer at Patterson Field, wrote a letter of recommendation for her stating that she "possesses an excellent temperament, unusual pilot instinct, and . . . her work in instrument flying has been exceptionally highly meritorious. . . . This officer recommends Miss Hope for any position involving aircraft piloting."

Hoping to continue her career as a pilot, Ginny took a job with a private company moving decommissioned planes for salvage. On December 7, 1944, she died as a passenger in a plane along with several other pilots when they crashed in Omaha, Nebraska. Very few of the WASPs were able to continue flying professionally.

Virginia Hope, Women Airforce Service Pilot (WASP). *MNHS Collections*

Building Planes

Kae Eisenreich enrolled in an inspection course while she was working at J.C. Penney's department store. She had graduated from high school in St. Cloud, Minnesota, and turned down a scholarship at the College of St. Benedict because her family could not afford room and board. Instead, she went to business college, taking courses in shorthand, bookkeeping, accounting, and typing. Although her job at J. C. Penney's paid more than her friend's job at a law office, Kae was eager to do even better. After completing the inspection class, she was hired by Char-Gale, a sheet metal and furnace company that had recently opened in St. Cloud. After the attack on Pearl Harbor, the company began manufacturing fuselages under a government contract. Kae tripled her salary when she started at Char-Gale.

In 1943, Kae moved to Minneapolis, following two friends who were working at Honeywell. They rented a small efficiency apartment with a pull-down bed and took turns sleeping on the bed and the davenport. Kae got a job at the airport near downtown St. Paul inspecting for Northwest Aeronautics, which had a contract to build gliders for the army. They built forty-eight-foot-long CG-4 gliders with wingspans of eighty-four feet. This unique aircraft could carry thirteen soldiers or a combination of troops, a jeep, or a 37mm anti-tank gun. The gliders were towed by

Women training to work at Northwest Aeronautics. *Courtesy Northwest Airlines via the Northwest Airlines History Center, Bloomington, Minnesota*

other aircraft to near the destination and then released so they could glide quietly into an area and the troops and equipment could land in closer proximity to their target than if they had parachuted in.

Northwest Aeronautics had to start up quickly to meet the army needs for gliders. The company used subcontractors and hired workers with little to no experience in manufacturing. Employees came from a wide range of previous occupations: writer, orchestra leader, chiropractor, violin maker, bond salesman, music teacher, band president, palm reader, coffin maker, and cabinetmaker. Kae was the first "girl inspector." She reviewed blueprints and used a micrometer and other instruments in inspecting holes in wing straps in relation to the center line and other specifications.

· · · · ·

In 1943, the same year that Kae was working at Northwest Aeronautics, Millie Bowers Johnson began work at the nearby Northwest Airlines Modification Center. Millie was born in Belle Creek, Minnesota, in Goodhue County, but when her father left, her mother moved the family, including Millie and her two younger brothers, to Faribault so they could be near Millie's grandmother. After graduating from high school, Millie wanted to go to art or beauty school, but there was not the money for that. Instead she took a first aid class and assisted the school nurse, checking on children and administering Mantoux tests for tuberculosis. Her mother was distraught by the news of the attack on Pearl Harbor because Millie's brothers were seventeen and nineteen years old. The whole town was concerned as men starting leaving for the military.

Millie and three other young women signed up for an architectural drawing class, hoping to become riveters. The classes were offered in Austin, seventy miles south of Faribault. They were given lodging in the Grand Hotel, and the classes were held during the day in the high school with lunch provided. The local paper noted that thirty women wearing slacks were being trained locally to help the US government "keep pace with its vast airplane production goal." The program was sponsored by the War Manpower Commission, which worked in collaboration with the United States Employment Service. The free training was offered in public schools in twenty-seven cities. Seventy courses were provided for war production industry jobs such as aviation mechanics, machine shop, radio communication, and welding.

After graduating from one of the courses, students found good-paying jobs almost immediately in St. Paul, Seattle, and San Diego. Men and women who had been barbers, plasterers, beauticians, retail sales clerks, garage mechanics, stenographers, and filling station attendants were looking for better jobs and better pay. One of the male course instructors who initially had his doubts about women workers found that "in technical work and accuracy they are positively the equal of men."

The women were free in the evenings, and Millie and her friends frequented a nearby ballroom to hear big band music. One of the girls decided she did not like drawing; she took a job in Austin with Hormel, where she stayed for thirty years.

When they completed the course, which lasted two months, Millie and her friend, Corky, went to Minneapolis. Millie was "petrified" and would not have gone up to the "Cities"—Minneapolis and St. Paul—alone. Corky, who lived in Northfield, told Millie to get on the bus in Faribault. She would join her in Northfield and they would ride to the Cities together. Millie was willing to follow her friend, but if Corky had not gotten on the bus in Northfield, Millie would not have gone on alone.

The women stayed with Corky's aunt and her two little girls in Minneapolis off of Lake Street. The aunt's husband was working in Alaska; she was glad to have company, so Millie and Corky lived there for free in exchange for a little help around the house. They took the streetcar to Holman Field, where Northwest Airlines, which employed 881 workers nationwide before the war, had grown to a workforce of thirty-six hundred by fall of 1942 and projected needs as high as ten thousand employees. Northwest initially hesitated to hire women because doing so involved adding separate restrooms, buying smaller coveralls, and adjusting sick-leave policies. Unions presented a barrier as well, initially resisting to enroll women.

Eventually, Northwest Airlines hired many women at the modification center. The company also hired fifteen blind employees and Asian workers. One man wore a button that stated "I am Chinese" to prevent people from thinking he was Japanese.

The airline converted a maintenance facility it owned at Holman Field into a top-secret center where workers modified B-24 Liberator bombers. After President Roosevelt's call for private industry to become an "arsenal of democracy" during his fireside chat on December 29, 1940, Ford automobile plants began producing airplanes. The Ford plants and other facilities producing aircraft were able to maintain high production levels if they did not attempt to customize the planes. Bombers were customized to allow for better performance in certain climates and to add specialized equipment. B-24s from Ford's Willow Run plant near Ypsilanti, Michigan, were flown to Northwest Airlines Modification to add photo-reconnaissance, fuel transport, anti-shipping equipment, and the top-secret H2X radar system. The facility was highly secured, and employees were not allowed to talk about their jobs.

Millie enjoyed life in the big city and her work. She was assigned to a team of six people. The crew boss was always a man. They worked three different shifts in two-week rotations: 8 AM to 4 PM, 4 PM to midnight, midnight to 8 AM. Millie placed rivets according to the drawings. She had to be nimble. Her team typically worked on gun turrets for B-2s. She made fifty dollars a week, which was good pay. Her work was interrupted when she had surgery for an appendectomy and had to return home to recover for a few weeks. During downtime, Millie and her friends went to movies and the Prom Ballroom, where they heard big bands and the Andrews Sisters. Millie loved the Andrews Sisters. She worked at Northwest Airlines for a year.

· · · · ·

Ferne Chambers came to the Twin Cities to work as well. She was an accomplished riveter at DePonti Aviation Company, a contractor for Northwestern Aeronautical. Ferne riveted glider torque tubes, which need to be exactly alike because they lift the ailerons, the edges of wings.

DePonti Aviation Company was located at Wold-Chamberlain Field, later known as the Minneapolis–St. Paul International Airport. Northwestern Aeronautical contracted with DePonti Aviation Company for welded fuselages and tail surfaces for the Waco CG-4A gliders. Villaume Box Company, another Twin Cities business, provided wooden wings and rudders.

Born to Canadian parents in Minot, North Dakota, Ferne moved to the Twin Cities for a job and to go to school. She had graduated from high school and attended the teachers' college in Minot, taking all of the art courses available, but due to the Depression she could not find employment. So she moved to Minneapolis, got a job at Woolworth's in downtown St. Paul, and took classes at a commercial art school two nights a week. When the United States entered the war, she got work at DePonti Aviation riveting fuselages.

Ferne and another woman were a two-person team riveting torque tubes until the woman left. She was replaced by a man who was ineligible for military service because he had a punctured eardrum. Ferne taught him how to rivet the sections. On payday she learned that he was being paid more than she was. She thought this policy was unfair. He claimed he should be paid more because he had a wife and he was a man. Further, he suggested that if she thought she was so smart, she should join the army. She said she would not join the army; if she did anything, she would join the "lady Marines." On her way home near the university, driving in her old Chevrolet, she stopped at the marine recruiting office, and within a week she was a "lady Marine."

The marines were the last branch of the military to recruit women. The Marine Corps began accepting women in November 1942 and gave them comparable rank to men. They were not given "cute nicknames." General Thomas Holcomb said, "They don't have a nickname and they don't need one. They get their basic training in a Marine atmosphere at a Marine post. They inherit the traditions of the Marines. They are Marines." They were called the Marine Corps Women's

Reserve (MCWR). To be accepted, a woman could not be married to a marine or have children under the age of eighteen. She had to be at least sixty inches tall and weigh at least ninety pounds. Black women were not barred, but they were not actively recruited. Some men treated them poorly, making obscene remarks, but this behavior was not tolerated overall. Initially, the marines made miscalculations in staffing, thinking it would take two women to replace every man. The leadership quickly learned that the women were capable and efficient. At the start, women were assigned to traditional roles as office workers and in food and housekeeping, but they also broke ground as radio operators, gunnery instructors, mechanics, and chemists. Eighteen thousand women ultimately filled 85 percent of the enlisted jobs, and they covered one-half to two-thirds of the permanent personnel at major marine posts.

· · · · ·

Ferne's basic training for the marines took place at Camp Lejeune, North Carolina, where she and other recruits got up at the "crack of dawn" and marched, marched, and marched. They were tested to determine their assignment. Ferne was enrolled in a celestial navigation course. She quickly felt she was in over her head. Some of the other women were teaching mathematics at the college level. She asked to be transferred to DoALL machine training, which was back in Minneapolis. The DoALL company made industrial saws, and during the war, they ran a school. When Ferne completed the training, her boyfriend from Crosby, a submarine sailor, came to Minneapolis on leave, and they were married. After a week together, she got on the train for California and he left for assignment in New London, Connecticut.

Ferne was assigned to the Aviation Women's Reserve Squadron 3 station at the Marine Corps Air Station El Toro in El Centro, California. Ferne quickly learned that El Centro, located ten miles from the Mexican border, is in the Sonoran Desert and is very hot during the day. Squadrons of fliers arrived to train at night when it was cooler. They would stay for three or four months and then depart.

Four hundred marine women reservists were on the base, along with twenty women from the navy. Women on the base were truck drivers, bookkeepers, stenographers, librarians, photographers, supply and mail clerks, parachute packers, and gunnery instructors.

The climate was conducive to crickets. One of the women marines wrote a poem about the conditions and sent it to Walt Disney Studios requesting a logo. Disney complied. A cricket-like logo was created for the women marines of Aviation Squadron 3. On weekends they often went to Palm Springs to swim and have dinner. Sometimes they would cross the border into Mexico for inexpensive steak dinners. Overall the food was good because so much fruit was grown in California. Ferne appreciated the fresh cantaloupe and watermelon.

Ferne was assigned in a shop operating the DoALL saws, but the men who had been there before she arrived were faster on the machines than she was. Another position opened up in the battery shop, but Ferne barely knew what a battery looked like. The shop was in the back of a large hangar where propellers were repaired. The captain explained that the sergeant who had been responsible for the shop was leaving and he was putting her in charge. He handed her an army manual explaining how to charge batteries. The chargers were about two feet square and could charge two airplane batteries at a time. The captain showed her how to hook them up—positive to positive and negative to negative—and warned her not to let the battery acid drip on her clothes because it would eat right through the material.

For the next two years, Ferne charged batteries. The acid did drip on her uniforms. She was given boondockers, a durable military boot. Every month she was given new clothes "because a lady Marine cannot wear clothes with holes in them." She got tired of sewing new stripes on her jackets every time she was given a new one, so she started using red fingernail polish to paint them on. Pilots would come in and ask for the sergeant in charge, and Ferne would reply that she was not a sergeant but she was in charge. They would say, "A girl in charge of a battery shop?" It was a bit disconcerting for some of the marines to encounter a woman with stripes painted on her jacket running the battery shop. She took good care of the batteries and logged them in. The men made a small desk for her and gave her a radio, one they had taken out of a plane no longer used. Months later she heard the announcement of President Roosevelt's death on this little radio.

Another woman from Minnesota, Martha Kushner from the Frogtown neighborhood of St. Paul, had followed a path similar to Ferne's. Martha worked at Montgomery Ward until she found better-paying work at Northwestern Airlines building gliders. Her job was to glue the fabric on the frame of the plane. After a while, she tired of the three shifts. She and a friend decided to become Navy WAVEs (Women Accepted for Volunteer Emergency Service), but the recruiter was out to lunch when they arrived. The marine recruiter was in his office, so they joined the marines. After training at Camp Lejeune, Martha was sent to Marine Corps Air Station El Toro and assigned to drive buses on the base as well as cars for officers.

· · · · ·

Ruth Johnson became an officer in the marines. She grew up in Lake City, Minnesota, where her mother raised three children as a housekeeper after she was widowed. Ruth was valedictorian of her high school class in 1934. She went on to graduate from the University of Minnesota and taught high school in Preston for three years. When the war broke out, Ruth thought that it was her "patriotic duty to enlist." After officers' candidate school, she became the executive officer of the women's marine battalion at Camp Matthews in La Jolla, California.

A group of gunnery sergeants challenged Ruth to qualify as an expert with the M1 Garand rifle, probably in jest. They showed her how to shoot it since she had not been trained to use a gun. Ruth successfully hit the target several times. Impressed, they handed her a .45 automatic pistol. She scored over 90 percent with the rifle and 96 percent with the pistol and became the first woman in the history of the marines to qualify as expert with two weapons. After the war, she married a fellow student from the University of Minnesota who had served in the army. Their wedding regrettably coincided with President Roosevelt's death, April 12, 1945.

. . . . .

Patty Berg was probably the most famous woman from Minnesota to join the marines. She was raised in Minneapolis; her father was a grain dealer and a member of the Chicago Board of Trade. In an attempt to dissuade her from pursuing football, which she enjoyed playing with boys from her neighborhood, including Bud Wilkinson, who went on to coach at the University of Oklahoma, her parents encouraged her to try golf. Three years later, at age sixteen, she was the Minneapolis women's golf champion, and the following year she won the 1935 Women's Amateur championship. She went on to play with the University of Minnesota golf team, which won the Curtis Cup against the British. She turned professional in 1940 after winning twenty-nine amateur contests. There was no professional women's golf circuit at the time, so she played exhibition matches and gave clinics for Wilson Sporting Goods, which created a "Patty Berg" set of clubs.

In 1941, Patty was in a car accident that severely injured her knee. Unable to golf for an extended time, she enlisted in the marines. In 1942, she was commissioned as a lieutenant and assigned to be a procurement officer with the eastern procurement division in Philadelphia. Patty dedicated much of her time using her celebrity status to recruit women. After serving, she returned to a successful golf career, winning the Women's Open in 1946.

8

SEMPER PARATUS, ALWAYS READY

Natalie Peake Blanch, an Ojibwe woman from White Earth, began working as a machine operator at the Twin Cities Ordnance Plant in February 1943, after her husband entered the military. She earned much more money from employment at the plant than she received working for the Work Projects Administration (WPA) as a writer and librarian, and yet she was able to continue her passion for writing in her off-hours. The well-known activist and writer Meridel Le Sueur was Natalie's mentor, encouraging her writing and involvement in activist groups. Natalie met Meridel when she was a reporter covering the 1934 Truckers' Strike in Minneapolis. This small truckers' organization changed the economic history of Minneapolis when it maintained a six-month strike that resulted in its recognition as a union, breaking the city's nonunion status. Natalie's income from her factory work plus the military family allotment from her husband's service allowed her to provide for her mother and young daughter.

Natalie's younger sister, Emily, shared their small apartment in Minneapolis. Emily had also left a WPA job, working at the Minneapolis Public Library. She found a better-paying job assembling parachutes at Honeywell Corporation. Emily was called a "whiz" by friends in high school, where she took the commercial course, including typing, shorthand, and accounting. She also took two years of French. She wanted to attend the University of Minnesota but needed to get a job after graduation from Central High School to help support her mother and niece. Her real dream had been to study dance at MacPhail School of Music and Dramatic Art, but that pursuit was not feasible for financial reasons. Once Emily had the job at Honeywell, she was able to afford evening classes at the university.

The third woman in their household, Natalie and Emily's mother, Louise Peake, known as Amie, was committed to nurturing the Native American community in the Twin Cities. She started the Na-gu-aub (Rainbow) Club in 1943 to help young Ojibwe women who were coming to the Twin Cities looking for war production jobs. The women met every Saturday at the Peakes' home, sharing their frustrations, fears, and ambitions, supporting each other over tea and homemade cookies as the war continued. In her modest and small apartment, Amie also took in Ojibwe people who needed a place to stay.

· · · · ·

Emily Peake, 1940. *MNHS Collections*

Natalie's employment at the Twin Cities Ordnance Plant triggered a background check. The FBI investigated her membership in the Young Communist League and her role as a librarian at the Minneapolis Labor School, which had a reputation for employing Communists and followers of Leon Trotsky. On June 14, 1943, under the signature of John Edgar Hoover, director of the FBI, an order was issued to detain Natalie.

Natalie may have sensed there was a problem. She suddenly gathered her poems and essays, packed a small bag, and left. Several days later, Amie received a call from Wauwatosa State Hospital notifying her that Natalie had been admitted to the facility. The Milwaukee police found her "dazed and disheveled." Emily took the train and brought her sister to Minnesota State Hospital in Anoka, where she was admitted with a diagnosis of schizophrenia. She was soon transferred to Rochester State Hospital, where their father, who had suffered similar symptoms, had been admitted a decade earlier after attempting suicide.

. . . . .

With her sister being cared for, Emily wanted to move on with her life. Influenced by the patriotic spirit around her, when the recruiters came to town, she decided to join the women's reserve of the US Coast Guard Reserve called *Semper Paratus, Always Ready* (SPARS), based on the coast guard motto. This reserve organization was the only option for women wishing to serve in the coast guard. Although it was the smallest branch of the armed services, eleven thousand women enlisted in the SPARS during the war years, and they served in a wide range of positions. The most untraditional roles were parachute rigger, radioman, coxswain, gunner's mate, musician, photographer, radarman, quartermaster, and chaplain's assistant.

In September 1944, Emily began training at the Biltmore in Palm Beach, Florida. As a *bootie*, a shipboard beginner, she had mess duty in addition to attending classes on coast guard history and terminology, Red Cross instruction, and swimming lessons. Her unit also made excursions to the ocean to swim and collect seashells. In some ways, these first days in the coast guard seemed like summer camp. She advanced to being a *boots*, seaman first class. For a woman who could only afford inexpensive clothing, the leather two-inch heel shoes, terrycloth robe, and pink pajamas she was issued were luxurious. She continued on to advanced yeoman school and succeeded at all of the classes, leading to her promotion to yeoman. She was then assigned to work in the captain of the port's office in New Orleans, Louisiana.

Emily found acceptance and success in her SPARS job. She fit into the more racially diverse New Orleans region, often being mistaken for white. Being able to pass as a white person and the notice she received wearing her uniform caused Emily to feel more respected than she ever had in the past. She was at ease working with the coast guard ship and sailor records. She had enough time in the evenings to take a zoology class at Tulane University and a ballet class, which allowed her to continue with her passion for dancing.

· · · · ·

While Emily was away, her mother, Amie, continued building community in Minneapolis. She nurtured the Na-gu-aub Club, got involved with the League of Women Voters, and took care of Natalie's growing daughter. Emily was discharged in November 1945, and she quickly enrolled and began taking classes at the University of Minnesota on the GI Bill, which would lead to completion of a degree and substantially better employment opportunities than she had held in Minneapolis in the past. Her service in the SPARS gave her background and experience that she would utilize to make significant contributions to her community.

Emily completed her bachelor of arts degree in psychology from the University of Minnesota with the financial assistance provided by the GI Bill. She was hired by General Mills and worked as a secretary in the advertising department. Her salary supported her mother, her niece, and herself. Her sister, Natalie, was still a patient at Rochester State Hospital, but one of the stories she wrote before being hospitalized, "Ollie," was published in *New Masses*, a well-known leftist literary magazine. Emily, Amie, and Jackie, Natalie's daughter, appreciated Natalie's presence and legacy through the publication of that story. The three of them also began to spend more time at White Earth, which allowed Emily and Jackie to pursue a deeper understanding of their Ojibwe culture.

In addition to her job at General Mills, Emily began sharing her passion for dancing by teaching children. She gave lessons at the Elliot Park Neighborhood House, a community center that drew children of many ages and races. Emily found ways to get tap shoes and ballet slippers for the children.

Through her work at General Mills, Emily met a French woman who helped her improve her language skills. Through the woman's family, Emily was invited to live in Paris to study abnormal psychology at the Sorbonne, her interest in the field undoubtedly inspired by her father's and sister's mental illnesses. After studying in Paris, in 1951, Emily went to Vienna to learn German. She worked as a secretary for the US State Department supporting the Four Power Council, the entity comprised of the United States, the United Kingdom, France, and the Soviet Union—the occupying forces of Germany.

Fluent in German, French, and English and accomplished in office skills, Emily earned ever more money, more than she would have in the United States. She continued to support her mother and niece at home, and she had the opportunity to enjoy the music, museums, and ballet of Vienna. But part of her past put an end to this productive and fulfilling time.

In March 1952, during the anti-Communist investigations led by Senator Joseph McCarthy, representatives of the US Army Intelligence began questioning Emily about her affiliations with un-American organizations. She thought she had answered them sufficiently, but a detailed investigation was ordered. Her name appeared on the past membership lists of American Youth for Democracy, Youth Progressives of America, and the Minnesota Student League for Democracy, all considered subversive by the US House Un-American Activities Committee. During extensive interviews of her high school and college classmates, coworkers from Minnesota and in Vienna, and a man she was dating, the FBI heard that Emily was intelligent, hardworking, and of sound moral character. They concluded that "there was no question as to [her] loyalty to the United States." Regardless, her contract with the State Department was not renewed, and Emily had to return to the United States in July 1953.

Emily moved back with her mother and niece. She opened a secretarial and translation service business. On August 1, 1953, US House Resolution 108 was signed by President Eisenhower. The bill intended to integrate Native Americans, to "set the American Indian free" by reverting civil and criminal jurisdiction to the states, and to merge the Bureau of Indian Affairs health service with the US Public

Health Services. The goal of the legislation was to "make the Indians ... subject to the same laws and entitled to the same privileges and responsibilities as are applicable to other citizens of the United States, to end their status as wards of the United States." Native Americans leaving reservations were given bus tickets, a two-week stay in a motel, and a modest food allowance to give them time to find a job and housing. The White Earth population fell by 50 percent, and the number of Native Americans in Minneapolis grew.

This rather sudden influx of Native Americans to Minneapolis caused challenges. At about the same time, Emily decided to take a secretarial position with a paint company to help support her mother and niece with less struggle than owning her own business. This job allowed her to resume work with children in the Waite Neighborhood House, previously known as the Elliot Park Neighborhood House. She started organizing regular programs for children, and Amie expanded her club activities for Native American women and children. They all came together to support each other and their culture.

In 1961, Emily became very involved in establishing the Upper Midwest American Indian Center, an organization by and for Indian people. The center sponsored powwows and drum clubs and provided a gathering place for the Ojibwe and Dakota of Minneapolis. Still, many Native Americans missed the sense of community that places like White Earth offered, and they returned to their reservations.

With increased visibility of Native Americans in urban areas and intensifying scrutiny of what it meant to be "American" in the post–World War II era, tensions rose. The burgeoning civil rights movement and the Vietnam War added to the volatility. Emily persevered, working to support her culture. She began teaching American Indian history in the Minneapolis schools. She was appointed to the Minneapolis Housing and Redevelopment Board. In 1970, she took advantage of her veterans' benefit to buy a small house. She worked on expanded programming at the Upper Midwest Center for senior citizens, health, housing, and employment and helped establish an Indian Guest House. She was a well-respected member of the community, seeking justice wherever she encountered injustice. She was awarded the Distinguished Citizen Award by Minneapolis mayor Charles Stenvig in 1977.

In 1993, Emily was diagnosed with liver cancer. She had survived breast cancer years earlier. Around the time of her diagnosis, she learned that during the Cold War in 1953 the army spread zinc cadmium sulfide over many cities, including ninety-one chemical releases in Minneapolis neighborhoods, without notifying residents. In what became the last weeks of her life, she visited Senator Paul Wellstone and asked for his assistance. Senator Wellstone demanded an investigation. The appeal to Senator Wellstone was Emily's last act to nurture and protect her community. She died on April 19, 1995.

9

LIVES LOST ON US SOIL: THE ALEUTIAN ISLANDS

On April 23, 1944, marine honor guards "maintained a constant watch" over four caskets draped in US flags in the Chapel of the Deep on a military base in the Aleutian Islands. Two of the caskets held the bodies of Ensign Helen Roehler and Ensign Ruby Toquam, navy corps nurses and best friends from Fairmont and Bricelyn, Minnesota. A local newspaper reported that the two "pals were united in death" when a navy plane crashed into the sea during a flight to inspect a hospital.

Many Americans were unaware of the military activity in the Aleutian Islands, a thousand-mile arc stretching from the tip of Alaska to three hundred miles from the Kamchatka Peninsula of the Soviet Union. The islands lie between the frigid Bering Sea and the warmer water of the Kuroshio Sea, the atmospheres from which mix to cause thick fog and sudden and violent storms to form. Forty-six volcanoes exist among the islands along a schism between two plates of the Earth, making the terrain even more volatile.

This region of rich marine life, including seals and blue fox, is the native home of the Aleut people, who call themselves *Unangan*, meaning "we the people." The islands were appropriated by the United States as part of the Alaska Purchase from Russia in 1867, and although the location had strategic potential, no military activity had materialized on the islands involving the United States, Japan, or Russia until World War II. The nearest islands were only an eight-hour bomber's flight from Seattle, Washington, home to a Boeing plant and a US Navy yard. The islands provided passage for supply lines to the Soviet Union under the Lend-Lease agreements, allowing US companies to provide equipment and supplies to the Allied forces before the United States declared war. In late 1941, the United States built secret air bases on the Alaska Peninsula and Umnak Island, disguising them as fish cannery companies. More than five thousand US troops were assigned to defend the area.

In May 1942, the United States intercepted Japanese plans to bomb the Aleutian Islands as a decoy to a larger attack on Midway Island in the Pacific Ocean. Heavy fog made it difficult for the US military to detect the Japanese until right before they bombed the important Dutch Harbor on June 3, 1942, and several days later a force of twenty-five hundred Japanese landed on Attu and Kiska Islands, where they took ten US weather crewmembers, forty-two Aleuts, and an American couple hostage. The Japanese shot the man, assuming he was a spy; his wife, Etta Jones, was held in Yokohama and Totsuka along with Australian women taken prisoner in Papua New Guinea until they were found by a US Army unit in September 1945. The forty-two Aleuts were imprisoned in Otaru on the Japanese island Hokkaido. Half of them died of tuberculosis and other illnesses, weakened by the sudden loss of their high-protein diet and fresh food.

The US War Department had been aware of the impending attack and was considering evacuating civilians, but the discussions were tangled in bureaucracy. The Office of Indian Affairs, the Fish and Wildlife Service, and the Division of Territories and Island Possessions were all involved in relocating the Aleuts from the islands. All white women and children, most of them military families, had been removed months earlier. At first, the conclusion was that the Aleut people would survive better if they "take to the hills"; this line of thought considered them to be self-sufficient because they "could never adjust themselves to life outside of their present environment."

After the attack, the US military hastily evacuated 876 Aleuts from all islands west of Akutan. They were told to pack only one suitcase and a roll of blankets. The US military burned the villages, including homes and churches, to reduce the likelihood that Japanese troops would try to occupy the area. Some of the homes that remained standing were subject to "wanton destruction of property and vandalism," apparently by armed forces personnel and civilians: "Clothing had been scattered over floors, trampled and fouled. Dishes, furniture, stoves, radios, phonographs, books . . . had been broken or damaged." The Aleuts also lost sacred religious icons, family heirlooms, and boats and fishing equipment they needed to make a living.

The Aleuts were taken to camps created in abandoned gold mine or fish cannery buildings in southeastern Alaska, structures that had little or no plumbing, lighting, or heating. About fifty of the Aleuts were hospitalized almost immediately. The conditions were crowded and dirty. Epidemics of influenza, measles, pneumonia, and tuberculosis swept through the community in the two to three years they were kept in these conditions. More than eighty Aleuts ultimately died during their incarceration.

· · · · ·

In June 1942, the month the Japanese invaded Attu and Kiska, Helen Roehler enlisted in the Navy Nurse Corps in Bethesda, Maryland. She had graduated from high school in Fairmont, Minnesota, and from nursing school at Bethesda Hospital in St. Paul. She was sworn into the navy in Faribault in July and reported for duty at US Naval Hospital in Corona, California.

In May 1943, US troops began attempts to retake Attu and Kiska Islands from the Japanese. They conducted a bloody battle on the ground and in the air. By May 30, they had retaken Attu Island, and by the end of July, Japanese forces had

FAIRMONT GIRL ENSIGN BURIED IN ALASKA—The casket at the reader's left contains the body of Ensign Helen Roehler, daughter of Sheriff and Mrs. Wm. Roehler of Fairmont. Next to it is the casket containing the body of her companion and friend throughout her service with the United States Navy, Ensign Ruby Toquam of Bricelyn. The other caskets contain the bodies of two more comrades, killed in a fatal airplane crash somewhere in Alaska April 23rd.

Pals United In Death

Navy ensigns Helen Roehler and Ruby Toquam, killed with two comrades in the Aleutian Islands. Fairmont Daily Sentinel, *May 27–28, 1944*

abandoned Kiska Island. US forces began reestablishing their presence on the islands.

In July 1943, after nearly a year's service at the US Naval Hospital Corona, Helen was approved for a seven-day leave, but her leave was canceled two days before it was scheduled to begin. She and her friend Ruby Toquam were suddenly reassigned for duty on a base in Dutch Harbor of the Aleutian Islands. They arrived in the region shortly after US troops had reclaimed it. They provided nursing services on the base and at installations throughout the region.

· · · · ·

Many lives were lost in the Aleutian Islands, including those of Ensigns Roehler and Toquam. On April 23, 1944, during a flight to check on hospitals and infirmaries on the island, their plane crashed into the sea. Their bodies were buried in Dutch Harbor until the end of the war, when they were returned to Minnesota. Helen was buried at Fort Snelling, and Ruby was buried near her hometown.

The Home Front

10

BETTY CROCKER, WIVES, AND MOTHERS

In February 1942, President Roosevelt told American women, "the eyes of the nation are upon you. . . . In far-flung outposts, in the military isolation of camps near home, men at sea, men in tanks, men with guns, men in planes, look to you for strength." Homemakers were urged to follow Eleanor Roosevelt's example and sign the US government's Consumer Pledge for Total Defense: "As a consumer, in the total defense of democracy, my country ready, efficient, and strong; I will buy carefully. I will take good care of the things I have. I will waste nothing."

Homemakers were confronted with rationing and shortages as they tried to feed their families. Rationing began on May 5, 1942. Weekly allowances were established for sugar (eight ounces per person), coffee, butter, canned and frozen foods, and red meat over the next year. Many women turned to Betty Crocker for assistance. A "representative" of General Mills in Minneapolis, Betty Crocker provided advice on the radio and in women's magazines, daily newspapers, and recipe booklets distributed in grocery stores.

She appealed to women's patriotism to reduce resentment toward the rations by explaining, "food rationing at home helps to save lives of American servicemen." She suggested a recipe for fresh fruit shortcake, which required no sugar to be added. She suggested mixing Wheaties cereal with hamburger and milk to create an "Emergency Steak" that would stretch red meat rations. Her booklet *Your Share: How to Prepare Appetizing, Healthful Meals with Foods Available Today* included fifty-two menus, 226 recipes, and 369 tips for shopping, preparing, planning, and serving meals. She provided inspirational calculations: if every household saved a single slice of bread from waste, one million loaves of bread would be saved a year.

Emergency Steak

1 pound fresh hamburger or ground round steak
1/2 cup milk
1 cup Wheaties
1 teaspoon salt and 1/4 teaspoon pepper
finely chopped onion (if desired)

Broil 8–15 minutes at 500 degrees. Brown other side and finish cooking.
6 servings

Betty Crocker's *Your Share: How to Prepare Appetizing, Healthful Meals with Foods Available Today*, 1943. Author's collection.

In addition to helping women conserve, because an unprecedented number of women in the United States were employed outside the home during the war, Betty Crocker offered suggestions for saving time preparing meals. One suggestion was to use General Mills' Bisquick, a premix including flour, sugar, baking soda, oil, and salt, which allowed women to make biscuits more quickly and without using any of their sugar rations. The booklets also included ideas for entertaining and etiquette. The brochure opened with a patriotic call to women so they could say, "I worked for freedom today." Betty also found ways for the twenty million people who were growing 40 percent of the nation's vegetables in their gardens to use their produce in their meals. She gave her innovative recipes patriotic names: Service Cake, Victory Pancakes, Yankee Doodle Macaroni, and Parachute-Landing Supper. Her suggestions focused on preparing a balanced diet given wartime constraints.

At Christmastime in 1942, Betty created a special recipe for "Military Christmas Cookies," which could be made in the shapes of tanks, battleships, and sailors. During the war, Betty received four to five thousand letters every week, many of them from women worried about losing their boyfriends, husbands, brothers, sons, and even sisters and daughters. They carried this weight while caring for their families, often single-handedly, and a third of them worked outside of the home at some point during the war. Betty responded, "Millions of us are praying for this awful war to end so all these young people serving their country so unselfishly may come home to peace and happiness."

In addition to creating recipes, writing columns, and answering letters, Betty was frequently on the radio. In 1944, she was featured on the *American Home Legion* radio program. She encouraged homemakers to join the legion at no charge. More than seven hundred thousand women signed up and received the "Homemakers Creed" of the Home Legion, pledging their beliefs that "homemaking is a noble and challenging career . . . an art requiring many different skills . . . [home] reflects the spirit of the homemaker . . . [and] should be a place of peace, joy and contentment. . . . [A] homemaker must be true to the highest ideals of love, loyalty, service and religion."

In 1945, the Office of War Information invited Betty to be the daily host for its radio program *Our Nation's Rations*. For four months, she provided updates on food shortages, instructions for sending packages overseas, and information about Red Cross blood drives and war bond sales. The US government placed their confidence in Betty to inspire and educate Americans in campaigns on the home front, which could not be ignored during an extended time of war. In 1945, *Fortune Magazine* named Betty Crocker the second most popular woman in America, right behind Eleanor Roosevelt.

· · · · ·

Who was Betty Crocker? She was a fictional persona created by a team of advertising men at Washburn-Crosby mill who found themselves responding to letters from women wanting cooking advice. In 1921, in response to a puzzle published in the *Saturday Evening Post* with an ad for Gold Medal flour, their award-winning product, they received several hundred letters with questions about baking and homemaking. Eventually, in 1924 the company hired Marjorie Child Husted, who later became the personality and driving force behind Betty Crocker.

Marjorie Child was born in 1892 in Minneapolis. Her first business success occurred as a young woman when she sold incubators at the state fair. Her father, an attorney, had obtained the inventory in lieu of cash payment from a client. While she was at the fair, she visited a fortune-teller who predicted she would someday make her own money. Marjorie went on to complete a degree in German at the University of Minnesota in 1913 and a degree in home economics education in 1914.

Marjorie worked for the Infant Welfare Society until World War I broke out; then she began working for the Red Cross. Subsequently, she became the director of information at an organization dedicated to helping parents groups

Marjorie Child Husted. *Couresty General Mills Archives*

prevent juvenile delinquency. In 1923, she turned to advertising and merchandising at the Creamette Company in Minneapolis. The following year she was hired to be a home economics representative for the Washburn-Crosby Company, the flour mill that produced the award-winning Gold Medal flour.

Even before the war, Marjorie created and produced *Betty Crocker's Cooking School of the Air* on a local Minneapolis radio station. On the show she shared cooking tips and kitchen-tested recipes. She was appointed director of the Home Service Department in 1929. By then a corporate merger formed a new entity, General Mills. In 1936, artist Neysa McMein created an image for Betty Crocker, who until then had been a "voice without a face."

Under Marjorie's leadership Betty Crocker's reputation grew. In addition to her business perspective, Marjorie could empathize with the women she was supporting with advice. Her husband was overseas with the Red Cross during the war, leaving her alone and worried for his safety. After the war, her staff totaled forty people, and she was recognized by the Women's National Press Club as woman of the year in 1949 for her business success. She received her plaque from President Truman on stage with Eleanor Roosevelt, who also received an award from the press club. Marjorie's astute leadership and marketing expertise contributed significantly to General Mills in a role equivalent to a vice president, an astonishing accomplishment in the 1940s. Marjorie Child Husted managed to support women during the war years and simultaneously rise to unprecedented heights in the corporate world. Her success endures through the Betty Crocker brand, which has continued for more than seventy-five years after the war.

· · · · ·

Women at home faced many challenges beyond cooking within the constraints created by rationing. Hilda Rachuy was a single mother with two young children, Dean and Doretta, ages three and four, when the war began in 1941. She worked at the federal government office of Immigration and Naturalization Service in St. Paul. When the munitions factory in New Brighton and other factories began hiring women at high wages, it became almost impossible for Hilda to find childcare. Her parents lived in northern Minnesota and were not close by to help. Women and men seeking high-paying jobs in the Twin Cities also created a shortage of affordable housing. Hilda scrambled to have a reasonable place to live and to secure childcare as one caregiver after another found work in the factories. Early in 1942, she was transferred to the central office of immigration and naturalization in Philadelphia. Fortunately, her sister and brother-in-law came to St. Paul from Bemidji to care for the children while he worked in the city, but Hilda missed her son's fourth birthday that year.

After returning to St. Paul, Hilda's attempts to provide housing and day care for her children continued. She even considered placing them in foster care. Eventually, she found the Walker Day Nursery, but it required a long commute on the streetcar and a long walk. There were happy moments, too. Dean and Doretta loved romping in their snowsuits. In the evenings, they went for walks and stopped at the White Castle fast-food restaurant for hamburgers.

In 1943, Hilda was offered an opening in the Grand Forks office. She took it and was able to find affordable housing and day care in the smaller town until the war ended in 1945, when the housing shortage intensified. She lost the house she was renting because it belonged to a returning serviceman. She took her children to stay with her parents in Bemidji until she could find somewhere to live. Finally, in 1947, after she transferred to the West Fargo office and saved enough money for a down payment on a small house, her family had a stable, comfortable life. Despite the struggles, Hilda was grateful for the kind, helpful, good people who assisted them along the way.

· · · · ·

Lavina Stone from Shelby County, Kentucky, was also living in St. Paul during the war. She had followed her aunts to live in Minnesota, and met and married Jim Murray in 1941. They had a daughter in June 1942, and in the same year, Jim was drafted into the US Army but never deployed overseas due to a ruptured eardrum.

Lavina moved in with her in-laws while Jim completed basic training at Fort Snelling and was transferred to Utah. She moved to Sioux City, Iowa, while Jim was stationed there in 1943. They had a small apartment off of the military base, and Jim could stay with his family most evenings. She returned to St. Paul when Jim was transferred to a base in Alabama. He was adamant that she not follow him there.

Lavina got a job pricing and stocking merchandise at Schuneman's department store in St. Paul. Her aunt worked there and told her about the position. African Americans were not allowed to work in sales behind the counters. It was a good job, better than the housekeeping jobs typically held by black women in the city. Most customers and employees treated her well, but there were some prejudiced people who made remarks. One of the white women, an elderly woman, always spoke up for her and encouraged her. At a low point, Lavina considered quitting, but the woman told her, "Don't you let anybody ever run you off of a job! You're as entitled to a job as much as anybody. You're an American citizen." Lavina felt that woman was always in her corner.

At home, Lavina's mother-in-law took care of the baby and did most of the housework, including cooking while Lavina worked. They did the best they could making meals with the rations, but very little meat was available, so they got used to eating a lot of SPAM instead of bacon. They grew tired of SPAM, but Lavina thought it was better than nothing.

Eventually, Lavina left the department store for a job as an elevator operator at the St. Paul telephone company. All of the elevator operators were black women. In this job, too, most people treated them well, but Lavina felt some of them were "snobs" and there were some racist rules. The black women had a break room that was dedicated to them. They were not allowed to eat in the company cafeteria because the white telephone operators had priority. At first the elevator operators were not even allowed to stand in line for food in the cafeteria. They were expected to go to a side door of the kitchen until the cooks insisted, "Let those girls come right through the line with the others."

In addition to working, Lavina attended the Pilgrim Baptist Church on Grotto Street in St. Paul. The pastor and congregation at that church meant a lot to Lavina while she dealt with the loneliness of being separated from her husband and the anxiety of the war. She felt when she went to church on Sunday, she could get through the week. Jim came home in 1945 after the war ended. Lavina stopped working outside the home for a while, but she sensed that working while her husband had been away made her more independent.

·····

Marianne Hamilton worked to support women whose husbands were away serving in the armed forces. Before the war, she had been a singer. At age thirteen, she began performing on many radio shows, including a taped one called *The Adventures of Buddy and Ginger*, which played all over the United States. She took the bus to the WCCO studio at the Nicollet Hotel in downtown Minneapolis. She studied French, Italian, and Spanish at the University of Minnesota when she was seventeen years old, but she did not complete a degree at the time because a course of study in the humanities had not been created. She did not mind because she enjoyed her radio work and singing in clubs.

Marianne married, and by September 1944, when her husband was drafted, they had two young children. Feeling lonely and fearful when her husband deployed, she wrote a letter to the editor of a Minneapolis newspaper suggesting that servicemen's wives needed a way to meet. In response to her letter, representatives from the newspaper called her and offered to let the women meet in their auditorium. On March 7, 1945, a thousand women showed up to the first meeting. Marianne was promptly named president of the G.I. Wives Club. She was interviewed on the radio to promote the club and was introduced as "radio actress, Army wife, nightclub singer, the mother of two babies, the president of the G.I. Wives Club, and a busy homemaker."

The purpose of the wives' club was to keep up the women's morale, keep up their husbands' morale, aid in the national war effort, and ensure a better world for the women. It was open to all servicemen's wives regardless of race, creed, or husband's rank. Veterans' wives and widows were also welcome. The group held events and offered childcare so women with children could attend. They divided into groups and met in different parts of the city to allow for flexibility in activities. They met in American Legion halls, at YWCAs, and at the Northeast Neighborhood House.

The club provided support for women in more traditional roles during the war, in contrast to the women who decided to work outside the home or join the military. At one meeting a professor from the University of Minnesota gave a talk titled "Adjustment Problems of the Wife Left at Home." He impressed upon the women the importance of writing to their husbands as much as possible to keep them dreaming of life after the war. He suggested they tell their husbands about the GI Bill and the money that would be available to buy a home to give the men something to anticipate. Servicemen were too busy to learn about the GI Bill, so their wives needed to learn about it for them. He warned them that their husbands would be "tired, very tired" when they came home and it behooved every wife to find out what was going on in the world and be prepared to help him make adjustments. He also implored them to advocate for peace when the war ended. He said, "We just can't have another war."

Mayor Hubert Humphrey worked with the club to address the housing shortage that arose in Minneapolis as servicemen came home. Many women, like Hilda

Rachuy, were facing eviction as servicemen needed the homes and apartments they had leased out while they were in the service. The mayor's committee considered creating housing in fire stations and schools that were not being used, and they sought Quonset huts and trailers that were being retired from military use.

The club also opened a day nursery at Wesley Church on Grant and Marquette Streets in Minneapolis. All GI babies up to six years old were welcome during the hours of 9 AM to 5 PM. There was a twenty-five-cent registration fee; if the child needed lunch provided, a small amount would be charged for the meal. The intention was for mothers to have a place for their children while they went to the dentist, shopped, or ran other errands.

Although Marianne's husband was drafted late in the war, he was in a unit that landed in Normandy and later fought at the Battle of the Bulge. He came home disillusioned, and together they started the United World Federalists, advocating to make laws against going to war. He wanted her to give up working outside of the home, which was fine with Marianne. She stayed home with the children and enjoyed it very much. Her husband got work in advertising art with one of the newspapers and struggled with drinking, likely exacerbated by his deployment.

11

ON THE FARM

In 1939, Ruth Storlie Rosten was left to fend for herself on a small farm near Glenwood, Minnesota, after her husband died of cancer. She lost the farm but was able to rebuy it from creditors after a year. Many farms had been repossessed during the Depression, and lenders were holding farms they could not sell. Ruth had three sons who helped her with the farm before the war started. The oldest son was drafted in 1942, and the middle son enlisted because so many men in the area were going into the military.

Ruth and her youngest son, only thirteen years old, worked the farm. They did not have a tractor. Instead, Ruth and her son farmed with four horses. Her son harnessed the horses before he left for school in the morning, and she hitched them to the wagon. During the harvest, she picked corn and loaded hay until he came home from school each day. The principal let him leave early to help during peak times. They grew wheat and oats for the animals. They had a dozen milking cows and some chickens. They used their old Model T car to drive their milk, cream, and eggs into Glenwood to sell. Prices were not good. They got only six cents for a dozen eggs. They could barely buy what they needed with the proceeds.

Ruth had always wanted to have sheep on the farm, but her husband never bought any because his brother had trouble with predators attacking them. Ruth bought eight ewes and started a herd that she kept fenced close to the house. Every fall they had wool, which sold for a good price, and sheep to sell as well. The income from the sheep helped make the payment on the farm mortgage. They did not have electricity or a refrigerator until after the war, and they heated with wood. Kerosene lamps provided light. Since there were only two of them living at home, they got by fairly well when rationing was implemented.

Ruth's oldest son was in some of the worst fighting in North Africa. He was an ambulance driver with the army. He picked up the injured men, many from his own unit, with bombs flying past. It was a tough duty. Her middle son was on the USS *Ticonderoga*, which was bombed badly in the South Pacific. He came home nervous and smoked a lot. Both sons went in the service in 1942 and came home in 1945.

· · · · ·

Linda James and her husband, William Benitt, owned Apple Acres, a two-hundred-acre farm in Washington County, near Hastings. Linda had been born nearby in

Newport in 1891. After completing her bachelor's degree at the University of Minnesota in 1914, she taught science for one year at Monticello High School before going east. She became the first woman to graduate from the Harvard-MIT School for Health Officers. She worked as a medical social worker at Massachusetts General Hospital and as the director of the after-care division at the Harvard Infantile Paralysis Commission. Her life took a turn in 1922, when she married William Benitt, an attorney originally from Goodhue, Minnesota. The couple returned to the state, and both of them completed master's degrees in the College of Agriculture at the University of Minnesota, seeking to pursue a lifestyle working on the land.

Linda and William bought Apple Acres in 1930, a difficult time economically to begin farming. They tended to eight hundred apple trees and one thousand laying hens themselves. They had no electricity or running water. They collaborated with their neighbors to demand federal funding to bring electricity to Washington County in 1938. The following year, Linda was hired by the Agricultural Adjustment Administration (AAA), an agency created by the New Deal in 1933 to increase farm income by limiting production. The agency later began authorizing farm loans and offering crop insurance on wheat. Linda's job was to educate women from town on farm challenges and the impact they had on everyone. For four years, from 1939 to 1943, she traveled the state coordinating distribution of information and programs with women from all eighty-seven counties in Minnesota.

In February 1942, Linda was on a panel of the state federation of women's clubs intended to facilitate a discussion between city and farm women: "Are Food Prices Unreasonably High?" Three hundred women from all over Minnesota participated. The chief focus of Linda's work was to bring an understanding to farm and city women alike of what the food situation was under war conditions, and to get their cooperation in making food supplies best serve the national need and the needs of nations fighting alongside the United States. She believed that the Midwest was the food arsenal of a good part of the world, and she felt privileged to play a part in securing food for victory. She was frustrated that some people regarded "the war as a personal nuisance, interfering with their comforts and desires. Only a bomb dropped on their heads" would change their minds. She found it incredible that "with the world flaming all about them they still think ... preparations for survival as only a nuisance to them personally."

As the winter of 1942 continued, Linda was on the road almost constantly, doing all she could to impress upon farmers the responsibility they had in producing food for the arsenal of democracy. She was simultaneously trying to convince city dwellers of the necessity of understanding what the food program was and how they could cooperate to make it effective. The program was a complex series of price and production controls focused on maintaining high enough prices to keep farmers in business without creating an unsustainable burden on consumers. She trained and inspired eighty-seven county field women to do the same. She used facts like "For every boy of ours on the front there are eighteen of us back home required to keep him supplied."

In the meantime, Linda's hens were doing their share, laying more than four hundred dozen eggs a week in a "patriot fever." Her husband, who served during World War I, dug "in a little harder for longer hours with his jaw set a little more square to produce more food if it is possible, thinking always of the lads on the front."

By mid-1942, Linda felt torn between her job with AAA and being needed on the farm. Gas rationing and rubber shortages threatened to limit her work, so she began traveling by bus and train. As she considered how to spend her time, she decided that each person must find the niche where they feel they can serve.

In addition to the challenges on the farm and with her work, Linda was troubled by the ominous presence of training planes endlessly circling the farm from dawn to dark. They were big bombers leaving for destinations unknown. Linda attended a meeting of the Civilian Airplane Spotter's Service at Cottage Grove. Members volunteered to serve but would not be called to duty unless the area was threatened by planes. Linda learned at the meeting that the enemy placed Minnesota third in importance. The Panama Canal was first, the Soo Locks were considered second, and Duluth Harbor in Minnesota was third because of the iron ore and concentration of war plants.

On the farm, Linda and her husband were challenged by not being able to hire people to help them. Two local boys, ages ten and thirteen, were working on the farm, including driving the large tractor. They had four thousand pounds of apples to process. In the fall, fifteen women and two men from the nearby town of Hastings worked six days a week at Apple Acres. Linda was grateful that the women were helping them, but she wondered how they could work nine to five with their homes and families to care for.

As the war years continued, Linda participated in Red Cross blood drives by donating blood herself and recruiting others to give. She also recruited knitters for the Red Cross. On holidays, she refrained from calling friends and relatives to leave the lines open for military families. She canned produce from the farm with the goal of having enough to get through the winter, so all other food could go for the military. Linda was also involved in civil defense; she helped organize Minnesota's first stateside blackout test on December 16, 1942.

In the fall of 1942, two prisoners of war from Germany wearing large "P. W." letters on their shirts and trousers were working at Apple Acres. Linda observed that they were good workers and hearty eaters, but "it gave [her] an awful shock to see those men working in [their] fields and eating at [their] table. All the time, all [she] could see was the awful misery and suffering they had let loose upon the world." The men came from one of more than fifteen POW camps in Minnesota housing

Linda James Benitt. *MNHS Collections*

German prisoners. In total, 1,275 German POWs of the four hundred thousand that were held in the United States were assigned to camps throughout Minnesota. The prisoners were given farm, lumber, and canning factory work, for which they were paid in accordance with the Geneva Convention agreement. The Geneva Convention restrictions prohibiting contact between prisoners and the public was enforced, especially with regard to American women.

• • • • •

While women like Ruth Storlie Rosten and Linda Benitt were farming during the war, Josephine "Jo" Skavanger was working in the rural town of Alexandria, Minnesota, for the local board of the Selective Service System, the federal agency responsible for drafting men. She had been born in Keene, near the western border of North Dakota, in 1916. Her parents farmed there during the dust bowl and a grasshopper infestation. The dust storms were devasting, but the grasshoppers were almost worse. At one point, the government gave her father a poison, probably arsenic, to spread out on their land to kill the grasshoppers. Farmers were told to bury what they did not use, and quite a bit of the unused inventory might have been buried near Morris, Minnesota. People in the area later questioned the impact the buried poison had on their water supply. Jo was born into this rather harsh land and circumstances.

Jo went to school in North Dakota and attended one year at Concordia College before entering the workforce. Her parents moved to Minnesota and settled on a farm near Brandon, where they started raising sheep. Jo and her sister worked in Alexandria. When the draft began, Jo started working for the Selective Service System. She was involved in registering all the men in the area, including collecting their questionnaires and information from their physicals. Extensive rules and regulations had to be applied to the various types of classifications and deferments. It was challenging work because the rules kept changing. The staff collected information on farms, including the size of the crops and livestock production. Farms had to be at certain production levels to qualify for deferments. Men classified as 1A were prospective inductees, 2C was for farm deferments, and 4F was for men disqualified for physical reasons. There were more than sixty classifications. Representatives from the state board of the Selective Service System frequently came and audited the records to ensure the local staff and board were following the deferment rules.

Occasionally Jo had to travel to St. Paul for meetings, and for a while she was designated to be a troubleshooter, requiring her to travel throughout the state. Because of the gas and rubber rations, she had to use buses and trains, which were very crowded. When hotels were full in some of the towns, she stayed in private homes.

At one point, Jo considered entering the military. She had no brothers, and she wondered if she should enlist on behalf of the family. The head of her office convinced her she was doing important war work with her job supporting the Selective Service Board.

Jo was very aware of the labor shortage on the farms around Alexandria because so many men had been drafted. At one point, the county extension service put out a plea for help, and Jo and five other women volunteered to shock corn for farmers after work. Shocking involved bundling the corn upright so it would dry before being stored. The women went out two nights a week and shocked corn.

A few businessmen from town came out to the farms and helped, too. When the women first arrived, the farmer was not sure what he was going to do with "girls" on his farm, but most of them, like Jo, had grown up on farms, and he was soon convinced they knew how to shock corn.

Jo was grateful for her job with the Selective Service. She learned how to deal with people. After the war, the local draft boards were closed and all of the processing took place in St. Paul. Jo was offered a job in St. Paul but turned it down because she did not want to go to the big city. Instead, she got married in 1948 and as Josephine Skavanger Sletto spent the rest of her career working for various government offices in Alexandria: the office of equal opportunity, the immigration department, the senior citizen's office, and the department for adult education.

· · · · ·

One little-known perspective during World War II is that of Mexican migrant workers, especially women. According to the census in 1900, there were only twenty-four Mexicans living in Minnesota. This number grew to seven thousand Mexican migrant workers by the end of the 1920s to meet the need for labor in sugar beet farms and production facilities. The numbers grew further in the 1930s because the AFL and CIO tried to unionize sugar beet workers and in response the companies, including the largest sugar beet producer, American Crystal, recruited Mexicans who would seek the work even at poor wages.

Alice Sickels, through the International Institute, which assisted Japanese people in relocating to Minnesota, also documented and advocated for the Mexican people living in the state. The institute and its volunteers and staff encouraged Mexicans living in Minnesota to seek US citizenship through naturalization. Citizenship had the potential to give them protections and access to education and health care. The wages they earned in beet fields and through other manual labor opportunities were not sufficient to maintain safe and affordable housing and food. The institute was also concerned about a federal ruling that women with US citizenship who married an alien prior to 1929 could lose their citizenship.

During the war, demand for domestically produced sugar increased after the Japanese took control of the Philippines, which had been a major source of sugar. Employers, including American Crystal in Minnesota, encouraged Mexicans to cross the border because of the labor shortage caused by the draft. A formal agreement, the bracero program, evolved between the US and Mexican governments in 1942, allowing workers from Mexico to enter the United States temporarily.

Despite the corporate and government support for their labor, Mexicans were called "wetbacks" and considered a threat to the "American way of life." They still were not able to afford decent housing and did not have access to health care. In addition to the efforts of Alice Sickels and the International Institute in the Twin Cities, the National Council of Churches' Migrant Ministry and the Home Missions

Council of North America advocated to improve the working and living conditions in many Minnesota cities, including Crookston, Moorhead, Fairmont, and Owatonna.

Mexican women found it difficult to secure jobs. Some were employed in ammunition and other types of factories. But they were not as welcome in roles traditionally open to women: teachers, typists, salesclerks, or waitresses. They were also discouraged from participating in any of the training programs that were available during and after the war. They did work in the fields and took care of their families. Ultimately, very little is known about Mexican women's experience in Minnesota during the war since memoirs or interviews appear not to have been collected or preserved.

12

BETWEEN "BOOGIE WOOGIE BUGLE BOY" AND "SOMEWHERE OVER THE RAINBOW"

On January 31, 1941, Universal Studios released the movie *Buck Privates*, which included the song "Boogie Woogie Bugle Boy," sung by a trio originally from Minneapolis, the Andrews Sisters. The movie was a comedy about army life starring Bud Abbott and Lou Costello. On September 16, 1940, President Roosevelt signed into law the selective service registration act, which required all men between the ages of twenty-one and thirty-five to register for one year of service in the military. Later that year, men began service, and *Buck Privates*, a lighthearted view of military life, was released soon after. The film was a hit for Universal Studios, grossing more than $4.7 million at a time when tickets were twenty-five cents. The Andrews Sisters were already one of the most popular groups in the United States, but this movie and the four songs they sang, especially "Boogie Woogie Bugle Boy" and "I'll Be with You in Apple Blossom Time," received excellent reviews and a high ranking on US *Billboard*'s lists of songs played on the radio and records sold.

· · · · ·

The Andrews Sisters got their start in the entertainment business in 1931 during the Depression. LaVerne, Maxene, and Patty Andrews entered a talent contest at the Orpheum Theater in downtown Minneapolis over their Easter break from school. The competition was sponsored by a band leader who was looking for new talent to travel with his orchestra on the vaudeville circuit. The girls took first place, and Larry Rich asked their parents' consent for them to travel with his show. Their mother came from a musical family and was supportive, but their father was more reluctant because the girls were so young. Patty, the youngest, was only thirteen years old. He eventually relented, and the girls boarded a bus to join the vaudeville troupe in Atlanta, Georgia.

LaVerne, Maxene, and Patty were born in Minneapolis in 1911, 1916, and 1918. Their father, Peter Andreos, changed his name to Andrews after immigrating from Greece. Their mother, Olga Sollie, was born in Norway. The couple moved around the Minneapolis area and occasionally lived in Mound, where two of Olga's brothers owned a grocery store. Peter was an ice cream maker in 1911, when LaVerne was born. He subsequently owned a pool hall, a restaurant, and a fruit company.

The young Andrews girls were inspired by the Boswell Sisters from New

Orleans, the first female vocal group to attain national recognition. They heard the Boswells perform on Bing Crosby's radio show. They started singing three-part harmony like the Boswell Sisters, with Patty, the youngest, singing lead and LaVerne and Maxene singing soprano and contralto or bass. They sang at schools, political meetings, and hospitals.

The Andrews Sisters quickly learned to engage their audiences and maintain a strong stage presence while they were with the vaudeville troupe in 1931 and 1932. After that tour, they moved with their parents to New York City. Vaudeville was being replaced by the big band sound. The sisters performed in New York and toured with their parents in a 1931 Packard driven by their father. The women sat in the back and rehearsed while they drove. Often they traveled with a dog as well because Maxene loved dogs.

In 1937, the Andrews returned to Mound, Minnesota, and stayed with family. Their father thought his daughters should give up entertainment and enroll in business school; they could have stable careers as secretaries after enduring six years of living on the road. LaVerne, Maxene, and Patty loved show business and wanted to continue, so they moved back to New York, this time to Tin Pan Alley. Initially, they got mixed reviews and endured hard times. They cooked meals in the hotel and sometimes shared a cafeteria meal and coffee three ways. They began to sing at some clubs and on the radio. A manager offered to work with them, and they began recording with the Decca label. They were searching for a B side song to go with "Nice Work if You Can Get It" when they came across the Yiddish tune "Bei Mir Bist Du Schon (Means that You Are Grand)." This filler song on their single quickly became the number-one song on *Billboard*. They sold three hundred fifty thousand copies of that song in one month, and soon sales topped a million. This was the song that propelled the Andrews Sisters to fame.

The Andrews Sisters sang with Bing Crosby and the Glenn Miller Orchestra in person and on the radio. Their ability to harmonize and sing a wide range of musical genres allowed them to continually invent new sounds while retaining a musical identity. Swing, boogie-woogie, jazz, classical, folk, gospel, Dixie, and blues songs were among their repertoire. Their "cohesive harmony and perfectly timed syncopations . . . set them apart." This success led to making movies and the "Boogie Woogie Bugle Boy" hit when *Buck Privates* was released in early 1941. Only *Gone With the Wind* had grossed more in sales.

Even before the release of *Buck Privates*, the Andrews Sisters began supporting the troops. In 1940, they participated in a lineup of stars performing on the radio to benefit the American Red Cross. Their songs were so well known that the US Air Corps began naming fighter planes and bombers "Pistol Packin' Mama" and "Shoo Shoo Baby." Wherever they toured, they added on shows at army camps and naval bases. Once after a show in Seattle, they went down to a dock and sang for servicemen on a ship as it pulled out. They frequently sang at the military hospital at Fort

Snelling when they were home visiting family. They gave as many as six shows a day at the military locations as well as munitions plants and other war factories to ensure they supported those contributing on the home front, including women. They also sang at canteens across the country, including the Hollywood Canteen and the Stage Door Canteen in New York. The women did not shy away from stopping at hospitals, where they visited the amputee wards, which most entertainers, especially women, avoided.

Touring in their car became more challenging after the United States became involved in the war and gas and tires were rationed. Most people were limited to three gallons of gas a week unless they could prove they needed the fuel for their work, so the Andrews family had to be careful about booking shows in cities close together. Once they were under contract with Universal Studios, the production company was able to supplement their rations for driving to shows. They were also challenged by rations on coffee.

The Andrews Sisters were frequently on the Armed Forces Radio Service. These shows—*Mail Call, G.I. Journal,* and *Command Performance*—were transmitted overseas and recorded and could be played at military bases and Red Cross facilities internationally. The shows included Bob Hope, Dinah Shore, and other well-known performers. The Andrews Sisters and other stars, including Frank Sinatra and Bing Crosby, volunteered to record songs specifically for the troops, twelve-inch records called V-Discs (Victory Discs). Many of these same people participated in war bond rallies, including a cross-country trip by train in 1942. The train stopped at towns and the performers would sing and encourage audiences to buy war bonds.

In June 1945, the Andrews Sisters were finally allowed to go overseas with the United Service Organizations (USO). In preparation, they were given briefing materials that informed them of the USO expectations and army regulations because they were under army discipline. They were required to wear their USO uniform any time they were not performing. Only within the privacy of their quarters were they allowed to wear civilian clothes. They could only use army transportation and were instructed to go to and from the performances and their quarters without making any side stops. One briefing memorandum clarified that USO entertainers were "civilians attached to the Army," meaning that they had "no privileges of rank" but were "under obligation to obey Army regulations and . . . under the provisions of the Articles of War." The Andrews were also given a full slate of vaccines, including for smallpox, typhoid fever, and tetanus. The protocols and rules made them feel as if they had "enlisted in the Army itself instead of volunteering to serve in the USO."

The USO also provided entertainers with a booklet, "A Guide to the Foxhole Circuit," which included helpful advice from some of the thousands of performers who had toured before them. The brochure also encouraged entertainers to follow the army guidelines so they did not "unknowingly . . . play into the hands of the enemy." They were given a long list of things they should pack to take with them that would not be available at the PXs (post exchanges) on bases such as bobby pins, cold cream, cosmetics, and hair bleach. The brochure noted that "GIs are not trying to be blondes. So either take along your own peroxide or make up your mind to stay brunette until you get back home." The brochure also gave advice about keeping their performances "clean" and in good taste as well as suggestions for interacting with soldiers in the hospitals they would visit.

The Andrews Sisters and all USO performers were required to sign an "Oath of Secrecy" contained in the Espionage Act, promising not to divulge any information to persons not entitled to receive it. This restriction included "the movement, numbers, description, condition, or disposition of any of the armed forces, ship, aircraft, or other war materials of the United States" or any plans or military operations or "any other information relating to the public defense which might be useful to the enemy."

Despite a somber tone, the USO brochure also noted that "When you sign up for an overseas tour, you are giving yourself an opportunity to serve your country and your fellow Americans. In this great war for freedom, you are putting your name down on the list of those who have fought to win. . . . When peace comes again to the world, it will be good to know that you found your place in the struggle."

Even at this late stage in the war, after victory in Europe (V-E day, May 8, 1945), travel plans were kept secret. The Andrewses were not told where they were going. They reported to Fort Dix, New Jersey, and in the middle of the night were driven to LaGuardia Airport, where they boarded an air corps plane. Once on the plane, they were allowed to open their itinerary. They had assumed they were going to northern climates because they had been issued winter uniforms at Saks Fifth Avenue, which distributed clothing for the USO. Instead, they were scheduled to perform in Italy. This sort of confusion had affected other performers, too: Jinx Falkenburg had arrived in the Caribbean in her winter uniform and a fur coat.

The plane stopped in Newfoundland first. Maxene was excited to see a country she had only read about in geography classes in school, but it was just a refueling stop. They were not allowed off the plane, and the windows remained covered for security purposes. Next, they landed in Casablanca, and the windows were uncovered. They saw the beautiful city and landscape as the plane descended. The passengers—the Andrews Sisters, thirty young second lieutenants, and the pianist and accordion player—were told it was another refueling stop, but as they sat in the hot plane a major leaned in and asked, "Which of youse guys are the Andrews Sisters?" When the women responded, he said, "Are youse guys ready?"

"Ready for what?" He told them they were supposed to be performing in a town with a name they had never heard of. They were a little reluctant to get off the plane at a place that was not listed on their itinerary, but they did not want to get in trouble or be seen as uncooperative. The USO tour meant a lot to them, so they hopped into the major's jeep and were whisked out into the desert. They stopped in a desolate-looking place, but there were seven thousand soldiers waiting. They began yelling when they saw the Andrews Sisters, who "put on a show right there, with no notice or rehearsal." They put on ten shows in Casablanca over the next two and a half days. Then, with an hour notice, they were told to pack and be ready

The Andrews Sisters performing at the Orpheum Theater in Minneapolis, 1943. *Minneapolis Newspaper Photograph Collection, Hennepin County Library*

to leave. Maxene noted it was not difficult to pack quickly because they did not have much clothing and had been performing in their winter uniforms. They were quickly flown to Naples, where the major there was extremely upset because the major in Casablanca was not authorized to keep the Andrews Sisters. It had been intended to be only a refueling stop. The Naples major was furious and "chewed" them out.

Their first official performance was in Caserta, Italy, in a well-known opera house. They were able to bunk with nurses stationed there. They performed to large crowds, the largest being seventy thousand servicemen held in a racetrack Mussolini built, five performances for groups of fourteen thousand soldiers at a time.

During one of the USO performances, the Andrews Sisters were on the same program as a band of black musicians. It was an outdoor concert, and all of the seats were taken except for the first three rows, which were reserved for officers. Maxene asked where the band would sit when they finished. The second lieutenant said they would find seats somewhere. It was clear to the women there were not seats available, so they insisted that the band be given seats from the vacant rows reserved for officers. The second lieutenant refused. The Andrews Sisters kept the crowd waiting for nearly half an hour while the officer got approval from his superiors for the band to sit in front.

During their USO tour, the Andrews Sisters sang in hangars, tents, and open fields, and they added impromptu concerts for small groups of GIs they encountered between scheduled performances. "Rum and Coca-Cola" was the most requested song and was called "the national anthem of the GI camps." By the end of the eight-week overseas tour, they had performed for one hundred eighty thousand soldiers.

On their return, the Andrews Sisters resumed their weekly radio show and live performances. They took time out between performances in New York City to sing for free in Times Square to crowds lined up to buy war bonds to encourage sales and entertain those waiting in line.

The Andrews Sisters, who contributed so much to the troops and war efforts, continued to record hits. By the time their careers wound down in the 1950s, they had recorded 113 singles, sold 75 million records, and recorded more than 1,800 songs, including eight that hit number one on the charts and nineteen gold records. They also appeared in twenty-two films. By some counts, they could be considered the most successful pre–rock and roll group in the United States.

·····

Another well-known woman from Minnesota also performed extensively during the war. Judy Garland, born Frances Ethel Gumm in Grand Rapids in 1922, secured her reputation as the star of *The Wizard of Oz* when it debuted in 1939. Judy grew up with her two sisters in Grand Rapids, singing and performing at their parents' theater, the New Grand. Her parents were performers who had met at the Orpheum Theater in Superior, Wisconsin. Ethel Milne played piano, providing background music for silent movies; Fred Gumm, originally from Tennessee, sang popular songs while the reels were changed. They moved to Grand Rapids after they were married when Fred was hired as the manager of the New Grand theater. Judy was only two years old when she first climbed onto the stage with her sisters during a Christmas performance. The family left Grand Rapids when Judy was four and began their climb, especially Judy's ascent, to Hollywood careers.

In 1941, Judy volunteered to make several appearances to promote Treasury bonds. In December of that year, she and her husband, David, traveled three hundred miles from their home in Los Angeles to Fort Ord in northern California to perform for the troops. They were there when Pearl Harbor was attacked. In January, she and her husband were among the first entertainers to respond to the War Department's request to provide morale-boosting performances at army camps. They traveled east doing three shows a day and added performances in towns along the way to encourage war bond sales. After visiting five military camps and a hospital, Judy collapsed of exhaustion and strep throat at Camp Wolters, Texas. She went home to recover and returned in the summer of 1942, performing at camps in seven states. She and David celebrated their first anniversary at Camp Robinson, Arkansas.

Movies were considered important for boosting morale at home and among the troops. General Eisenhower ordered, "Let's have more motion pictures!" Millions of people—70 percent of the American population—went to see a movie every week during the war, but producing movies was becoming more difficult. By 1941, many of the men making them were in the armed forces. In addition to live performances on military bases and to promote war bond sales, Judy performed in radio shows transmitted to the front lines, including *G.I. Journal, Mail Call,* and *Command Performance,* hosted by Bob Hope. She also performed at the USO Hollywood Canteen in southern California, which became one of the best clubs in the country during the war years, a gathering place for servicemen on leave or waiting to go overseas. In the fall of 1943, Judy joined the Hollywood Cavalcade, a train full of stars including Fred Astaire, Betty Hutton, and Mickey Rooney, which traveled ten thousand miles over twenty-three days, entertaining seven million people and inspiring more than a billion dollars in war bond sales.

· · · · ·

The United Service Organization (USO), a private agency formed in 1941 under the direction of the army and navy, had as its objective "to make sure our soldiers, sailors and other young people who are drawn away from their homes by military service and defense work are provided with wholesome recreational activities and an opportunity to maintain their ties with civil and religious life." The USO was the collaborative effort of six service organizations: the International Committee of Young Men's Christian Associations (YMCA), the National Board of Young Women's Christian Associations (YWCA), the Salvation Army, the National Jewish Welfare Board, the National Travelers Aid Association, and the National Catholic Community Service. The USO sought to "aid in the war and defense of the United States and its Allies by serving the religious, spiritual, welfare, and educational needs of the men and women in the armed forces and the war and defense industries of the United States and its Allies." The USO was built on shared belief in "a supernatural power that exists beyond any that is upon this earth; faith in the brotherhood of man; belief in the individual dignity of man; belief in the existence of positive ethical standards of right and wrong that exist apart from the will of any man."

Over the five war years, a million people volunteered their service to the USO and a billion people attended its programs. Its budget of $200 million was funded by voluntary contributions, and the military units built many of the facilities and stages. The USO had permanent clubs where servicemen and -women could go to hear bands and dance and get snacks and cigarettes. Alcohol was not permitted. The organization also provided mobile units that could get out to areas where troops were guarding bridges or staffing antiaircraft units and were unable to come to clubs. It also sent entertainers like the Andrews Sisters and Judy Garland to perform on stages set up across the United States and overseas, virtually everywhere there were US troops, all the way from the Arctic Circle to the equator.

General Eisenhower noted that winning the war relied on "the cooperation of nations and of people within nations. The USO has given an impressive demonstration of the way people in our country of different creeds, races and economic status can work together when the nation has dedicated itself to an all-out, integrated effort."

In addition to the tours and concerts the Andrews Sisters and Judy Garland gave throughout the United States and abroad, local women supported a USO service club in St. Paul. In May 1942, Work Projects Administration (WPA) workers cleaned out rubble from the old Machinist's Hall and began transforming the place into a USO facility. Once it opened, the club provided refreshments, pool and billiard tables, board games, desks for writing letters, deep chairs for reading, and a jukebox for dancing. According to a newspaper article, "Plenty of pretty hostesses" were on-site as well. Men and women home on leave and stationed at Fort Snelling came to relax. A day nursery was established for service members' children. In its first year, the facility served 89,431 visitors, and when it closed in March 1946, it had been open thirteen hundred days.

13

RADAR RESEARCH AND NAVY INTELLIGENCE

While some women joined the military, worked in untraditional venues, kept farms running, maintained their homes, and supported the war effort through the American Red Cross and USO, Julia F. Herrick, a biophysicist working at Mayo Clinic, was invited by the US War Department to conduct research on radar. In 1942, she was granted a leave of absence by Mayo Clinic to allow her to become a civilian working at the Army Signal Corps Engineering Laboratories in Fort Monmouth, New Jersey. During her nearly three years of research, she was also assigned to the radio direction finding receiver subsection of the equipment subsection at the Evans Signal Laboratory at Bradley Beach, New Jersey.

Dr. Herrick's research focused on radio direction finding, which allowed military units to determine their own locations and to find enemy transmissions. Her team was charged with designing a direction finder that could be transported in a small vehicle and of a size and weight three men could set up and make operational within twenty minutes. Development began in August 1943 and concluded in August 1945. The project was successful for its intended use of radiocommunication direction finding, and she and her team found that "it may also have important application to homing and navigation for position finding for rescue operations."

· · · · ·

Julia Herrick's path to radar research began early in her career. She was born in 1893 in North St. Paul. After completing a bachelor's degree in math from the University of Minnesota in 1915, Julia taught high school math, chemistry, and physics in Pine City and Ely, and in Minneapolis at a private high school later known as Blake School. She returned to the University of Minnesota, and in 1919, after completing a master's degree in physics, she became head of the physics department at Rockford College, Illinois.

Frustrated by the lack of funding for her lab and changes in the curriculum that discouraged students from taking physics, Julia applied to Mayo Clinic. In 1927, she was accepted as a fellow in biophysics there. By 1931, she had completed her doctorate and became an associate in experimental surgery and pathology, conducting research in Mayo's Institute of Experimental Medicine. She studied the impact of ultrasound on bone and made important contributions to the development of the thermistor, a device used for physiologic thermometry by biophysicists,

ANTENNA
AN-45-E

LOOP
ASSEMBLY

RADIO RECEIVER

HEADSET
HS-29-E

MICROPHONE
T-35 (CHEST)

TRIPOD LG-15-A

POWER
CORD

LIGHT SHIELD

CHEST CH-113-A

Julia F. Herrick and her team helped design this direction finder radar unit. *Institute of Radio Engineers,* © 1949 IEEE. *Reprinted, with permission, from L. J. Giacoletto and Samuel Striber, "Medium-Frequency Crossed-Loop Radio Direction Finder with Instantaneous Unidirectional Visual Presentation,"* in Proceedings of the Institute of Radio Engineers, *September 1949*

anesthesiologists, and experimental surgeons. She had thirteen years of experience working in the field of biophysics when the war broke out.

When Dr. Herrick first arrived at Fort Monmouth, she was assigned to a technician with a few college credits and a couple of years' experience in electronics, Gustav Shapiro. He said Julia "was a fish out of water, but a smart woman. She had a lot of mathematics, and that's why they assigned her to me. She was able to supplement what I didn't know. I started to work on cavity resonators (what did I know about cavity resonators?). I had the feel, but not the mathematics. Between the two of us, we managed to figure things out."

Gustav Shapiro also got to know her personally and learned about her background:

Dr. Herrick came from a Minneapolis banking family. There were three children, two sons and she was the daughter. When the father died, he left control of the bank to her because he trusted her common sense more than that of his sons. She was a smart gal in her late forties I would say, and prematurely gray. She was an extremely good looking and appealing woman and it was very easy to get along with her. She had the common touch. We once had a Thanksgiving party at our house and played charades. When it was her turn to act out something, she took a long-stemmed flower in her hand and stretched out on the floor facing the ceiling with her eyes closed. She was enacting [a nineteenth-century minstrel song]. She was a regular person.

Dr. Herrick was considered an excellent, hardworking member of the signal corps research team. By all accounts, she was a dedicated, strong woman, and yet on September 13, 1944, Dr. Herrick reported to the infirmary "nervous and crying" after being notified that her nephew, a paratrooper, had been killed in the Normandy invasion.

Dr. Herrick's tenure in the radio direction finding branch of the Eatontown Signal Laboratory at Fort Monmouth lasted from her appointment in May 1942 to June 1946. Her job title was radio engineer. Another engineer, Julius Rosenberg, who had recently graduated from City College of New York with a degree in electrical engineering, was hired by the signal corps in 1940. In 1942, the same year Dr. Herrick arrived at Fort Monmouth, Rosenberg was assigned to Fort Monmouth as an engineer inspector. He was fired in February 1945 for suspected membership in the Communist Party. Rosenberg was later accused of running a spy ring, and two other engineers also working at Fort Monmouth fled to the Soviet Union. Julius and Ethel Rosenberg were convicted of federal espionage charges. They were executed in 1953.

After returning to Mayo Clinic in 1946 from her military assignment, Dr. Herrick continued research on the biological effects of microwaves, ultrasound, physiologic thermometry, and the circulation of blood. She began to study engineering as well. She joined the Institute of Radio Engineers (IRE) and became the first editor for the *Medical Electronics Professional Transactions.* Throughout her career, she published more than 130 articles and attained full professor status at Mayo Clinic. After retiring from the clinic in 1958, at age sixty-five, Dr. Herrick began working for NASA in the Jet Propulsion Laboratory in Pasadena, California, contributing to its space research programs during the first years of its formation until 1965, when she returned to the Midwest and continued working in the medical field until her death in Rochester in 1979.

While Dr. Herrick was on the East Coast working with the Army Signal Corps, Veda Ponikvar became one of eighty-one thousand women to join the navy in the Women Accepted for Volunteer Emergency Service (WAVES). She was assigned to analytical and intelligence work in Washington, DC. Veda was born in Chisholm, Minnesota, a small town on the Iron Range, in 1919. Her father was a miner, and her mother was a homemaker. Veda enlisted in March 1943 and was sent to officers' training at Smith College, Northampton, Massachusetts.

Julia Herrick, Mayo Clinic biophysicist. *Used with permission of Mayo Foundation for Medical Education and Research. All rights reserved.*

The officer who interviewed Veda noted that she was "a rather heavy-set young woman of Slavic origin, [but] her personality makes one unaware of an average appearance. She was a member of several honorary societies, and culminated a college career of activities and debating by being made editor of the year book. This is an outstanding honor at Drake and carries with it a full tuition scholarship." The interviewer also marked attributes on the "personality appraisal sheet," noting that Veda's grooming was inconspicuous and in conversation her volubility was well regulated, not rambling or garrulous. On a personality scale of 4.0 to 2.0, she was given the moderately high score of 3.5.

Veda had been the editor in chief of the *Chisholm Tribune Herald* at the time she enlisted. She set editorial policy and wrote all of the editorials. She was in charge of the reporters and press employees. She wrote several sections of the weekly paper. She had also been the representative for the Sixtieth Legislative District in Minnesota, temporarily replacing a male senator who was in the armed forces. In that role, she was a member of the committees for rehabilitation, labor, and rules and taxation. Perhaps her most valuable credential was her competency in languages. Veda was able to read, write, interpret, and speak fluently in six foreign languages, including several Slavic languages, French, and German.

After completing the eight-week navy officers' school at Smith, Veda's first assignment was in the Office of Procurement and Material in Washington, DC. In that role, she was the editor of secret publications and in charge of other writers. After two months, she was transferred to the foreign branch of naval intelligence. In this position, Veda was the chief analyst of morning conferences and head of the Yugoslav and Albanian desks. During the time she was in this role, the region known as Yugoslavia was contentious, fraught with internal conflict as well as having been defeated early in the war by Hitler. The Allied forces wanted to regain the region. Veda served as an interpreter and oriented naval attachés assigned to posts in Slavic regions. During this fourteen-month assignment, she was frequently involved in security updates given directly to President Roosevelt at the White House. Once when she arrived, the president asked how the WAVES managed to keep their ties so straight. Veda replied, "Mr. President, I cannot tell you. It is a Navy secret."

As the war in Europe began to wind down toward the end of 1944, Veda was reassigned to the office of the inspector of naval material in Detroit, Michigan. There she was the transportation and assistant security officer, in charge of transportation priorities. She also assisted in security and was a member of the coding board.

Veda's active status ended in August 1946. She was interested in continued service and so remained on inactive status but not officially discharged in the event her skills would be needed. She was not discharged until 1959. Her extended discharge date might also have related to the classified nature of her work. The navy was known to keep personnel and records secret by extending discharge dates.

Upon her return to Minnesota, Veda, who had wanted to run a newspaper since she was in fifth grade, started the *Chisholm Free Press*. Nine years later, she bought the competing paper in town because it was basically run by the mining companies and did not reflect the workers' perspectives. She said she knew "a newspaper was a powerful force—for good or bad." She made up her "mind to be positive, but [she'd] be honest." She'd do her "homework and get [the] facts straight." She was

Veda Ponikvar, navy intelligence. *Chisholm War History Committee records, Minnesota Discovery Center, Chisholm*

heavily involved in politics and was considered a formidable influence in the region. Some people said she not only ran the newspaper; she also ran the Iron Range, leading to her nickname: the Iron Lady. Among her accomplishments was her role in establishing the Boundary Waters Canoe Area, to protect a million-acre wilderness from development, including mining. On a smaller scale, but of great importance, was her work in creating a facility for developmentally disabled people. She spent a lifetime committed to helping the underdog.

Veda returned to the White House on two occasions, meeting Presidents Gerald Ford and Jimmy Carter, to receive awards for community work and volunteering. In the 1989 movie *Field of Dreams* starring Kevin Costner, the main character's obituary is read at the end. Dr. Archibald Graham, the real person upon whose life the movie is based, practiced medicine in Chisholm after his baseball career. When he died in 1965, Veda wrote his obituary and published it in her newspaper. Actor Anne Seymour plays Veda in the movie and reads the obituary.

Veda wrote more than forty-three hundred editorials throughout her career. She said, "Once you get printer's ink in your veins, you can't replace it. It isn't blood—it's ink." But in addition to her civic involvement and newspaper work, she was also known for her baking. Her walnut potica was said to be the reason many politicians and three-star generals would appear at events she hosted.

· · · · ·

Another woman who would eventually live in Minnesota worked in navy intelligence in Washington, DC, during the same time that Veda did. A large installation of "code girls" was assigned to decipher German and Japanese code throughout the war. Helen Friedline from Jennerstown, Pennsylvania, worked with the large deciphering machines. Her mother raised her and her three brothers after separating from their father, who was a mine supervisor. The Depression had hit the coal mining town in Pennsylvania hard, like it did the Iron Range in Minnesota. Helen's family lived in poverty, and food was scarce. Helen did not attend her high school graduation ceremony because she did not have shoes. The school provided a good education, though, and in addition to the core curriculum, Helen learned to play the piano and cello. After graduation, Helen waited tables and worked as a housekeeper for a local woman.

After the United States entered the war, Helen worked for Westinghouse Electric as an armature winder. She and some friends decided to join the navy, where they knew they would receive adequate clothing and food. Helen was assigned to naval communications as an "operator of special equipment. This duty required a high degree of accuracy, alertness, manual dexterity, and some proficiency in record keeping." The machines were large, filling rooms, and they were loud. Helen suffered hearing loss in her right ear as a result.

Helen was not sure why she was given this post. When she enlisted, she had requested an assignment in nursing. She must have scored well on the enlistment exams, plus the ability to play musical instruments was sometimes correlated with math aptitude.

Whatever the reason, Helen and the other WAVES provided a critical service decoding messages. Helen was described as "a capable, conscientious, willing, and adaptable worker" by her captain in the Naval Communications Annex. The navy booklet containing her record also noted that "The individual was employed in a position of special trust and no further information regarding his duties in the Navy can be disclosed. He is under oath of secrecy, and all concerned are requested to refrain from efforts to extract more information from him." She received the

Navy Unit Commendation award for her service, but it was directed that due to the "nature of the services performed by this unit, no publicity be given to [her] receipt of this award." Several hundred women worked in the Annex, where armed guards were present outside and inside. Decades later, the assistant chief of staff for the Naval Security Group Command noted that "Never in the history of American intelligence had so many people kept a secret for so long." It is likely that Helen was working on the famous Enigma code that allowed the US Navy to decode German ciphers.

Another letter sent by the deputy chief of naval communications said, "You may take real pride and satisfaction in the part you have played in bringing about the victory that has come to us. The Navy will always be grateful for your loyalty and devotion to duty."

During her assignment in Washington, DC, she met a navy pharmacist mate from St. Paul, Minnesota, at the Pepsi Center, where men and women in the service were given refreshments. He was a marine about to deploy on missions against the Japanese in the South Pacific and to rescue POWs in China. They decided if he survived and if she liked Minnesota after spending time there, they would get married, which is what happened. Helen attended Gustavus Adolphus College on the GI Bill and finished a nursing program at Bethesda Hospital in St. Paul. She soon had a son, who years later followed in his parents' footsteps with an assignment in special operations with the marines during the Vietnam War.

14

LIFE OF A WAC STATESIDE

On June 19, 1944, just days after D-Day, Anne Bosanko told a friend she was joining the Women's Army Corps (WAC). After attending the University of Minnesota in Minneapolis for two years, she put her education on hold because she wanted to contribute to the war effort. When Anne began a liberal arts program at the University of Minnesota, the United States had been at war for just over a year. At first, she was impressed with how women were able to become more involved in the campus newspaper, the yearbook, and student government with the male students away. The USO held mixers at the student union for the men assigned to the navy's V-12 officers' training program, the army pre-meteorology unit, and German- and Japanese-language units in the Twin Cities.

In the spring of 1944, while Anne was finishing up the semester at the university, the news about the war in the European and Pacific theaters worsened. She felt that young, single women with no family responsibilities should not be sitting comfortably at home, business as usual, when fellows their age were being called into service and dying on beaches and in deserts. She wanted to do more than roll bandages for the Red Cross. She visited recruiting offices and enlisted in a new medical corps branch of the army.

Even though factory work paid much better, $150 to $200 per month in comparison to the $50 a month that WACs were paid, Anne chose the military, possibly because of her father's commitment to military service. Anne's father taught at Blake School, a private prep school for boys. He had a law degree from Yale and was admitted to the bar in Connecticut. He enlisted with the British Army during World War I; the US Army had rejected him because of his eyesight. Fluent in French, he served in Paris as a telephone operator. So, after the attack on Pearl Harbor, it was no surprise when Anne's father found a way to serve. Despite his recent surgery for an ulcer, he joined the Minnesota State Guard, which was created to provide back-up support at home because the Minnesota National Guard had been activated for the war. At age fifty-one, he was one of the oldest recruits.

Anne might also have been influenced by British priests who had come to her high school during the early months of the war in Europe, when she was a senior at an Episcopal girls' boarding school in Faribault. The priests visited and told vivid stories about the battles and hardships in Europe during the years before the United States was directly involved in the war.

Anne chose the WAC because the other branches, especially the WAVE recruiters, were so disparaging of it. She did not want to be part of a snobbish organization. She signed up for the duration of the war plus six months. On May 15, 1942, President Roosevelt had signed legislation creating the Women's Army Auxiliary Corps (WAAC). Women were enlisted with less authority, lower rank, less pay, and fewer benefits than men in similar positions. In July 1942, the navy began Women Accepted for Voluntary Emergency Service (WAVES), on the same basis as male reservists. Perhaps in response to the navy's position and increasing competition in recruiting, in June 1943, WAAC became Women's Army Corps (WAC), dropping "auxiliary." With the change in name, women were given equal rank and pay. Anne was entering the more equitable version of the women's unit with the army.

· · · · ·

Anne had a physical exam at Fort Snelling and was sworn in on her twentieth birthday, September 20, 1944, the youngest age for women to be accepted into the army. After the ceremony, her family celebrated with dinner at one of their favorite restaurants, the Covered Wagon, complete with Manhattan cocktails for toasting. Her father was especially proud that she was continuing the family tradition of army service. Her only sibling, a brother, was too young to enlist.

On October 8, 1944, Anne arrived at Fort Des Moines, Iowa, for basic training. She and the other recruits learned to march and were tested on guard duty, articles of war, and world history. She adjusted to the ill-fitting uniforms, living in barracks, and "putrid chow, no room for my stuff, obnoxious Southerners, pushups, and KP." She wrote home that she felt "pretty low at 5 a.m. on Saturday morning while cleaning out the grease trap over Number 3 mess," but her spirits improved later that evening after spending time singing and having a couple of beers at the PX with friends.

Upon completion of her basic training, Anne was sent to William Beaumont General Hospital at Fort Bliss, El Paso, Texas, where she began medical classes: anatomy, nursing, first aid, and pharmacy. She woke every day at 5:30 AM, made it to reveille by 6 AM, and ate breakfast by 6:40 AM at a coed mess hall, where the men whistled at the women constantly. Anne and her family wrote to each other to share their respective challenges at home and in the military for the duration of her service. Anne's mother, concerned for her safety, worried about her dating too much or drinking too much. Anne replied that the streets of El Paso were "crawling with MPs who would come" to her rescue. Her mother finally relented, agreeing that Anne had "plenty of balance and common sense to manage." Through her letters, Anne asked her parents and brother to keep up their busy social lives and happy times. She asked them not to share their inner feelings of concern or fears for her. She was counting on them to keep up her morale.

Anne Bosanko with her
father, Paul Bosanko,
a World War I veteran.
MNHS Collections

Through other letters, her parents reported on their victory garden, canning efforts, and challenges coping with rations. One coupon book noted the reasons for the rations: "1. Soldiers need the sugar more than civilians. 2. Ships normally bringing sugar into the United States were now needed to transport military supplies. 3. Labor shortages exist at sugar refineries because labor is needed for war production. 4. Beet production has decreased. 5. Demand for sugar for canning has cut into general sugar supplies." One advantage that Anne had was access to some goods in the PX that were difficult or expensive to buy at home. She often sent cartons of cigarettes to her parents, which they appreciated. In return, they sent her anything the PX was short of. Once she wrote and asked them to send clothes hangers immediately.

Her mother also shared news that in January 1945, the Episcopalian bishop for

Japan was at their cathedral. The Nisei choir from Fort Snelling, consisting of the Japanese men in the military language installation and several Japanese WACs, sang. The bishop spoke about the hope of eradicating racial prejudice. He commended the Twin Cities for accepting relocated Japanese people.

· · · · ·

After two months of training at Beaumont Hospital, Anne became a surgical technician, proficient at assisting in surgery, sterilizing instruments, and injecting patients. She was assigned to LaGarde General Hospital in New Orleans on February 9, 1945. She began caring for patients in the bedside and postoperative areas. In March, she was transferred to Birmingham General Hospital, Van Nuys, California. Her surgical cases included bone and skin grafts, wound revisions, hernia repairs, hemorrhoidectomies, finger amputations, appendectomies, nephrectomies, and colostomy closures. Doctors performed a gallbladder operation on Madame Aurora Quezon, wife of the president of the Philippines. However, the number of servicemen being evacuated was declining. On the bright side, this location was a bus or streetcar ride from Hollywood, which made up for the circumstances at the hospital. Anne and her coworkers could frequent one of the largest and best-known USO locations, the Hollywood Canteen, where celebrities such as the Andrews Sisters performed. Beyond performances, celebrities could be seen serving sandwiches and milk and signing souvenir postcards.

Within a month of Anne's arrival, President Roosevelt died. At the hospital, staff observed a five-minute period of silence but continued their work. After the war in Europe ended in May, as the workload lessened and the sense of urgency abated, Anne's morale dropped. After celebration of Victory in Japan (V-J) Day (August 15, 1945), morale plummeted further as the workload continued to decrease and the purpose of fighting an enemy was gone. Many WACs, including Anne, would be in the service at least six more months, as dictated by their enlistment terms. Anne worried that she would be twenty-three by the time she was discharged and she was no longer sure about continuing her education when she returned. She never "felt more useless, never [had] life seemed more futile."

The deaths she witnessed also had a cumulative impact on Anne. One weekend a seventeen-year-old merchant seaman was brought in after an auto wreck. Anne thought the surgeon did a marvelous job, but the young man died the next morning. In another accident, German POWs were injured when their truck overturned on the way to a farm; three of them died. Perhaps most memorable was the young serviceman who hanged himself in a grove outside the post. He had been depressed about his heart condition, a consequence of rheumatic fever.

Anne decided if she had to stay a WAC for nearly another year, she would take on something different. The need was shifting from nursing to occupational therapy, to help injured troops in rehabilitation. She transferred to Halloran General

Hospital, Staten Island, New York, for training. She was thrilled to be in New York, with opportunities to visit Times Square and take advantage of a plentiful array of entertainment options. In her new role, Anne taught crafts and, at one point, managed a unit dedicated to weaving. In New York, the blue WAC uniform was similar to that of the civilian mess hall workers. Anne was frustrated when she was mistaken for a kitchen worker. This hospital had not utilized WAC medical assistants previously. Upon the WACs' arrival, Anne wrote, they were perceived to be "queer neolithic creatures, or a third set."

· · · · ·

On February 8, 1946, Anne was assigned to Madigan General Hospital, Fort Lewis, Tacoma, Washington. During her first week there, she experienced an earthquake. An explosive noise shook the windowpanes. She felt the building rock back and forth, and the wall lockers almost fell over. Despite this frightening jolt, Anne found the landscape to be pretty and familiar, reminding her of the North Shore along Lake Superior in Minnesota, with huge pine trees and views of the water. As she tried to develop a plan for her future, she had many locations to compare to her home state: Des Moines, Los Angeles, New York City, New Orleans, El Paso. When she was homesick, she recalled Minnesota weather, even the winters, fondly. She compared the people she met from many other regions of the country to the people she knew at home. In the end, Anne concluded Minnesota was a mind-set, a worldview, and not merely a physical place.

· · · · ·

In March, Anne's father, who had written to her often, mentioned in a letter that he was having problems with his stomach again. He had had surgery a couple of years before for an ulcer. She also received news that a WAC she knew well had been assigned to Bushnell Hospital in Utah and, shortly after her arrival there, had attempted suicide. She had been crying for hours on end, and the WACs in her unit were worried about her but never intervened. Anne suspected that months of hard physical labor with no days off and being "bitched at by those fool nurses just broke her down." The woman took an overdose of sleeping pills but was found in time. Her stomach was pumped and she was moved to a neuro-psychiatric ward, where she continued to cry and laugh excessively and was eventually diagnosed to be manic-depressive.

On May 12, 1946, Anne was told to see her sergeant. She worried she was in some sort of trouble. Instead, the sergeant asked her to sit down and gave her a telegram from her mother: "Dad died suddenly early this morning. Please wire if you can get home for the funeral." Shocked, Anne arranged for a leave through the Minnesota Red Cross. She returned for the funeral by train.

Anne learned that her father died of stomach cancer. The surgery he had in the past was not for an ulcer, but for cancer. Her parents decided not to tell Anne and her brother. While she was home, Anne was able to spend time with friends, many of whom were on leave from the military or recently discharged. After the funeral leave, Anne returned to Fort Lewis and worked until she was discharged in August 1946. Several people she knew were planning on continuing their education at the University of Chicago, so Anne decided to apply there as well, thinking she needed a change of venue from Minnesota.

Upon her discharge, she stopped in Chicago to register for classes at the university on her way back to Minneapolis. Before the semester began, a man from home she had known before going into the service proposed and she changed her plans. They both registered for classes at the University of Minnesota, using GI benefits to cover the cost of tuition and books. After their marriage, Anne put her career on hold to raise three children. Her husband continued his education through law school and became a practicing attorney. Anne was active in community organizations, including the League of Women Voters. She waited until 1959, when their children were older, before she returned to school through an experimental continuing education program at the University of Minnesota. She earned a degree and spent her career as a school psychologist.

Reflecting on her service, Anne felt the war did not turn her into a feminist; she had been a feminist since she took an American history course in tenth grade. She knew that women could contribute more than housework and Barbies. It did not occur to her that a large part of humankind did not want women to contribute and were in fact threatened by the idea. She reported, "Joining the WAC gave me the chance to be more than a spectator in the worldwide upheaval that touched everyone's lives."

The War in Europe

15

D-DAY AND THE LIBERATION OF PARIS

Writing for Time-Life 1942-44

Mary Welsh, a journalist from Walker, Minnesota, who had been covering the war in Europe since 1938, wrote a story for *Life* magazine in February 1942 about American army units in northern Ireland. She noted that the first man off the ship was a private from Hutchinson, Minnesota. The US Army cook was distressed, claiming that they had "gone back 20 years. No refrigerators, no electricity, no mixing machines."

During 1942, Mary covered American troops and wrote many articles for *Time* and *Life*. Her husband, Noel Monks, covered British action for other periodicals. They were not together very often, and in mid-1942, Time arranged for Mary to visit the New York office for a break. Her first stop on her return was to see her parents in Thief River Falls in northern Minnesota, near where she grew up. She was relieved to find them living comfortably but modestly in a clapboard white house with a lawn and garden. They were feeling the impact of the food and gasoline rations. After her visit, the sight of them on the train platform, waving goodbye to her again, stayed with her.

The local paper published an article, "London Writer Visits Parents in Thief River Falls," and included a quote from the Time bureau chief, who described Mary as "without a doubt the ablest female journalist in London," noting that "until Dunkirk she was the only woman correspondent with the R.A.F. in France."

In New York, she was given an office on the seventeenth floor of the Time-Life Building, overlooking Rockefeller Center. She was assigned to do a piece she considered rather trivial about tensions between the American soldiers and the British Tommies. Years into the war, the British forces did not have the same resources, even down to cash to use in pubs. The piece did not generate much reaction externally from readers, but Mary discovered that it "ignited a small intramural brushfire" within Time-Life. At this time, men were the writers and women were restricted to researching. The men resented the encroachment on their territory, and the women were upset that Mary was allowed to write an article when they were not. After that, only a few people from the office would socialize with her.

In addition to the alienation she experienced in the office, Mary felt more like an outsider in the stores and restaurants. Meals at restaurants were served with much more food than people in Britain and France received, and, worse, plates in the United States were often returned to the kitchen with food on them. The opulence disturbed her. Passport issues kept her in New York three months longer than she intended to stay.

Finally, on January 1, 1943, Mary headed back to London. After six months in the United States, she was distressed by the gray, weary nature of her colleagues and friends in Britain. She felt guilty about the relatively plush life she had in New York. She also had to adjust again to her close proximity to the military action. During a small dinner party in her neighborhood, her friends continued talking casually while guns blasted nearby and Mary sat on her hands to hide their shaking.

While Mary was acclimating, President Roosevelt and Prime Minister Churchill were meeting in Casablanca under trellised bougainvillea. Her husband passed through London, visiting her briefly before heading to North Africa as well. They acknowledged that circumstances of the war kept them apart more than they expected, and they knew their plans to start a family had to be delayed. They missed long walks and quiet evenings together. Mary gloomily accepted the news from friends a few weeks later that Noel was "squiring a pretty girl" in Cairo. She decided to not worry about it and resolve any issues they had later, after the war.

In the meantime, Mary received a letter from her parents notifying her that they were moving from northern Minnesota to Chicago, where they might be of more use during the war. Mary was not sure what her father would be able to do there and considered it a "gallant gesture and foolhardy," but there was not much she could do from overseas beyond accept the reality of the situation.

In September 1943, Mary had an opportunity to attend a concert in Royal Albert Hall, where she heard the American composer Marc Blitzstein conduct a small orchestra of servicemen. He opened the concert with "Freedom Morning," a piece he had just finished writing, a tribute to the black American servicemen he heard singing around his unit, the Eighth Air Force. Also on the program that evening were pieces that resembled military-sounding Sousa marches juxtaposed with religious melodies. A chorus of servicemen sang, some of the pieces in a cappella: "From the darkness the rolling liquid song which could only be American emerged, 'Joshua fit the battle of Jericho, Jericho, Jericho . . . Joshua fit the battle of Jericho. And the walls . . . came tumblin' down." By the end, tears poured out of Mary.

Mary adjusted to rationing but sometimes struggled to preserve her food. A piece of wartime cheese, a very low-quality morsel, went bad in her refrigerator, which had stopped working. She tried to eat it anyway to avoid wasting it, but it made her sick, so she threw the small bit away. Within a couple of days, a man appeared at her door with a summons to appear in court for disposing of food. She had to hire an attorney to represent her. He explained to the judge that Mary's refrigerator had stopped working and she was trying to get it repaired. The judge cut him off and dismissed the case, noting that while the British people had managed for centuries without mechanical refrigeration, it was obviously a necessity for Americans. Mary also heard of a woman who had been arrested for throwing bread crumbs to the swans in Hyde Park.

Mary continued covering the war for Time-Life. In March 1944, she was "getting terrific, fulsome compliments from New York" on the King George cover story. She worked hard to gather information for her articles, and she had to relentlessly negotiate with the military censors to get her stories through. She picked up some of her tips from offhanded comments made by military officials living in her building, such as Admiral George Barry Wilson, General Eisenhower's aquatic division head. She socialized with American expatriates and other socialites, including William Saroyan, Irwin Shaw, and Alexander Fleming, whose efforts along with others' had resulted in the discovery of penicillin in 1928. She also worked closely with many notable photographers, including Lee Miller and Bob Capa.

Liberating France

In mid-1944, noting that several ports were closed off from civilian business and speculation was building that the Allied forces would soon be attempting to free France from Nazi control, Mary tried to determine when the attack might take place. She went to Foyles bookshop on Charing Cross Road and bought an almanac that listed all of the high tides in the English Channel. From this guide, she suspected that the Allied forces would cross the channel on June 4, 5, or 6. She shared her findings with a military officer who passively acknowledged that she was right but threatened to jail her unless she promised to keep the secret. The spring bombings of London intensified. There were thirteen major raids, with three hundred bombers in each.

One sunny, cheerful day in spring of 1944, Irwin Shaw took Mary to lunch at the White Tower. When they were seated on the second floor, Shaw pointed out that the large man across the room wearing a Royal Air Force (RAF) uniform was Ernest Hemingway. Mary had met his wife, Martha Gellhorn Hemingway, another journalist, a few months before at a cocktail party. The room was warm, and Mary took off her jacket, revealing her large chest. Shaw noted that they would probably have many men stopping by their table. He was right: several men stopped by to talk with Shaw and meet Mary. Soon Hemingway came over and asked Shaw to introduce him to her. Mary found his voice sounded younger than she expected. He asked her to join him for lunch in a few days, an offer Mary accepted. Shaw immediately predicted that something would come of the lunch with Hemingway. Mary said, "You're off your rocker."

At their lunch, Ernest noted his admiration for the RAF and admitted he did not initially understand the accents of the people he encountered nor the flying jargon. He was writing for *Collier's*. During their conversation, Mary noted there were gaps in his knowledge of the RAF and the outcomes of many battles, including the Battle of Britain. She filled him in and recommended some background reading. He took notes and seemed to seriously consider her information and advice. He mentioned he had met her husband during the Spanish War and thought he "was a great guy, 'classy.'" Mary thought the lunch was very businesslike and did not expect to see Hemingway again.

But Mary did see Ernest again, on multiple occasions in London among gatherings of her friends and colleagues. The encounters were not by chance; it seemed he was finding ways to see her. One warm evening, he arrived at her friend's flat and they sat in the dark, due to the blackout, while Ernest told her long stories about his family. At the end he said, "I don't know you, Mary. But I want to marry you. You are very alive. You're beautiful, like a May fly." She did not reply. He continued, "I want to marry you now, and I hope to marry you sometime. Sometime you may want to marry me." Again, she did not reply. Eventually, she told him he was silly and reminded him they both were married.

By this time the Allied forces were bombing France daily, trying to get control of the country from Germany. One morning, Mary had the opportunity to ride in a Mitchell with a radial engine. She was strapped into the bombardier's seat, and the plane shot up twelve thousand feet. The crew flew along fighters as they came into formation. She was witnessing one of the highest-powered armadas England had ever known. When the pilot turned back, he dropped the plane suddenly at a forty-five-degree curve. Mary wildly looked for something to hold on to, sure they were about to crash. Instead, they leveled off and returned just above the treetops.

In late May, after the couple had been separated nearly a year, Noel returned to London. They spent time with friends and together, but Mary sensed something different about him. She didn't bring up the rumors about his girlfriend in Cairo, and he didn't mention "any carryings-on" of hers in London. During this time, Mary heard that Hemingway had been injured in a car accident. She took him a bouquet of daffodils and tulips, and he asked her to visit him again in a couple of days when he would be discharged.

Landing on Normandy

On the morning of June 6, 1944, a military friend called and told Mary, "Take the curlers out of your hair and get going." She did not have any curlers, but she did get going and was soon aboard a C-47 with others from the press. The air tour ended up not being very newsworthy. She returned to the ground and waited. About a hundred bombs fell daily as Allied troops exhibited strength in the air and troops landed and secured Normandy beach.

While the press and citizens of London waited to see the outcome of the intense air and ground fighting at Normandy, including one of the bloodiest confrontations on Omaha Beach, Mary and Ernest had lunch. As they talked, they discovered a common interest in boats. Mary recalled her fond memories of being on the water with her father in northern Minnesota. They both had friends among Native Americans. This time together was the beginning of a courtship. Hemingway promised to dedicate a book to her. She wondered how many similar promises he had made to women.

By mid-July, Mary's request to accompany a medical corps in Normandy was finally approved. She was disappointed to learn that a small group of women would be transported together. Mary was accustomed to traveling alone, which usually permitted her to be closer to the action. With these women, she would be billeted in a hospital with less opportunity to move freely. The feature stories she wrote for *Life* were more in-depth than the wire stories these women would be sending back. She did not want an escorted tour.

Mary managed to disengage from the group almost immediately after arriving in Normandy. Using her connections, she was able to get the commanding officer to approve for her to go forward to battalion clearing stations and then along the line of evacuation. Her first night at the transit camp was cold and damp. She slept in her full uniform within her sleeping bag with additional padding, and yet she felt deeply chilled and found the dried egg breakfast with unrecognizable coffee to be little consolation. She wondered how the GIs tolerated the conditions.

Her military escort and driver stopped periodically so Mary could look at the abandoned battlefields, vast and desolate but cluttered with gas masks, helmets, canteens, food rations, rifles, and even dead soldiers. At one field she followed the familiar scent of death to two young men lying in a ditch, one whose blue eyes stared up at the gray sky. The top of another soldier's head was missing. When she arrived at the battalion station, she walked the rows of beds in the evacuation hospital. She was "struck by their terrible anonymity. Name, serial number, blood type, army unit. . . . Nobody knew . . . which of the bodies had been high school football captains or presidents of the local drama club, or hot men on the guitar." She felt an urge to comfort all of them but did not know how she, as a whole person, could comfort a soldier who had lost a leg or worse.

Liberating Paris

After a few days, Mary returned to London and spent some time with Ernest while writing a cover story for *Time* about supply lines. There was less bombing in the city now thanks to antiaircraft guns along the southeast coast, which stopped about half of the incoming fire. Despite the relative comfort and ability to track important decisions being made in London, Mary yearned to return to Paris, where she had been in the early months of the war, to see and cover the city's liberation.

In late August, Mary got the necessary approvals but had to wait because there was a shortage of jeeps. She had packed light in case she would have to carry her load on her back. She took a sleeping bag, good road maps, candles, matches, her helmet, a water bottle, her proper uniform (skirt, shirt, and battle blouse), and her typewriter, of course. She wore her khaki trousers, field jacket, and flat shoes, which she found much more comfortable, especially when she had to stand around and wait for hours. Finally, the colonel who agreed to take her with him was ready to depart. As they left the Normandy airfield, Mary quickly determined that he did not seem very proficient at reading army maps. She wrote to her parents about the trip:

> Since he was the senior officer in the jeep, I had to be polite about it and not intrude my views about routes. I let him go five miles out of his way before suggesting he have a look at my map, which showed me very clearly which way we should go, but it indicated very little to him since he had never learned, apparently, to read a map. By now it was raining furiously with about a bucket a minute coming through the roof of the jeep where there was a big tare [sic] and landing on me, giving me that [sic] appearance of a drowned rabbit which is not much help in persuading Full Colonels that I know better than they do how to navigate a jeep through France.

Eventually they made it when the colonel began to take some of her advice and confirmed their directions at every crossroads with the military police. When they arrived, Mary dropped her knapsack, typewriter, and bedroll at a small hotel and walked a short distance to Hôtel Scribe, where the press was gathering. Along the way, Parisians hugged and kissed her when they saw her uniform. Oddly, her first assignment in Paris this time was to cover Parisian fashions and what had happened to prestigious houses such as Chanel and Vera Borea. Occupation by the Germans and a shortage of materials kept these big names dormant, but it was clear they had survived and were beginning to emerge from behind a shuttered existence.

The press and public waited for Charles de Gaulle, escorted by French general Philippe Leclerc and the US Eighty-Second Division, to return to Paris. Mary recorded everything she saw and heard from Place de la Concorde, along Champs-Élysées, and at Arc de Triomphe. The crowd roared, "Vive la France" and "Vivent les Américans!" Thousands continued on for a mass of thanksgiving at Notre-Dame, where bells rang loudly. Mary entered the crowded cathedral, where she heard the choir and a few accidentally discharged rifles. In the article she wrote for *Life*, Mary described what she saw under the title "PARIS IS FREE AGAIN!" and the photographer captured images of people hanging out of windows and sitting on rooftops as they watched the Allied troops and dignitaries pass by. Farther back in the magazine, Mary had a short piece titled "The Fashions." Primarily, she noted the enormous hat styles and earrings "as large as oranges, from ear to shoulder." Paris was returning to its old and new self.

The day ended with a late-night dinner with Ernest Hemingway and his translator. He spoke mostly of his memories of Paris when he had first moved there, and he began calling Mary by the nickname "Pickle." They spent the night in his room at the Ritz. They maintained separate rooms on different floors, but the manager, a stickler for propriety, did not seem to notice that they spent the next several days in one room.

Mary took a break from reporting, and she and Ernest reacquainted themselves with the liberated city. They lunched and visited with friends, including Paul Cézanne, Sylvia Beach at her bookstore—Shakespeare and Company—Pablo Picasso, Gertrude Stein, and Marlene Dietrich. Perhaps the most touching moment occurred when Mary saw Yehudi Menuhin walk onto the stage of the Opéra of Paris for the first time after the liberation. She watched as he played "La Marseillaise." The deafening applause shook the hall. The orchestra joined him first in playing Mendelssohn's Concerto in E Minor, then a French piece, and ended with Beethoven. The music and being in the midst of an audience of people who had just emerged from a bloody war filled Mary with emotion. And yet, Britain was still under siege.

For the next couple of weeks, Mary and Ernest lived and worked out of their quarters at the Paris Ritz. He wrote poems to her while she resumed reporting. In early September, Ernest rejoined the Fourth Army Division, but they wrote to each other steadily, the permanence of their relationship growing.

The Battle of the Bulge and Entering Germany

In late October, Ernest's son, Jack Hemingway, a lieutenant in an intelligence unit of the army, was wounded and captured in a mountainous region of eastern France still held by the Germans. Ernest wanted to go immediately using his press credentials to check on his son but thought better of it. If the Germans knew they had a celebrity's son in custody, they might try to avail themselves of the bargaining advantage it might give them. Instead, Ernest convinced Mary to go behind enemy lines using her press credentials to get as close as possible to Jack.

Once again, Mary was driven by a soldier so young she referred to him as her child-driver, but they made it through the countryside and up six thousand feet into the mountains. The captain of Jack's unit took her to the very spot where, among the pines, mud, and snow, Jack had been captured. Mary documented the surroundings and sent back cables to Ernest and the Time office, since she was allegedly working during this trip. She was a quarter of a mile from the front; she could see the entrenched German soldiers. While she was scouting around, looking for any information about Jack, the Germans fired several mortars, blowing up a piece of the hillside above her.

As Mary returned to the unit with her escorts, she thought it seemed "incongruous that people should be trying to kill each other across that pretty, tranquil valley; that bones and boys' blood might at any moment disfigure the Christmas-card scenery." She verified that Jack's shoulder had been injured and that he was being treated well. His only identification was his dog tags, so the Germans should not have suspected his identity.

As the Allies continued advancing toward Germany, Mary began covering the Allied countries as they positioned themselves, acting like victors planning to divide up the spoils of war. She also covered trials of those found to be traitors to France during the war. She worked and lived with "water sliding icily from the hot tap six days a week," hot water available only on Sundays. Prices for goods more than doubled. During this time, Ernest began planning their future together in Cuba. During a cold, bleak December, they remained in Paris as the Germans mounted their last significant effort, the Battle of the Bulge. Ernest headed off to rejoin the division hosting him, but Mary stayed behind at the Ritz.

In the early days of the new year, Mary decided it was time to tell her parents that she was leaving her husband, Noel, and had met someone new, but she did not divulge Ernest's identity. She was also called back to London by her boss at Time. By the end of February, she had been released by the War Department and planned to return home. She wrote her parents, and this time she admitted that there were rumors circulating about her and Ernest Hemingway, but she could not talk about it until she came home. Ernest left for the States March 6.

The following day, the Ninth Armored Division crossed the Rhine into Germany, the first of four divisions to get across before the bridge collapsed. Mary found a way to fly overhead with a reconnaissance flight. Everything she saw was destroyed, except for cemeteries. Forests had been burned, villages leveled, and bridge buttresses broken. Smoke filled the air. She stayed to pick through the ruins of Cologne. She saw how the Germans had stored food in their cellars and how healthy their children looked. They had reaped the benefits of having the upper hand throughout Europe for the previous four years.

The article Mary submitted after this trip was one of the last pieces she wrote as a working reporter. She negotiated a year's sabbatical beginning at the end of March. On her way home, she and some Red Cross women shopped in Halifax for unrationed chocolate and nylon stockings. From there she went by train to New York, where on April 12 she was unpacking at the Ambassador Hotel on Park Avenue when she heard that President Roosevelt had died. She was asked to appear on Time's *March of Time* radio show that evening to comment on the impact the president's death might have on US military men and women.

Shortly after she left London, she received a letter from Major General F. L. Anderson, who wrote, "I am greatly appreciative of the wonderful job you have done for the Air Forces over here. Your understanding, your patience, and your good will have been invaluable . . . but your greatest characteristic . . . was your desire to present the true picture above all other things."

Marriage to Ernest Hemingway

Mary visited her aging parents, who now resided in Chicago, and spent some time with friends before joining Ernest in Cuba. She began adjusting to life in his compound, learning the Spanish language and about Cuban customs. There was a constant stream of family and friends, including Jack, his son, who arrived after being released by the Germans at the end of the war. She worked on the paperwork related to her divorce from Noel. She felt herself sink "into depressions of spirit, no deeper than gullies" despite the excitement of her new life with Ernest. He convinced her not to continue in journalism, and she felt the loss of her independence and her new dependence on him financially and for all decisions about their living.

On June 7, 1945, she wrote in her journal: "The man has his house, his writing, his children, his cats. Nothing is mine. . . . I can't fight for area of personal domination. . . . I feel very much alone, knowing nothing of the pursuit of fish, animals and birds." She flew to Chicago, and on August 31, 1945, her divorce was finalized. Less than a week later, on September 2, the war ended, and the following year, on March 21, 1946, Mary Welsh married Ernest Hemingway, becoming his fourth and last wife, a marriage that would last for fifteen years, a period during which he wrote *The Old Man and the Sea* and won the Pulitzer and Nobel Prizes in literature.

Mary gave up journalism, in part, because Ernest told her, "you're a great reporter now, but when you get older you're not gonna have all these fellows eager to help you out with information." She enjoyed her career and thought she was lucky to have done what she did as a woman decades before the women's movement in the United States. She felt liberated and thought she experienced very little discrimination because she was female. She decided after living in Cuba with Ernest for a year that he was "fascinating and complicated and charming" and that she would prefer a life with him instead of continuing her career.

Over the years, Mary and Ernest traveled extensively, including on safaris through Africa. Mary wrote very little. Their marriage was filled with great joys and great strife, some of it related to Ernest's chemical dependency and depression. Mary took him back to Minnesota, her home state, to Mayo Clinic for treatment, but ultimately their marriage ended in 1961 with his suicide.

16

THE 28TH GENERAL HOSPITAL DURING D-DAY AND THE BATTLE OF THE BULGE

When the Allied forces started landing on Normandy Beach on June 6, 1944, and journalist Mary Welsh from Minnesota was trying to make her way to the action, the staff of the 28th General Hospital was on the southern coast of England across the English Channel waiting to care for casualties. As the one hundred and five army corps nurses, including Mabel Johnson from Eveleth, Minnesota, made their night rounds, they heard the constant drone of planes. They had been anticipating the attack for weeks.

The first casualty came in at 4:45 AM, a pilot from Nebraska who had dropped some of the first paratroopers. He had been shot on his return trip and suffered a gunshot wound and compound fracture of his left femur. In addition to confirming this was the military operation the staff had been waiting for, he said he was grateful for being able to complete his mission. He was hemorrhaging and was given blood plasma. The pilot was in surgery within forty-five minutes of arriving.

Hundreds of casualties followed. Many of them sustained shrapnel wounds. Once the debris was removed and the wound closed, skin grafts were done if necessary. One serviceman arrived with an extensive white phosphorous burn on his face, which occurred when his bomb-loaded boat hit a mine. His face no longer looked human.

During its twenty-three-month deployment, the 28th General Hospital, sometimes acting like an evacuation hospital, cared for forty thousand patients. Mabel acknowledged that they worked long hours, but she appreciated the opportunity to help the men "who were offering everything to hasten victory." Their courage and bravery inspired the staff to do their utmost in caring for them.

Mabel kept focused on her work in England even when she received the startling Red Cross cable a few months earlier notifying her that her sister, Alice, was critically ill with a strep infection. Once the infection spread into her bloodstream, doctors feared she would die. Mabel replied in another cable saying she was beside herself with worry and she hoped penicillin was being used. For the first time, Mabel seriously wished she had never joined the army. She wanted badly to be home with her family. Thanks to the penicillin, which had just become available for general use, Alice lived, as did many of Mabel's patients.

In addition to the frightening news about Alice, Mabel also received word that her cousin Kenneth had been killed in the fighting in France. His wife had been teaching radio code in the Sioux Falls, South Dakota, schools. Mabel had seen him once by coincidence when they were both stationed near London. Mabel managed to maintain connections with home, mostly by letter, even though she was very close to the front at times.

· · · · ·

Now a long way from home, Mabel had been born in 1905 on the Iron Range, in Eveleth. In the fall of 1943, she was assigned to the Army Nurse Corps at Station Hospital, Fort Riley, Kansas, and subsequently the 28th General Hospital in Swannanoa, North Carolina. That unit departed on December 22 on the former luxury liner the *Queen Mary*. They arrived in Britain, where they trained and treated patients in various locations until they moved to the coast of the English Channel in April and began taking patients from the D-Day fighting in June.

Mabel and the staff of the 28th General Hospital stayed along the southern border of England for a few months, accepting the stream of casualties that came in from the European fronts. The nurses unloaded patients from trains upon arrival and then escorted the injured in ambulances to the hospital. They wore fatigues, not their standard nurse's uniforms during this time. As the troops moved into France, so did the 28th General Hospital. The staff arrived in Normandy in mid-August, where they stayed until they moved to Liège, Belgium, in late September. At first, they were not as busy as they expected to be, but the nurses were required to work ten hours a day regardless. To keep busy, the women folded gauze until they were almost cross-eyed.

Some of the servicemen Mabel encountered as patients were memorable. One young man was blind and needed to be led everywhere he went. Many of the men had trench foot, an infection caused by the wet conditions. Their feet were covered in blisters or blue from the lack of circulation. In severe cases, amputation was necessary. When the hospital was busy, German prisoners of war would be assigned to assist on the wards, especially with heavy lifting. Mabel admitted she felt some "disgust and hatred" toward them, although many of them looked like kids. She thought, "Hitler must be reaching the end of the rope" if he is recruiting such young soldiers.

Once, hospital staff cared for a seven-year-old boy named Ernest, who had been hit by a US command vehicle. He had a broken leg and a head injury. He had lost blood and was in shock. He remained unconscious and required surgery to relieve the pressure from a subdural hematoma. He recovered well and became very popular on the unit. Other patients would read or sing to him, and his family brought fresh flowers and eggs, which were a welcome surprise. The staff had only eaten powdered eggs for most of the deployment.

In late November, tensions increased in the region as Germany attempted to retaliate against the losses it had incurred in France. On December 16, 1944, the Battle of the Bulge began. While D-Day was an important and well-known military operation, the Battle of the Bulge became the bloodiest single battle of World War II for the Americans. Fortunately, it was the last major German offensive campaign. It began in the heavily forested areas in east Belgium and involved 450,000 German troops. There were 89,000 American casualties and 19,000 deaths.

Mabel and the 28th General Hospital were only twelve miles from enemy lines. The location became dangerous when the Germans began using the first guided missiles ever deployed, V-2 rocket missiles. Many US hospitals in the region were hit, and on December 26 and 28, Mabel's hospital was bombed. Within ten minutes, every nurse was at her post to comfort and care for the patients. Ironically, the only death in that attack was a German POW.

One of the incoming American soldiers told the hospital staff they were seven miles from Cologne. They often relied on patients to inform them of their location and the status of the war because these details were not shared with them for security reasons. Coincidentally, a patient arriving during this period turned out to be the husband of one of the nurses. Fortunately, his injuries were not fatal. The Battle of the Bulge ended on January 25, 1945, with the Allies winning but at great cost.

Memorial services were held for President Roosevelt's death in April. The Belgians draped black crepe paper over their flags. They also watched trucks of liberated soldiers, most of them French, pass by from Germany. Mabel felt proud the US troops had made their release possible. Some of the newly freed prisoners were brought to the 28th General Hospital for treatment. Mabel noted they looked pathetic after two years of imprisonment. On average, they had each lost forty pounds. Nearly all of them had bronchitis or pneumonia. The hospital staff used penicillin to treat cases of diphtheria.

In July 1945, the hospital relocated to Sissonne, France, where the census was six hundred when they first arrived. By August, the workload had lightened and the danger had abated, allowing Mabel and the other staff to get to the Riviera. The blue Mediterranean Sea, beautiful oleanders, and the sandy beach provided them with a much-needed respite.

After Victory in Japan (V-J) day in August, the nurses either hoped to go home or looked for another interesting assignment. Becoming a public health nurse in Germany was one option. Mabel felt a little bitter about the army. Its recruiters had promised her additional training and promotional opportunities, but that did not happen. Although she was honored to treat the servicemen and be a part of winning the war, most of her work had been tedious. After returning from a leave spent in Switzerland, Mabel found herself transferred to another hospital, one that was scheduled to return home soon. By December 1945, Mabel was back in Eveleth, Minnesota.

· · · · ·

Mabel Johnson on overseas deployment to Europe. *Mabel L. Johnson Papers, MNHS Collections*

Another army corps nurse from the Iron Range was still on duty when Mabel left Europe. Rose Polga was one of ten children of Italian immigrant parents who grew up in the mining town of Buhl. After graduating from high school and spending some time at the junior college, she went to Rochester, Minnesota, for nursing school. She attended the Kahler School of Nursing, associated with Mayo Clinic. Her diploma was signed by the Mayo brothers in 1938. She returned to work at a hospital near her home for a short time, and then she went to Los Angeles. When Pearl Harbor was attacked, Ruth visited home briefly and then enlisted with the Army Nurse Corps, beginning active duty in 1942.

Rose Polga (Bayuk) onboard the US Army Hospital Ship *Thistle. Courtesy Mark Bayuk*

Rose's first assignment was a trip across the Atlantic Ocean on the RMS *Queen Elizabeth*, a British ocean liner repurposed for military service from 1940 to 1946. She traveled with thousands of troops headed for duty in Europe. She was then assigned to US Army Hospital Ship (USAHS) *Thistle*. She traveled back and forth on that ship eleven times, from the home port of Charleston, South Carolina, to wherever it needed to pick up patients: Gibraltar, Oran, Naples, and Marseille. On its last voyage, the USAHS *Thistle* went through the Panama Canal to Honolulu, Manila, and Leyte before docking in Los Angeles.

On board, Rose and the other nurses cared for 320 wounded servicemen. They had a total of 454 beds and carried chaplains, surgeons, social workers, a psychiatrist, and corpsmen. She listened to the injured men while she cared for and reassured them. Occasionally, German and Italian prisoners of war were on board, too. The meals were basic, many dinners of potatoes and bacon. Merchant Marines ran the ship, which as a floating hospital was lit and unarmed as it made its voyages across the ocean. Rose was released from active duty in March 1946. She returned to Buhl and worked as a school nurse and later as the director of nursing in a nursing home. She married Ed Bayuk, had a son, and moved to White Bear Lake, where she worked and remained active with the Red Cross for many years.

17

LIBERATION OF DACHAU

On May 3, 1945, two weeks after President Roosevelt's death and days after Mussolini was killed in Italy and Hitler committed suicide in Berlin, two nurses from Minnesota entered Dachau concentration camp outside Munich with their units. The smell of rotting flesh hung in the air. Boxcars packed from top to bottom with dead bodies sat along the tracks and roads that had brought two hundred thousand people to enslavement and where nearly forty thousand prisoners died during the twelve years it was open. More bodies were stacked in piles outside the crematorium. Beads of rain ran off the motionless faces. Dead dogs lay in kennels, shot by American soldiers after prisoners warned them the starving dogs were trained to attack. The army restored water, light, and disposal systems that hadn't been working for several days, contributing to the deplorable conditions. German people in the area helped load the bodies onto carts to take them outside the gates for internment in mass graves.

The 116th and 127th Army Evacuation Hospitals converted the German SS barracks, scrubbing them down with creosol, emitting another pungent smell that Dorothy Wahlstrom and Vera Brown would remember for the rest of their lives. Dachau began holding ten thousand prisoners, but by the time the Allied forces arrived, the camp had grown to thirty-five thousand prisoners, most of them severely undernourished and ill due to overcrowding and poor treatment. The 116th and 127th Evacuation Hospitals were set up to accommodate twelve hundred patients each. They brought X-ray equipment, a pharmacy, two operating rooms, a sterilizing unit, and a dental clinic.

Even the living looked near dead: skeletal, shaved heads, protruding eyes. Some did not move, either too weak or scared. Typhus was rampant. Dichlorodiphenyltrichloroethane (DDT) teams dusted the patients and premises daily to try to stop the spread of typhus via lice and rodents. Patients were first dusted with DDT and six hours later given a thorough bath, dusted again, put in pajamas, cataloged, and assigned to a ward. In addition to typhus, nearly a third of the prisoners had tuberculosis. Malnutrition was the largest problem, and many prisoners developed diarrhea when they began eating nutritious food.

The wards within the hospitals each held one hundred twenty patients, with two nurses to staff them during the day and one at night. The patients were Polish, Russian, and French. Some were priests. Jews had been brought for experimentation and extermination. Forty nationalities were represented. Language barriers were sometimes challenging for the nurses and patients. Soon patients were well enough to serve as translators. In one ward an Austrian doctor, quite ill with typhus, helped translate. The patients also started assisting each other as soon as they were strong enough.

· · · · ·

Emma Dorothy Wahlstrom was born in Gibbon, a small farming community in south-central Minnesota, in 1918. Her family moved to Clear Lake, Wisconsin, in 1925, and she graduated from high school there. Dorothy completed her nurse's training in St. Paul at Bethesda Hospital School of Nursing in 1939. After working at Gillette State Hospital for Crippled Children, Dorothy joined the Army Nurse Corps on July 23, 1941. She was assigned to the 127th Evacuation Hospital, which was activated in March 1944 at Camp Bowie, Texas, a unit of the Fourth Army Division. She and other recruits trained there, including caring for German POWs hospitalized in six wards of Station Hospital at Camp Bowie. They left for Europe by train on January 8, 1945, a trip that would eventually land them at Dachau.

· · · · ·

Vera Brown had been assigned to the Dachau liberation after being part of the 127th Evacuation Hospital. She had been in Paris for V-E Day and saw the celebration: people "swinging from the upper floors of the Opera House. They were so happy the war was over, they didn't know what to do with themselves." She also saw the French people dragging prisoners of war down the street unmercifully. She had been with the 103rd General Hospital in Perham Down, England, an hour outside of London, where the unit was set up in a rush, a sure indication that the invasion of France was about to take place. Two days after D-Day the hospital accepted a "flood of wounded young men." Vera administered anesthesia, mostly sodium pentothal and relaxants, sometimes nitrous oxide. Some of the more effective gases were not available because they were explosive. Vera and her colleagues worked around the clock trying to save men whose arms and legs had been shot off. Those who had been shot in the abdomen usually died. The nursing quarters were cramped, cold, and damp. Several of the nurses contracted tuberculosis while they were there. It was after these intense assignments that Vera Brown joined the evacuation hospitals at Dachau.

Vera had wanted to be a nurse from childhood. She pretended to wear a uniform and took care of other kids. Her dad discouraged her, saying she would have a career of emptying bedpans. She did her nurse's training at St. Joseph's Hospital in St. Paul. She loved the work and was offered a job at graduation in 1942 that promised to pay seventy dollars a week. When she saw that amount in her paycheck and found she was struggling financially, Vera joined the army, where she could make seventy dollars a week and get her room and board. She was assigned to Fort

Snelling, where she proudly wore her blue army uniform. She was at Fort Snelling until March 1943, when she was transferred to Fort Warren, near Cheyenne, Wyoming and then eventually posted overseas.

• • • • •

During six weeks at Dachau, Dorothy and the staff of the 127th Evacuation Hospital cared for 2,267 patients, most of them requiring treatment for a combination of diarrhea, malnutrition, typhus, and tuberculosis; 246 of their patients died. The 116th Hospital admitted an additional 2,057 patients, almost all of whom had typhus and were malnourished; 190 of those patients died. Dorothy felt as if they could not escape death. In the mornings, as she came to the hospital, seven or eight stretchers were lined up in front of each ward with those who had died during the night.

Dorothy and the staff of the 127th Evacuation Hospital stayed at Dachau until June 17, 1945. In addition to everything they witnessed, they carried the knowledge that Dachau was only one of the Nazi's twenty-seven concentration camps and eleven hundred satellite camps. And although nearly forty thousand people perished there from 1933 to 1945, more than 2.3 million men, women, and children—Jews, Jehovah's Witnesses, resistance activists, homosexuals, and other perceived enemies of the Third Reich—were imprisoned, enslaved, tortured, and abused; 1.7 million of them died across all of the camps and satellites. More disturbing is that the 1.7 million people who died in the camps are only a portion of the 6 million Jews who were killed by Nazis, shot in their homes, in the streets, in ditches and fields.

The evacuation hospitals were there while others celebrated the liberation of Paris and V-E Day throughout Europe. During their posting, the American flag flew

Dorothy Wahlstrom. *Clear Lake Wisconsin Historical Society*

at half-staff for President Roosevelt. Dorothy, Vera, and the other nurses were not the only women at Dachau when it was liberated. Elisabeth May Adams Craig, a journalist writing for the *Portland (Maine) Press Herald*, originally from Coosaw Mines, South Carolina, was there. Elisabeth May began as a super model for *Vogue* magazine and then studied photography. From behind the camera, she became a US Army correspondent for *Vogue* during World War II and visited four concentration camps, including Dachau when Dorothy and Vera were there.

On June, 17, 1945, the 127th Evacuation Hospital moved by motor and train to Camp Philadelphia in France, where its staff was stationed for two months caring for war casualties as troops began returning to the United States. They returned to Camp Patrick Henry, Virginia, and the unit was deactivated on November 30, 1945, in Fort Benning, Georgia. Dorothy remained with the Army Nurse Corps for another year, until August 3, 1946, completing five years of service before being discharged at Fort Sheridan, Illinois.

Vera remained at Dachau for three months before she was reassigned to a women's hospital near Wiesbaden. Finally, in December 1945, she had enough points (a measure of age, time served, service overseas) to be discharged. She boarded an Italian freighter so full the passengers had to sleep in shifts. They encountered a severe storm in the north Atlantic, and the ship pitched back and forth. They could see the propellers come out of the water, and one of the portholes burst. They landed in New York after fourteen days, and Vera took a train to Fort Des Moines for discharge. By the time she arrived, she had the flu, but once her paperwork was complete, she left in a car with her sister and brother, who had come to get her. On their way to Morris, they were caught in a terrible snowstorm. They drove as far as they could but eventually had to abandon the car and walk the last three and half miles in the storm. A big celebration had been planned to welcome Vera, but it was three o'clock in the morning when they arrived, and everyone had gone home.

· · · · ·

The war did not end on V-E or V-J day for Dorothy Wahlstrom. Upon retiring in 1981 due to arthritis, she concluded a thirty-five-year career with the Veterans Administration, St. Croix County, and other employers. Dorothy read about a Holocaust commemoration event being planned in St. Paul, Minnesota. She contacted a man mentioned in the article and was invited to speak at the event, held on April 18, 1985, at B'nai Emet Synagogue. Candles were lit in memory of the six million Jewish people who lost their lives in the Holocaust. A tribute was given to the liberators, and veterans responded. Dorothy also spoke:

> I am aware that I am looking into the faces of many who survived the unimaginable darkness of these death camps. . . . I could describe the smells and sights and silence of death [in Dachau]. Only those who were there

can truly recall them in all their vividness. In truth, one cannot escape from these thoughts even when one desires to do so. It was certainly a calculated attempt by the Nazis to desecrate not only the body, but also the mind and spirit! . . . It was truly a humbling, distressing experience to see our brothers and sisters in this terrible dehumanizing state.

I share with you vicariously that sense of profound sadness that seems to be touched off like a computer in the mind at similar sights and sounds around us, at any time and in any place. . . . Yours was the unmitigated pain and suffering and sorrow and loss and anguish and degradation—mental, emotional and physical. Truly you are living memorials to the fact that you have been sustained and have taken the victory over your suffering and anguish. You have raised sons and daughters, you have excelled in the professions and the arts and in the world of business and commerce. You have risen above tragic circumstances and blessed a world that hasn't dealt kindly with you . . . flashbacks of the terror of the "Holocaust" victims have endured. . . . I find no comfort in what has happened, but rather that Sacred Scriptures record that the Lord will vindicate His Israel and that there will always be a House of David. I am truly grateful to the Lord for having allowed me to serve you, His people. Thank you for letting me come to you tonight to mingle my tears and my memories with yours. The Lord of Heaven and earth bless you and keep you and protect you now and forever.

Dorothy's words that day reveal the pain and sorrow she felt for decades after her service, suggesting that nurses were susceptible to post-traumatic stress disorder. She died the following year and was survived by her brother and sister and several nieces and nephews.

18

WAR BRIDE

Allies Move Through France

About 2 PM on August 28, 1944, three American tanks arrived in the small town of Guignicourt, France, north of Paris, close to the Belgian border. These were the first troops to come through the area after the Allies landed on Normandy Beach in June. The townspeople poured out of their homes and businesses, laughing and crying, taking bottles of champagne out of hiding to celebrate. The soldiers handed out cigarettes, chewing gum, and chocolate. Although the Americans were tired and dirty, they looked beautiful to these French citizens who had suffered under the German occupation for four years. Several people, including Nelly Bettex, climbed onto one of the tanks to have their photo taken. The unit continued to liberate more towns on their way to Germany. Nelly heard later that some of those tanks were blown up in subsequent fighting, but they would not be forgotten by the people of Guignicourt.

Nelly Bettex was a secretary to the mayor of Guignicourt, assisting with his city work and his insurance business. She routinely rode her bike into the countryside to deliver documents or collect premiums for him. She frequently had to stop and jump into ditches when planes flew overhead.

· · · · ·

Nelly had been born in this rural area in 1926 and knew it well. Her mother owned and ran a small café, and her father had a repair shop and made weather vanes out of copper, zinc, and steel. Nelly began experiencing the war in 1940, when she was fourteen years old. German planes began bombing the airfield near her village, Juvincourt, fifteen miles from Reims, France. Some of the bombs fell on houses, killing the occupants. Nelly was afraid but thought the French and English soldiers would keep her community safe.

The Bettex family and their neighbors watched refugees from Belgium go through town in cars at first, and then on bikes and on foot. Within weeks, her parents sent Nelly and her sister to Paris to stay with an uncle. They took their bicycles, too, in case the wagon could not make it all the way. After two days of traveling by wagon, the girls found one of the last trains going to Paris. The next day, the mayor ordered the evacuation of their village. Nelly's mother and other relatives got rides on another farmer's wagon, but the fighting had already intensified.

When the German planes flew overhead, everyone "took to the ditches or under trees, as they were shooting at the refugees . . . some died and were buried on the spot." Her father refused to leave, thinking they would all be able to return in a few days.

Nelly and her family, except for her father, stayed in a crowded apartment in Paris with her uncle. The Germans were bombing Paris, primarily factories and military targets, but there was also collateral damage in neighborhoods. On June 14, 1940, the Germans arrived in Paris. Curfews were implemented. Everyone needed to carry identification. After a few weeks, Nelly's father appeared at the door, dirty and with a long beard. The Germans had arrested him at home and made him cook for them at a camp until he managed to escape.

Nelly started school in Paris, where she was able to learn English and German. She had been interested in learning English after meeting British soldiers who patrolled in her town and stopped at her mother's café before they had to evacuate. Because of the curfews and bombings, she had plenty of opportunity to study. During this time, neighbors kept to themselves because they "could not trust anyone for fear that they might be 'collaborators' helping the Germans. . . . The Jews, in particular, were persecuted and forced to wear the Star of David on their clothes continuously. They could be picked up in their homes or walking down the street. The Germans separated men, women and children and put them in different trucks on their way to trains sending them to concentration camps, and the gas chambers."

Down the street from where Nelly and her family were living, a Jewish family lived in the top apartment of a large building. One day, German soldiers stopped at that building. When the Jewish family saw them coming, they knew they would be arrested, separated, and sent to camps to die. Instead they all jumped out of a window to their deaths.

As Nelly and her family tried to keep to themselves and endure the frightening and difficult circumstances, her father discovered that work was hard to find. After a long search, the only job he could secure was at a German ammunition factory that required a two-hour commute each way. It was exhausting and dangerous since the Allied forces were bombing Paris. Although they were trying to target military sites, they sometimes missed and hit houses. The sirens sounded almost every night.

Nelly also wanted to help her family financially, so she talked her parents into letting her attend a secretarial school. She took business courses and continued to learn German and English from the international faculty at the school. Shortly before graduation, she began part-time work for a lawyer. She worked during the day and finished her coursework at night.

The French Resistance

Raymond, a young man Nelly was fond of, joined the French Resistance. The resistance fighters rescued American pilots and crews when their planes went down, blew up bridges, and did as much as they could to thwart the Germans. Sometimes Nelly and her family hid Raymond and his friend with them. Other times, the men stayed with Raymond's friend's sister and her husband. Once when they had been staying there, German soldiers knocked at the door and searched the residence. The two resisters, who had been cleaning their guns at the time, escaped through a back window. When the Germans discovered a bullet that Raymond and the other resister had accidentally left behind, they shot the woman and her husband but left their three-year-old child unharmed.

Eventually, Raymond was captured by the Germans. He was allowed to send one postcard before he was executed, and he sent it to Nelly, professing his love for her and hoping she would find a good man to marry. He was proud to be dying for France. Nelly was shattered. Later, one of her uncles who also joined the resistance was executed by the German forces.

In late 1943, Nelly's family had the opportunity to return to the town of Guignicourt, near where they had lived before the war. They rented a vacant house, and her father opened a repair shop. Nelly found a job working for the town mayor, who also ran an insurance business. Often she rode her bike through the countryside to collect bills from farmers. She enjoyed getting out of the office, but her travels were dangerous. She had to watch for planes overhead.

When she was not working, Nelly volunteered for the Red Cross. A woman in Guignicourt organized it. Volunteers learned first aid and ran to help after a bombing when people were hurt. Once the nearby airfield was bombed and citizens who had been clearing the area from a recent bombing rushed to the hangar for shelter, but the hangar was hit and caught fire. Nelly and the first aid volunteers ran to help, but the German soldiers would not let them assist. They felt "helpless and dejected. Some of the wounded could have been saved."

Although radios were forbidden, many French people kept them secretly. On June 6, 1944, the British Broadcasting Corporation (BBC) announced that the Allied forces had landed on the beaches at Normandy. The citizens of Guignicourt were elated, not knowing the significant casualties that occurred. The Germans used the nearby airfield to support their troops in Normandy. They pulled planes and tanks out of the woods where they had been hidden. They also loaded a train at the station in Guignicourt with tanks and ammunition. Two Allied planes circled the town and destroyed the train with machine-gun fire. Projectiles flew, hitting houses.

Liberation and Work with the American Troops

By mid-August, it was clear that the German troops were withdrawing. Nelly's mother began sewing an American flag out of scraps of material. On August 28, the American tanks arrived in Guignicourt and Nelly and the townspeople welcomed them with champagne.

One day, a sergeant belonging to an American intelligence unit walked up to Nelly as she stood in the doorway of her house. Unexpectedly, the American addressed her in French. Sergeant Victor Croes had been born in Nice, France, and immigrated as a young man to the United States, where he was hired to be a personal chef for Jay C. Hormel, owner of the Hormel meatpacking company. An American citizen, working in Austin, Minnesota, Victor was drafted into the service and found himself back in France. The American unit needed to verify their location, meaning they were lost and needed directions, which Nelly was able to provide in French and in English.

The American unit and Sergeant Croes stayed in the area for several weeks, using the nearby airfield. He and Nelly saw each other often, including at a dance the townspeople put on to celebrate their freedom. When it was time to leave, he told Nelly he wanted to marry her. She was not ready to get married, but they began a long correspondence.

· · · · ·

In the spring of 1945, an American officer with a French translator appeared at Nelly's workplace and offered her a job as a translator. The pay was very good, so she arranged to work half days at her office job and the rest of the day for the American military.

Nelly felt she was treated like a queen. The unit staff sent a car to bring her to and from the office every day, and they showered her with gifts of soap, chocolate, and cigarettes, which her father loved. She enjoyed the work translating documents and dealing with the French authorities on behalf of the Americans, and she became friends with two American Red Cross nurses on the base.

On May 7, 1945, in a small red schoolhouse in the town of Reims, only fifteen miles from Guignicourt, Germany surrendered to the Allied forces, ending the war in Europe. General Eisenhower represented the United States in that meeting, and later, as Nelly was typing in her office, everyone in the room suddenly jumped to attention. Nelly stood up, not sure what was happening until the door opened and in walked General Eisenhower. He was there for a short visit, but a memorable one for Nelly.

The American unit found ways to have fun in addition to the work. A large room was built so the soldiers could relax and enjoy refreshments provided by the Red Cross. The GIs organized a small orchestra and included some German

Nelly Bettex (Croes) and others on tank, celebrating the liberation of France, August 1944. *Mower County Historical Society, Austin, Minnesota*

prisoners from the camp who could play. The dances were on Saturday nights, and Nelly was asked to go with an officer to visit the mayors of all of the surrounding towns to recruit "nice" girls to the dances. The young women needed to be accompanied by at least one parent. Donuts, coffee, and Coca-Cola were served. Some of the mothers who came brought their knitting and looked on.

In 1946, the American unit moved to Germany. Nelly was offered work with the Criminal Investigation Department (CID) and the Central Intelligence Agency (CIA). She chose the CID and began working with the US military and French police. Many of the cases involved the black market, situations where GIs sold government equipment and supplies to civilians. There were some criminal cases and some situations where prostitutes came to the office to report information they gathered while working. Nelly was protected by agents while she translated information to and from informants.

Marriage and Moving to Minnesota

For two years, Nelly and the French American soldier Victor Croes exchanged letters. Over time, Nelly discovered she appreciated his warmth and fell in love with him. He asked her to marry him and come to Austin, Minnesota, which she did. He sent her an airplane ticket and met her in New York. They were married December 1, 1947.

Nelly was warmly greeted by Victor's bosses, Jay C. Hormel and his wife, Germaine Dubois Hormel, a French woman. Jay met Germaine Dubois while he was serving in France with the US Army during World War I. They married in 1922. A few years later, Jay Hormel was traveling in Nice, France, on business. He met Victor, who was working in a popular hotel. Knowing Germaine Dubois would appreciate a French chef, Hormel hired Victor, and he came to work for the family in 1927.

Victor and Nelly had two children, a boy and a girl. In 1951, Nelly began working at Hormel, where she remained employed for forty-two years. She did various types of office work, including secretarial work for the industrial engineers and in the corporate offices. She was also the corporate translator when company leaders needed someone who understood French.

19

CIVILIAN RELIEF IN ITALY AND AUSTRIA

After ten months in Cairo and Alexandria at the beginning of the war, working in an administrative role at the American Red Cross (ARC) service clubs, Louise Boie from Plainview, Minnesota, was reassigned to the sort of work she initially desired to do the most: civilian relief. She was transferred to a rural area in southern Italy after Allied forces took control. General Eisenhower was the overall commander of Operation Husky. From mid-July to mid-August 1943, US and British troops landed in Sicily, many coming from the secured North African countries and then proceeding into Italy, capturing the southern region of the country from German and Italian forces. The northern section of the country remained under Axis control. The Red Cross provided services alongside the Allied forces.

By late summer 1943, when it was still plenty hot and muddy in southern Italy, Louise was assigned to canteen service and civilian relief. One night she went out with one of the mobile canteen units to visit a battalion of rangers. They drove into the mountains at dusk and stood in mud six inches deep for four hours. Louise thought the mud looked like chocolate ice cream, felt like quicksand with bananas added, and dried like glue. The Red Cross staff talked with soldiers while they distributed donuts, hoping to encourage the men and show support. When they were done, Louise and the other Red Cross workers slept at an evacuation hospital, where they could see and hear flashes of gunfire at the front. She marveled at how peaceful and undisturbed the mountains and country roads looked in contrast to the destruction they witnessed in the towns.

Louise had crossed northern Africa, seeing the lush green in Tunisia and Algeria, Casablanca and Gibraltar, and then Sicily before arriving in Italy. The destruction in the towns she visited on her new assignment was almost overwhelming: buildings that stood like skeletons and entire blocks that had become fields of rubble. These were the beloved homes and towns of people who were now entirely homeless or without heat or water. Some of them had only the clothes they were wearing. The Red Cross, working in collaboration with the Allied Military Government (AMG), began to assess conditions for civilians in newly occupied areas and provide support as necessary.

Louise and her colleagues were instructed to make a survey of all hospitals, clinics, and institutions for the poor, orphans, and handicapped. They toured the facilities, or what was left of them, from "air-raid shelter to attic," making notes of laundries, toilets, storerooms, dormitories, kitchens, sources of funding, utilities, and availability of medicines. They tried to identify the greatest needs and determine what resources were available locally and what the Allied forces needed to supplement. All of the Allied government officials Louise met in the process were "doing tremendously difficult jobs with patience, shrewdness, kindliness, and devotion." She found it thrilling to see how it is possible to "slowly bite into confusion and disorder and begin to straighten out human problems, make a plan, and be in control of human welfare instead of lost in human disaster."

In addition to the Allied government staff, Louise was also in contact with the army troops as she had been when she worked in the clubs. She continued to admire them in their toughness and their gentle sides. They painted pet names on their jeeps, trucks, ducks, tanks, command cars—names of their home states, girls, comic strip heroes.

· · · · ·

Louise Boie (Saunders) with the American Red Cross civilian relief in Europe. *Mildred Louise Boie Saunders Papers, Sophia Smith Collection, Smith College, Northampton, Massachusetts*

By December 1944, Louise was in Vienna, Austria, working on civilian relief. The Allied forces had liberated France and many European regions. Again, the Red Cross staff began by surveying local agencies. They found twenty-seven institutions were delivering supplemental food to children, patients in hospitals, and pregnant and nursing women. They were helping ninety-three hundred people daily. In addition, the American Red Cross collected ninety-seven thousand garments, which were distributed in time to keep people, many of them without heat, warm as winter approached. Writing to her home chapter in Boston, Louise shared the "joy and astonishment of old ladies, mothers, children, and men at such beautifully made and warm garments . . . generously contributed by women in America." She also described how the Red Cross and US forces held Christmas parties in all of the children's hospitals and orphanages: "Each child got a garment, two chocolate bars, a roll of life savers, and a Christmas card from the Red Cross." GIs and nurses helped distribute the items. They also provided bed garments to people in the general hospitals, bars of soap to pregnant and nursing women, and boxes of food to the elderly in the US section of Vienna.

The ARC in Minnesota supported efforts like these by contributing to the production of sewn and knitted pieces of clothing as well as surgical dressings. Chapters were given quotas and sometimes donated materials. In the Hennepin County chapter alone, volunteers, mostly women and children, dedicated more than two million hours of service and completed 486,000 sewn articles, 56,000 knitted items, and 11.5 million surgical dressings. Most of their items were distributed for Norwegian and Russian relief. Many of the surgical dressings were used at the Veterans' and Fort Snelling Hospitals.

During Louise's time in Austria, she endured a personal tragedy. Her cousin, Millard Charles Boie, a marine, died in the battle for Sugar Loaf on the Japanese island Okinawa on May 13, 1945. US troops were advancing a major naval armada against the Japanese. The eighty-two-day conflict was conducted under relentless attack by Japanese kamikaze planes. There were many lives lost, including Millard's. Millard's wife lived in Plainview, where Louise's parents lived and she had grown up. There was not anything that could be done but to carry on, so that is what Louise did. She focused on what good she could do with the Red Cross and the Austrian people.

· · · · ·

Louise continued in war relief efforts in Vienna through the end of the war, into early 1946. In her Red Cross reports during this time, she noted the need to help "destitute Jews, who have housing, financial, food, clothing, and work problems." She visited an institution with six hundred twenty-five beds housing pregnant and nursing women, sick mothers and children, unmarried mothers, the very poor, and some patients with tuberculosis. She also worked with a home run by a Catholic nun for children of mixed marriages, Jewish and Aryan. It was burned by the SS and lost all of its possessions, including all of the children's clothing and shoes. The children were undernourished.

During her year in Vienna, Louise collaborated with Austrian and US government agencies, other international Red Cross associations, and some Jewish and Catholic organizations to bring basic food, clothing, and medical supplies to people in the city. Part of this work involved creating procedures and avenues of communication so distribution of supplies could occur efficiently and without redundancy to the people who needed it the most. Emergency feeding was the top priority, but these organizations also worked to establish healthier living in overcrowded conditions that lacked hot water and soap, breeding grounds for typhus. Louise described the destitution in her reports and strongly recommended that the ARC collect condensed milk, soap, toothpaste, towels that could be used as diapers, as well as Christmas toys and presents.

Louise and the Red Cross staff were constantly balancing the need to find and distribute food with challenges of finding persons in need, such as concentration camp prisoners, and a longer-term goal of trying to establish a sustainable program for the Austrian people. Conditions improved throughout the summer and into the fall, but then as winter approached, ARC workers were confronted with concerns about inadequate housing and a lack of coal for heating.

Louise's Red Cross reports, while always professional in tone, began to reflect her frustration as she noted that the "problems of civilians in Vienna are complicated not so much by supply as by distribution and inefficiencies of Austrian agencies." The ARC had established milk stations for children and mothers to receive extra rations, but delays in coming to agreement on the appropriate size of the rations resulted in no rations being distributed for a period. Her requests changed from a list of supplies to an appeal that the "military government work with Viennese authorities and agencies to encourage more efficient and reliable distribution operations."

The list of people who needed support continued to increase. Louise noted the needs of concentration camp prisoners; political prisoners; "U-Boat" people, who had literally gone underground in caves and cellars; and persecuted Jews, who wore the Star of David and had been unable to work, buy clothes, or get normal rations. Despite her frustration, Louise's reports always included her appreciation for their accomplishments and a record of the "astonishment and gratitude of the people" receiving assistance.

In one of her last reports, Louise described the expansion of the milk program to more children beyond those who had been markedly malnourished to all children and also to the elderly. ARC staff were feeding 9,300 people a day, and 891,302 feedings had been given from the time the program began in September 1945 to January 1946.

Despite the hardships, in a letter to friends sent in December 1945, Louise expressed the pleasure she and her colleagues had thinking of Christmas at home while they tried to provide some holiday joy in Vienna, where "no-one can get Christmas trees, the streets are decorated with rubble and ice, there are no gifts to be bought for love nor money, and the dinner for most will probably be bread and dried peas." They were able to provide some extra rations of flour and sugar so some cakes could be baked. They planned a party for all children between five and twelve years old, with strolling musicians and Donald Duck and Mickey Mouse movies. They intended to distribute some extra clothing, but when the shipment arrived from the American Red Cross, they discovered it contained only pajamas and underwear for men. All of Vienna's streetcars lined up to provide transportation to the party. US servicemen participated in the distribution because the children loved to see them.

Louise noted that, in addition to the pervasive malnutrition and lack of heat, many Viennese had been "corrupted by Nazism," and "their joy at liberation is confused by a combination of stunned apathy and weakness from hunger, the complications of division of the country and the city by the four powers, and a lack of mental, emotional and spiritual energy." She wondered if she would have the spiritual courage, if she were a European, to face the future. She recalled that Europeans had been through multiple upheavals in the past and endured. Still, she called for "real leadership, compassion, understanding and constructive and vigorous rehabilitation." She wondered where "are our child specialists, our real educators, our vigorous, energetic re-storers of faith in human life, in education, in the rebuilding of family joys and inner security . . . [for rebuilding] needs shining faith and understanding of the great burden of guilt and despair and fear and strain."

Louise left Vienna in late January 1946 and arrived back in the United States in plenty of time to help her twin sister, who was pregnant. Louise assisted with her sister's young son and maintained their household in North Carolina through the arrival of a new nephew in April. She subsequently spent time in Boston, New York, and Washington, DC, pursuing work as an editor and in social services. She published a volume of poetry, *Better than Laughter*, through the University of Minnesota Press in 1946. Carl Van Doren, Pulitzer Prize winner and critic, wrote "Some extremely lovely poems here, some extremely sharp and pointed ones. All finely intelligent." A reviewer for the *Christian Register* noted, "In these pages there is an exquisite blending of mind and heart. Clear-sighted, compassionate, with a deep feeling for human beings and a ready understanding—such is the spirit that finds utterance in a volume that the wise will treasure."

After returning to the states and ending her Red Cross career, Louise awaited the discharge and arrival of Lieutenant Colonel William Saunders from his military service. She and Bill had met during her Red Cross work. He was eventually appointed to Fort Bragg, North Carolina, as an engineer, and they were married in 1948. Louise desired to support her husband in his career and well-being and to have a family. They later moved to Durham, North Carolina, where Louise's sister, Maurine, and her family lived. Louise and Bill never had children, but she remained very active in her nephews' lives and committed to families and children in her community through volunteer work.

The Pacific Theater and End of the War

20

SERVING IN THE PACIFIC THEATER

Mayo Clinic Nurses

Dr. Julia Herrick was not the only one from Mayo Clinic making contributions during World War II. The clinic provided training sessions for more than fifteen hundred medical officers. A research team invented the g-suit and the M-1 maneuver, which allowed pilots to resist the effects of g-forces while in the air. Mayo scientists also worked in secret on procedures that resulted in improving survival rates for parachute jumps at forty thousand feet. Dr. Chuck Mayo, a descendent of the founders, began organizing a hospital unit for military deployment before the attack on Pearl Harbor. He recruited volunteers from the clinic and from physicians who had trained at the clinic and were practicing elsewhere. In January 1943, sixty-five doctors and seventy-five nurses of Mayo Clinic's 71st General Hospital were posted to Stark Army Hospital in Charleston, South Carolina. They drilled, received instruction in army medicine, and took long hikes for six months. In June 1943, the unit was divided into the 233rd and 237th Station Hospitals.

On December 8, 1943, the unit boarded a train in Charleston, not knowing their destination. Many of them packed winter clothing, worried they were headed to Europe. In Atlanta, their train turned west and they knew California was their destination. They spent Christmas at Camp Stoneman near San Francisco. On January 6, they boarded the *New Amsterdam*, a luxury passenger ship that had been converted to a troop ship. They were at sea for sixteen days on rough waters, causing rampant seasickness. They landed at Sydney, Australia. A month later, the 233rd was relocated to Nadzab and the 237th moved to Finschhafen, New Guinea. The beaches were littered with American and Japanese equipment from a recent battle.

Immediately, the medical team started seeing patients: wounded troops from battles in the surrounding areas and POWs who had been taken prisoner by the Japanese and had been living in the jungles. One patient was one of their own: a nurse contracted cerebral malaria and went into a coma. They gave her massive doses of intravenous Atabrine. She surprised them by surviving. She also surprised them by refusing to go home.

The nurses were graduates of the Kahler and Saint Marys Hospital Schools of Nursing. They were well trained and hardworking, but they also found ways to relax. Beatrice DeLue and others enjoyed listening to records on a small phonograph,

Mayo Hospital unit nurses. *History Center of Olmsted County, Rochester, Minnesota*

including "Rhapsody in Blue," which she had brought along. They watched movies while sitting on bomb crates, often in the rain because it frequently rained for days. For entertainment when the fighting slowed down and moved north, Bob Hope, Jack Benny, and Irving Berlin performed. Beatrice's mother sent her sheet music so they could play the old piano on the unit. A dental student from the University of Minnesota who had been recruited to join them started a dance band. The music helped break the monotony. They heard news on the radio, much of it coming from Australia. They often picked up Tokyo Rose, the Japanese propagandist. They ignored her lies about wives at home being unfaithful and assertions that Japan was winning the war.

When they were not caring for patients or relaxing, they attended to house-keeping. The nurses appreciated having a washing machine. It was not large enough to accommodate the whole unit, so the men washed their clothes in the river. Regardless of how the laundry was done, the wet clothes had to hang out on lines waiting for a dry day.

· · · · ·

After fifteen months in New Guinea, the units were transferred to the Philippines, one to Clark Field, north of Manila, and the other to Batangas, fifty miles south of Manila. The medical staff remained there until the war ended; some had to stay months longer until replacements could arrive. Morale was low by the end while they waited for their turn to go home.

Serving with the American Red Cross

Mayo Clinic nurses were not the only women from Minnesota in New Guinea. Gertrude Esteros had arrived in Port Moresby almost a year earlier, in January 1943, with the American Red Cross. She had finished training in Washington, DC, to be a recreation worker in a field hospital. She had received an orientation to the armed services and some specific training in recreation therapy. Most useful, though, was the time she spent at St. Elizabeth Hospital, which had a large psychiatric ward. Gertrude become familiar with the symptoms and triggers related to mental illness. One of the lecturers said, "There is not a human being who doesn't at some point under certain circumstances . . . lose contact with reality. When the circumstances are severe." Gertrude appreciated the opportunity to work with psychiatric patients and doctors before her deployment.

Gertrude joined the American Red Cross instead of the military because she considered herself a pacifist. She could not see herself wearing a military uniform. She had been born in Cloquet, in northern Minnesota, in 1914, but her family moved after a horrific fire destroyed the town and surrounding area just after her fourth birthday. Her parents set up house a few miles away in Saginaw and farmed. Gertrude went to St. Paul for high school and completed a degree in home economics in 1936 at the University of Minnesota. She taught in a high school, at West Central Agricultural College in Morris, Minnesota, and at the University of Illinois.

Gertrude was teaching at Lindenwood College in St. Charles, Missouri, when the war broke out. As she sat in the auditorium full of women while President Roosevelt addressed the nation, announcing the attack on Pearl Harbor, she thought, "with all of this going on in the rest of the world, I can't sit here in the middle of the United States in a women's college and do nothing." She started seriously planning how she could be of service.

Gertrude was particularly moved by the growing war in Europe. Her parents had immigrated from Finland. Her father became naturalized soon after arriving in the United States, but her mother came later. Gertrude remembered going to naturalization class in the evenings with her mother. Gertrude was learning English at grade school while her mother was learning English and citizenship at night school. The family spoke Finnish at home and felt connected to relatives still living in Finland, which had been affected by the war since 1939.

Along with other Red Cross personnel, chaplains, and members of special and replacement teams, Gertrude boarded a lone ship, not in a convoy. Because Japanese submarines were active in the Pacific, her ship zigzagged across the ocean. It took them forty-three days to get to Brisbane. They were taken overnight to Sydney, where they arrived on Christmas Day 1942. They were processed and departed for New Guinea by plane. While she was traveling, Gertrude felt the impact of heading into the unknown. She did not know what she and her colleagues would face. She wondered if she would measure up. Could she do what she had been trained to do? These questions filled her mind to the point that she never felt fear.

· · · · ·

New Guinea was unlike any place Gertrude had visited before. The jungle climate was hot and humid. Gertrude had never seen people like the residents of New Guinea. Physically she noted that they were dark skinned and had "thick, very thick, black hair." She was surprised to hear the GIs refer to them as "fuzzy-wuzzies." The hospital environment in Port Moresby was different, too. Most of the service personnel there were waiting to go home. They were bored and anxious. Some of the patients were paratroopers who had been mistakenly sent to New Guinea. It quickly became apparent that the jungle was not an appropriate place to assign paratroopers, who had "disastrous" experiences jumping from planes and fracturing their legs in the dense vegetation.

Gertrude discovered that many of the other servicemen waiting to go home were not injured. They were gay. The army decided they were unfit to serve. Later in the war, when the military branches were desperate for troops, recruiters did not question anyone's sexual orientation. They needed every live body they could get. But in late 1942 and early 1943, these men were being sent home. Gertrude "had no experience whatsoever" with gay men, but she now "had an opportunity to know these people, as they were waiting to go home."

The camp's commanding officer said, "Look, your first job, your important job is . . . we need some kind of recreation program here." Gertrude did not have much for supplies or equipment, so she planned dances and theater. At first, she thought it would be challenging to create programming with only men, but she soon discovered that some of the men were willing to take the parts of women and even dress like women.

During her time at the facility at Port Moresby, she got to know the gay men. Although initially they tried to be discreet, after they had been singled out and directed to this hospital to be sent home, they were less concerned about hiding their sexual orientation. Gertrude found nothing "different about them. They were decent people . . . they accepted [her] and [she] accepted them. . . . Many of them were college graduates [and] good conversationalists. Intelligent people . . . so that there was nothing abnormal about it" to her. She thought many of them felt hurt about being discharged and some of them felt bad about their circumstances of being gay, something "over which they had no control." Being the child of immigrants and having felt rejected and judged when schoolmates would tease her about her accent or poor English, Gertrude empathized with them.

After a few months, Gertrude was transferred to a field hospital in Finschhafen, in the same location where some of the Mayo personnel would be posted a year later. When she arrived, there were no nurses, only navy corpsmen. There she worked with war casualties in teams with social workers and secretaries. The secretaries helped the servicemen keep in touch with family at home. In this location, Gertrude was able to set up a recreation tent, made out of bamboo with a thatched roof. It was much more comfortable than the hot military tents made of thick, heavy canvas.

In addition to setting up activities for the patients, Gertrude talked with many of them. They were often lonely. Many of them had received news that their wives had been unfaithful. Girlfriends married other men. Gertrude began to think there was not a single faithful woman left in the United States. Some of the men talked about their dogs, books they had read, or operas they had seen. Sometimes she helped with basic nursing care when the corpsmen were busy.

· · · · ·

After eighteen months in New Guinea, Gertrude was required to take a leave in Australia. After two weeks, her unit closed up in Finschhafen and moved to Hollandia. Her assignment ended up being to Leyte, in the Philippines, where the conflict was still active. On the way to Leyte, her ship was attacked by Japanese suicide bombers. The ship vibrated with the impact of the machine guns going off on the deck as the crew shot back at the Japanese planes. The Red Cross women watched the gunners at work and saw their torpedoes go up high into the sky. They saw flames and the tracers create tremendous fireworks. A Japanese plane came flaming down twenty meters from the ship's stern.

Gertrude worked with gravely injured men at the hospitals in Leyte. Once she took down the story of a young noncommissioned officer who was the last survivor of his whole unit. He was desperate to tell what had happened to everyone. Many of the men had acted with valor and deserved posthumous recognition. He told the whole story to Gertrude and died a couple of hours later.

She also worked with badly burned patients, who "were so desperately uncomfortable and nobody had time to deal with them." She gave them liquid. Most of their bodies had been burned. Even morphine did not help. They were miserable and dying. Often, she was simply sat with

Gertrude Esteros. *Hennepin County Library*

them. The nurses were too busy in surgery.

Gertrude stayed with them so "somebody was there." She was in "situations where nobody could have made a difference, other than that you could make that human being feel a little more human while he is still living. Then when he'd gone. He's gone."

Some of the patients could not take it anymore and broke down. Gertrude knew a man from Virginia, Minnesota, who had been in all of the important campaigns in the South Pacific. He was a medic. He brought the wounded and deceased in from the front line. It was amazing that he had never been injured, but he also never got a break. He was a large man, husky and over six feet. But he broke down. He was catatonic and hospitalized for eight months. He came out of it and returned to Minnesota, but he was never the same.

Gertrude was subsequently assigned to a large convalescent hospital outside of Leyte. The patients were not as critically injured. They were stable and waiting to return to service when they were sufficiently healed. This hospital was huge, with six thousand cots. She and other staff built a recreation facility they called the Giant Shed made out of bamboo with a thatched roof. In addition to crafts, music, and other recreation, they served Coke, which was very popular, even when it was lukewarm.

Gertrude was later assigned to a hospital in Panay. One night, as she was eating dinner with others in the unit listening to the radio with a speaker tied to the top of a coconut tree, as daylight was turning to the velvety dark of evening, they heard the announcement that the Japanese had surrendered. There was not any cheering. They just listened and said, "Oh, yes. So it's over." Although there was a lot to do for the next year, the volunteers and other workers seemed to lose some of their sense of purpose. Gertrude resigned from the Red Cross and returned home. Initially, she felt adrift. She joined the faculty at the University of Minnesota and found herself teaching a course she loved, Introduction to Related Art and Design, but she could not stand the paperwork, which seemed unimportant after her experiences in the war. It took time for Gertrude to adjust to civilian life, but eventually she did, and she taught at the university until her retirement in 1980.

21

CRYPTOGRAPHERS AND SPIES

While the Mayo Clinic nurses and Gertrude Esteros were serving at New Guinea and the Philippines, Josephine Downey from St. Paul, Minnesota, was also there as a cryptologist with the Women's Army Corps (WAC). Josephine, at thirty-six, was older than many of the young women who went into the military during the war. She had an undergraduate degree from the University of Minnesota, a master of arts degree in French from Middlebury College in Vermont, and fifteen years of experience teaching ninth-grade French, Latin, and Spanish at Maria Sanford High School in Minneapolis, where she also advised the drama club and coached plays.

Josephine completed her basic training, spent eleven months as a clerk, and trained for eight weeks with the signal corps at Camp Crowder, Missouri, as a cryptographic technician. Her training prepared her for a position encoding and decoding secret messages using manuals and machines. Josephine began her tour in New Guinea in August 1944, shortly after General Eisenhower's troops arrived and the Japanese surrendered. She and her cohort arrived on "ducks," amphibious vehicles, which crossed the water and rolled right up onto the beach and down the road. For the next year, she was part of the final stage of the war conducted in the Pacific theater.

The WACs anticipated rugged living conditions but were surprised to find new barracks with showers, electric lights, and ironing facilities. Their lodgings felt like a glorified summer camp. At night, they reclined like queens, sleeping under fine nets to keep the mosquitoes and malaria away. Their diet was disappointing, though, including mostly SPAM, which Josephine did not care for. To her surprise, one of Josephine's bunkmates turned out to be another woman from St. Paul: Elisabeth Manship, daughter of the sculptor Paul Manship. Elisabeth spent her free time making pencil drawings of her WAC companions.

In April 1945, after General Eisenhower's troops recaptured Manila, the capital city of the Philippines, Josephine's unit was relocated there. They traveled in a rugged, slow refrigerator ship that formerly transported bananas. Josephine slept on the deck because it was cooler than inside the ship. They were under complete blackout during the journey. After arrival and setup, the WACs caught a glimpse of General MacArthur when he arrived to address the Philippine Congress. They heard him congratulate the Philippine people for their courage through loudspeakers set up outside the crowded building.

While in Manila, in addition to cryptographic work, Josephine witnessed the trial of Japanese general Tomoyuki Yamashita in November 1945. She heard the painful testimony of many civilians. One witness broke down hysterically as she recalled the executions of her husband, son, and nephew. Another woman said her one-year-old and six-year-old children were "snatched out of her hand" and killed. One woman lost six children, an uncle, her husband, and brothers. Homes were burned to the ground. More than two thousand people were taken, three hundred at a time, down to the river, where they were bayonetted, beheaded, and thrown into the water by Japanese troops under General Yamashita's command.

The trial was covered in US newspapers and magazines. Josephine wrote home to her family and told them to read the coverage in the November 19, 1945, issue of *Time*. A woman Josephine knew

Josephine Downey, cryptographer. *Josephine Downey Papers, MNHS Collections*

was included in one of the photographs. When it was the general's turn to testify, Yamashita did not deny that the massacres occurred, but he claimed he did not order the deaths and that he did not know they occurred. In December, he was found guilty, and on February 23, 1946, he was hanged.

· · · · ·

By this time, the volume of messages requiring coding and decoding was dropping. The army staff had more free time, giving Josephine an opportunity to take classes at the Philippine University: Philippine history, the Tagalog language, and the cultural history of China and the Far East. The army was also hiring local women to help in the office to replace military staff. Josephine noted that the WACs had been given structured training to do the coding and they had a year's experience. It was a "pet peeve" of hers to hear the GIs say, "The dumb flips [Filipinos] are stupid," just because after two weeks they were not as efficient as the WACs. She felt as if she spent half her talking time trying to defend the Filipino women. Josephine thought some of the GIs appeared to despise Filipinos "because they are brown and resemble Negroes."

Many of the WACs were ready to go home. They were discharged based on a priority and points system. Women over forty were released first, followed by women whose husbands had been discharged, and women with a health condition such as jungle rot. Otherwise, they were released based on their Advanced Service Rating Scores (ASRS), which awarded points for time in the service with extra points for being overseas or in combat. Josephine's score was thirty-eight. Forty-four points were required to be discharged. Age was also a factor for the WACs, and as the age for discharge was lowered, Josephine's eligibility increased. Still, it was too late to get home in time to begin teaching in the fall, so she considered other opportunities.

When it also became too late to be home for Christmas, Josephine thought about extending her assignment. A one-year commitment was required to continue working in Manila. Opportunities in Japan required nine-month commitments, but assignments in China required only a six-month commitment. Josephine pursued opportunities in China so she could return home in time to teach the following fall and still see a new country in the meantime. She was assigned as a cryptographic technician with the American consul in Shanghai, where she stayed for six months, enjoying the rare chance to experience Chinese culture, including the opera. She returned to Minnesota and resumed her career as a language teacher at Johnson High School in St. Paul, where she stayed for twenty-nine years, resulting in a total of forty-six years of teaching by the time she retired.

• • • • •

Other women from Minnesota were also stationed in China during the war. Women employed by the Office of Strategic Services (OSS) were dispatched throughout Europe, and especially in the South Pacific and China. The OSS was established by President Roosevelt on June 13, 1942, by military order. The office was intended to contribute to "enforcing [US] will upon the enemy by means other than military action . . . [including] unorthodox warfare, guerilla activities behind enemy lines; contact with resistance groups; subversion, sabotage and unorthodox or 'black' psychological warfare." After the war, the OSS functions were reorganized into the Central Intelligence Agency (CIA) by an executive order issued by President Truman in 1946.

Of the thirteen thousand people employed by the OSS at its peak during World War II, 35 percent were women. Half of the total staff was posted overseas, mostly in Asian countries to complement the intelligence efforts of the British in Europe. Those working in Europe included Marlene Dietrich, who sang for the "black" radio programs broadcast in German, intending to foster suspicion and animosity among the Germans, Italians, and Fascists.

Jeanne Taylor, an artist originally from St. Paul, arrived in Kandy, Ceylon (Sri Lanka), at the OSS on Christmas Eve 1944. Julia McWilliams was in charge of the holiday celebration. Jeanne observed that Julia "swept down the broad stairway into the great open lobby [of the Queen's Hotel], waving and greeting everyone with her boisterous enthusiasm. Julia had used the last of her paper clip supply from Washington to decorate the Registry with loops and swags hung from the rafters, some interspersed with Frangipani [sic] flowers picked from some of the trees on the Detachment." Julia would later marry Paul Child, another OSS employee. They would move to Paris, where she would learn to cook and develop her career as the renowned chef Julia Child.

. . . . .

Jeanne Taylor worked primarily in the research and analysis branch, which collected public and classified information for use in covert operations. OSS also collected military classified information through its secret intelligence branch, conducted sabotage and guerilla warfare through its special operations branch, and spread disinformation in enemy territory through its morale operations branch. Other branches conducted even more specialized activities.

Jeanne was born in St. Paul in 1912. After majoring in fine arts at the University of Minnesota and studying painting and drawing at the St. Paul School of Art, she studied at the Art Students League in New York City and with a private artist in Geneva, Switzerland. Economic pressures during the Depression led Jeanne to return to living with her parents in St. Paul, where she became a supervisor with the Federal Art Project of the Work Projects Administration (WPA). In this position, she oversaw the "research, selection, and photographing of indigenous objects." After returning to New York City in various teaching and design jobs, including drafting electrical circuits at Bell Telephone Laboratories, Jeanne joined the OSS in Washington, DC, in 1941. As a member of the presentation branch, she created illustrations for posters, charts, graphs, and film animations presented to the joint chiefs of staff. She transferred to the OSS office in New York City, where she was a "drafts woman for small secret explosives devices, [and] inspector of those devices in the plants manufacturing them."

Jeanne arrived in Kandy on March 8, 1944, with Eleanor "Ellie" Thiry, another woman from Minnesota, along with Julia McWilliams, Cora DuBois, and five other women who had left on the SS *Mariposa*, a luxury liner requisitioned by the US military. The vessel headed for India with three thousand men and a few civilians. The OSS team prepared for the long voyage by attending multiple farewell parties in Washington, DC, and completed an orientation that included boat evacuation drills to assure they would not "think twice about going over the side, via ropes." Ellie noted they had to wear a ridiculous amount of gear and were expected to "strap to their bodies" fatigues, gas mask kits, and musette bags and top it off with a steel helmet.

The OSS group drew considerable attention as the only women on board and for their appearance, varying in size, shape, and age. Julia, more than six feet tall, towered over the men as well as the women; Ellie was petite; and Cora was in her

Jeanne Taylor. *Jeanne Taylor Papers, MNHS Collections*

forties, in contrast to most of the passengers, who were in their twenties. Julia fabricated a story that they were missionaries to deter the catcalls they endured. The women caused further disruption when they began sunbathing. The captain had to close off a portion of the deck exclusively for them to prevent further distractions.

Ellie may have adjusted to the living arrangements more readily than the other women since she was the eldest of nine children born on a farm in Rock Creek, near Pine City, Minnesota. She was accustomed to sharing bedrooms and a bathroom. The women slept in triple-decker bunks. They were allowed a few cups of salt water for bathing and washing their clothes in the tub. Everything had to dry on strings hung across their cabin. There was very little room to move around.

After weeks at sea, they stopped in Australia to resupply. A destroyer escorted the SS *Mariposa* as it zigzagged across the Indian Ocean to avoid Japanese submarines before docking in Bombay. Once there, the OSS team learned their orders to go to Calcutta had been changed to Kandy, Ceylon, just across the bay from Burma, where the war was active.

Further confusion ensued because the military staff handling their train arrangements did not know they were women before they arrived, and this realization caused the staff to scurry to find appropriate accommodations. While the women waited for the paperwork to catch up with them, they went shopping and sightseeing in Bombay, enjoying their "introduction to the Mysterious East."

After eighteen days, the women were put on a train for a four-hour journey through steep mountain valleys and dense jungle. They saw beautiful waterfalls and fruit bats the size of pigeons. Arriving in the city of Kandy, they were billeted at the Queen's Hotel, a colonial-style British building in great disrepair. They encountered a cockroach infestation and large lizards in their rooms. Soon several of them were hospitalized with dengue fever caused by mosquitoes breeding in the hotel's pipes.

Eventually, the women met up with the men in their small unit, including Paul Child, who would later marry Julia McWilliams. Their offices in Kandy were grass shacks called bashas in the hills beyond an estate where the British commanding officer, Admiral Lord Louis Mountbatten, had set up his headquarters amid lush tropical gardens on the grounds of a tea plantation. The men lived in bashas near the office. The women lived in the hotel a few miles away and were taken from the hotel to their offices by weapons carriers daily. One woman noted that she was able to look out her office window and see coconut palms, papaya trees, a terraced rice paddy, and a pagoda. She also described "Buddhist monks in bright saffron robes and shaved heads," oxcarts, rickshaws, silversmith shops, "and in the night sky, the new moon lying upside down in this hemisphere." The office huts were connected by cement sidewalks and barbed wire.

Cora DuBois was the head of research and analysis. Ellie was the commanding officer's secretary. Julia was in charge of registering and cross-indexing all reports coming in from Washington, DC, and OSS operatives in the area. During one month, she and her staff accessioned, cross-indexed, circulated, and filed six hundred pieces of information. At one point, she became frustrated trying to keep all of their code names straight so she requested that the office in Washington send "one of those books you have, giving people numbers and funny names like Fruitcake #385." She further threatened that if they did not send the book she would "fill the next Washington pouch with itching powder and virulent bacteriological diseases, and change all the numbers."

The unit overall, Detachment 404, was involved in important missions against the Japanese. They collected and disseminated 2,400 intelligence reports, trained 215 local agents, and launched 125 operations in Japanese-held territory. In addition, they trained operatives and disseminated disinformation to counteract Radio Tokyo, which was broadcasting in Thailand, attempting to convince the Thais that the Japanese were winning the war and that Thailand should align with them rather than remaining neutral. The OSS team also generated leaflets and printed them in a thatch and plywood building. Jeanne Taylor designed maps, charts, and visual aids for "agent survival in jungle environments."

One of their most unconventional projects was to stuff resistance propaganda and antimalarial pills into thousands of condoms, which they inflated and dispersed into the sea near the coasts in hopes of influencing the Indonesian people.

Ellie Thiry (Summers) when she was in the Office of Strategic Services (OSS) Detachment 404 in Kandy. *Courtesy Chris Summers*

One of the women who thought up the plan enjoyed the look on the OSS doctor's face when she requested five hundred condoms.

Immediately after V-E day in May 1945, the focus of the war shifted to defeating Japan. The OSS staff was reassigned, primarily to an advance office base in Kunming, China, four hundred miles south of Chungking (Chongqing), the capital of Free China, where Ellie Thiry and Colonel Richard P. Heppner were assigned. Their flight encountered a storm on the way from Ceylon to Chungking, but Julia McWilliams "calmly read a book" while the rest of them "were preparing to die."

On June 1, 1945, the OSS office in Chungking opened. The staff's primary goal was to pinpoint prisoner-of-war campsites where the Japanese were holding Allied prisoners. Rescue teams focused on these areas. Jeanne Taylor created headquarters war room presentations and reconstructed captured—and water-soaked—Japanese maps and blueprints. By piecing together these documents, she was able to identify the Japanese specifications for building a splinter fleet in the Hong Kong shipyards. The Allied forces successfully bombed these shipyards based on the information Jeanne constructed.

Despite the intensity of their work, the OSS staff found time to relax. They occasionally had parties on the balcony of Mei Yuan ("beautiful garden") hotel, where they played a hand-cranked record player and danced to USO-issued recordings of their favorite songs, including the Andrews Sisters singing "Don't Sit Under the Apple Tree."

Because the mess hall offerings were highly repetitive, including lots of SPAM and powdered eggs, they sometimes left the hotel and found ways to appreciate the area's beauty. One weekend Jeanne, Julia, Paul, and two other men drove a jeep up Burma Road and stayed at a small inn with a hot spring that, it was claimed, had healing powers due to the radium levels in the water. On the drive back they admired the view of rice fields and thick pines leading up to a monastery. Paul "felt inspired by the beauty and drama of China."

A month after V-J Day, in September 1945, OSS became part of search-and-rescue missions looking all over China for Allied prisoners who had been incarcerated by the Japanese. As this work wound down, "peace brought a sudden vacuum" to daily life in Kunming: "Up until [then] there had been purpose, urgency, importance in the work" they were doing; "Now suddenly [they] had no direction, and the prospect of returning to a routine life was difficult to imagine." Headquarters decided to "reduce civilian personnel for budgeting reasons and to reduce the female personnel to make the organization more homogenous and military prior to the move to Shanghai, following the signing of peace terms."

Many of the women in these OSS operations and the OSS office in China were commended for an "admirable record of heroism, resourcefulness, initiative and successful operations against a ruthless enemy." Colonel Heppner awarded Julia McWilliams the Emblem of Meritorious Civilian Service, and Cora DuBois received the Exceptional Civilian Award and the Order of the Crown of Thailand recognition.

In addition to being positively recognized internally, the women working for these OSS offices were celebrated by James M. Cannon, a foreign correspondent for the *Baltimore Sun,* who noted that "Detachment 404 was the first place in my experience where women were given professional responsibility and succeeded very well. They proved they could do the work as well as the men."

Still, some men resented the presence of women in the OSS. Captain Oliver Caldwell wrote, "If I were making arrangements for an ideal war, I would insist that no women were permitted in forward areas. Regardless of the gallantry and dedication of individual women, the injection of sex into a wartime situation established an intolerable obstacle to discipline, without which not much of anything can be achieved." He seemed to suggest that the presence of women challenged discipline in the men, and rather than address the issue with men, it would be better to exclude women.

· · · · ·

At the time of Jeanne Taylor's transfer back to Washington, DC, her supervisor, Paul Child, rated her as having superior abilities to work with others and superior leadership skills. He noted that she was a "splendidly trained and able person in general graphic work. She is cooperative and keen-minded, but given to moods which on occasion inhibit her capacity to work steadily through times of stress." During the deployment, Jeanne became romantically involved with Cora DuBois, and they returned to Washington, DC, as a couple. It is worth noting that her supervisor was at one point romantically interested in Jeanne. Was the reference to her being "given to moods" merely a sexist comment or retaliation for her rebuffing him?

· · · · ·

A few of the OSS women were spies, and one of the best-known among them, a woman from Minnesota, went by the code name "Cynthia." In mid-1943, General Eisenhower and the Allied forces were planning Operation Torch, a mission to reclaim the North African countries of Morocco and Algeria, which were controlled by Vichy France, the puppet government of the Nazis. The OSS was asked to obtain the French codebook from the Vichy French embassy in Washington, DC. Cynthia was chosen for the important mission.

Cynthia was born Amy Elizabeth Thorpe on November 22, 1910, in Minneapolis. She went by Betty. Her father, originally from Northfield, was a highly decorated Marine Corps officer. Her mother, Cora Edna Wells, was the daughter of a bank president, merchant, and state senator representing Morris, Minnesota. Cora graduated with honors from the University of Michigan, followed by study at the Sorbonne in Paris, the University of Munich, and Columbia University.

Although Betty's parents and their families had been grounded in Minnesota for generations, shortly after her birth, the family moved to Maine, where her father was appointed commander of the Portsmouth Naval Prison. From Maine, they moved to Cuba, where Betty's mother cared for their growing family, now three children, in their home on Guantanamo Bay Naval Base. Betty's mother, with her impressive education, was an aspiring socialite. She was happy when they relocated to Washington, DC, where Betty's father was posted to General Staff College. Intending to climb the social ladder, her mother hosted elaborate dinners, including one occasion when Vice President and Mrs. Coolidge dined with the Thorps.

Betty inherited her mother's sense of adventure and desire for life as a socialite. After studying at private schools in Washington, DC, and in France and spending her summers at Newport, Rhode Island, Betty married a British diplomat. They had two children, who spent most of their childhoods in boarding schools. Betty and her husband traveled abroad frequently, and Betty attracted admirers along the way.

Betty's marriage was not as satisfying as she had hoped. Through one of her fleeting affairs, she accomplished her first act of espionage in 1938 in Warsaw, where she and her husband moved when he was assigned to the British embassy. One of her lovers, a Polish diplomat, revealed to her Hitler's intention to target Czechoslovakia and Poland and "take a bite of the cherry." Betty's career as a spy began when she disclosed this information to British officials. Soon Betty was officially recruited by British intelligence to obtain information by manipulating men she seduced into revealing important military secrets. She went on to obtain German and Italian codes from diplomats.

Cynthia was just the spy OSS needed to obtain the French codes that would help assure that Operation Torch in North Africa would be successful. In March 1942, Cynthia collaborated with Colonel Ellery C. Huntington Jr. of the OSS security branch. She had been nurturing an affair with Charles Brousse, a diplomat in the Vichy French embassy in Washington, DC, for nearly a year. She had initially met him under the false pretenses of being a reporter wishing to interview him. She flattered him and quickly seduced him.

Brousse had been a bombardier with the French air force during World War I and was the co-owner of a leading regional newspaper in France. In mid-April 1942, a pro-Nazi politician was made head of Vichy France, and Brousse saw his government become a puppet of Nazi Germany. He decided working with the Allies was the best way to save his country, so he began forwarding French embassy reports to Cynthia regularly. She approached Brousse directly about getting the codebooks. At first he refused, thinking it was too dangerous. The consequences would be severe if they were caught.

Brousse eventually agreed to help, but he did not have access to the safes containing the codebooks. Cynthia proposed a plan. She suggested they pretend to meet for a romantic evening at the embassy after all the other staff left. The night guard, knowing Brousse, would leave them alone. They would crack the safe, sneak the books out, and copy and return them before the morning staff arrived. It took several attempts and involved a safecracker known only as "Georgia Cracker." They were nearly caught but eventually succeeded. The codebooks were copied in a nearby apartment by other OSS agents taking photographs of them. The ciphers were immediately sent to London and used to assist General Eisenhower's command, ultimately leading to Operation Torch's success, an important turning point for the Allies in North Africa.

After this mission, Cynthia continued working for OSS. She and Charles Brousse eventually married and lived in France until her premature death of cancer in 1963 at fifty-three years old.

22

THE MANHATTAN PROJECT

During the war, a thousand Minnesotans worked on a project so secret they did not know what the outcome would be until it happened. In October 1941, President Roosevelt created a top policy panel to oversee the production of a bomb more destructive than anything previously known. The president had been warned by refugee scientists from Germany, including Albert Einstein, who had immigrated to the United States in 1939 when Hitler came to power, that German scientists had discovered nuclear fission and they were pursuing creation of an atomic bomb. Military and university scientists across the country investigated the possibilities. The US Army Corps of Engineers took the lead, using offices in Manhattan and Washington, DC. In June 1942, the Manhattan Project was approved by the president.

The following month, Catherine Filippi from Keewatin, Minnesota, was among two hundred Women's Army Corps (WACs) interviewing at Fort Devens, Massachusetts, for what they thought were routine desk jobs. Within weeks, she found herself reporting for assignment at a closely guarded office building in lower Manhattan. The daughter of Italian parents, Catherine had graduated from Hibbing High School on the Iron Range. After taking some college courses in Hibbing and St. Cloud, Catherine decided to visit Europe, including family in Italy.

While she was in Italy, Catherine met a boy from home, Louis Piccolo, who was also visiting family. In May 1939, Catherine saw and "heard the fanatical utterings of the man with the little black mustache, Adolph [sic] Hitler." He already had the support of Mussolini in Italy. The US State Department was urging Americans traveling in Europe to return. Catherine was reluctant to leave because she wanted to see more of the continent before going home. The morning she entered Warsaw, Poland, the Germans also entered the city. In December, she boarded a ship in Naples with other Americans returning to the United States. They soon learned that one of the other passengers was a German spy; the ship stopped at Gibraltar, and British intelligence officers escorted a man off. The young man from home Catherine had met during the trip became stranded in Italy for the next two years. Once home, Catherine decided to join the WAC to do her share to fight totalitarianism and to satisfy her yearning to be on the go again.

·····

After working at the Manhattan office, Catherine was sent to officer candidate school at Fort Oglethorpe, Georgia. In February 1945, when she completed the

Catherine Filippi, assistant public relations officer, Manhattan Project, 1945. *MNHS Collections*

three-month training program, Catherine was assigned to a military installation at Oak Ridge, Tennessee, eighteen miles from Knoxville. Bombs destined for Japan were made in this facility. In addition, research on U-235, an isotope of uranium that can sustain a fission reaction, was being conducted by famous scientists, who came and went in disguise using code names. Catherine took pride in knowing that some of the first success isolating U-235 had been accomplished by Alfred Nier, a University of Minnesota physics professor. Catherine and a thousand WACs worked at this facility.

Catherine supervised the Manhattan Project classified files unit, oversaw the destruction of all outdated files, supervised staff, and ensured the preservation and proper maintenance of valuable, secret records and documents. In July 1945, she became assistant public relations officer. In this role, she prepared news releases, special articles, and photographs. She supervised the stenciling and mimeographing of all news releases, assisted with interviews and press conferences, and cleared articles for publication. In the month before the atomic bomb was dropped on locations in Japan, Catherine worked on a team gathering material for distribution to the public after the bombing.

· · · · ·

In May 1944, another woman, Frances Jacobs was busy typing the WAC Physical Training Manual when the section chief told her she was wanted in the classifications office. This usually meant a new assignment. Frances thought a reassignment would be exciting and she might not have to "spend the duration fighting the battle of Fort Des Moines after all." After multiple interviews but no specific news, one day she was called to the classifications office at 8 PM. Evening interviews were highly unusual. This time the officer interviewing her was a WAC from Washington, DC. The officer asked Frances, "If you were doing something of vital importance, and were not allowed to give an inkling to anyone concerning your work, could you refrain from doing so?" Frances said she could. The officer asked, "But, if someone scoffed and said you probably were not doing anything important anyway, would you have to prove how important it was by dropping at least a hint about your vital work?" Frances said no. Then the officer asked her, "Would you be happy away from civilization, night clubs, and movies? Can your family get along without you for an indefinite period of time? Can you work long and hard on an important task without recognition?" Frances thought she could.

After several days, Frances was told to pack her bags. At midnight, a truck arrived and picked up Frances and five other WACs. Once they were on the train, they received their orders, which were for Fort Sill, Oklahoma. They all had expected to go overseas. These dreams were replaced with visions of "sweating out the war in muggy Oklahoma." Upon their arrival, the women from Fort Des Moines were grouped with a lieutenant and thirty other WACs. They were told not to unpack and were not given any assignments. A few days later, the lieutenant came into the mess hall at noon, "blew her whistle and ordered, 'All my girls leave at once! . . . Get on the truck. . . . Talk to no one, and await further orders!' There was dead silence in the Mess Hall as she spoke."

The WACs were taken by truck to the train station; twenty-four hours later they arrived at Albuquerque, New Mexico, where a bus met them and took them to a state highway patrol station outside of Santa Fe. They were "unceremoniously shoved onto two Army trucks standing by . . . the WAC Officer told [them] to take a good look around because it might be a long while before [they] saw civilization again." They were greeted by the post's commanding officer, who welcomed them and told them not to try to send any mail until further notice. He divided them into two groups. After the first group left, two armed guards came to escort Frances and nine other women into an area surrounded with barbed wire fence. The women were told not to look around and not to say a word.

Once they were inside one of the buildings, the WACs were greeted by Dr. J. Robert Oppenheimer, one of the most revered nuclear physicists in the world. They were in the Technical Area of Los Alamos station. He told them they might not understand what they were working on, but that it was of the utmost importance and "the success or failure of the project . . . might well mean the winning or losing of the war for the Allied nations." The women were speechless.

Frances and another woman were introduced to one of the mathematicians, Dr. Donald A. Flanders. He told them they had scored well on one of the army's placement tests that suggested they would be good with figures. He would teach them what they needed to know to assist him. They could not even tell others on the base what they were doing. Those in the Technical Area would not be eligible for passes or furloughs. Anyone who needed to leave for emergencies or business would be accompanied by an armed guard.

Frances and the others went to work, completing the tasks they were given. They suspected they were working on a large bomb. They saw chemical laboratories, knew about the mysterious machines operating in the laboratory's basement, and were aware of the Monday morning meetings of the renowned chemists, physicists, and mathematicians.

To help alleviate the tension, dances and movies were available in the barn. In the winter, they could go skating on the frozen pond. Horses were available for riding. Frances was injured once while riding and had to be escorted by an armed guard to the hospital.

Frances was reassigned to work with Dr. Alvin C. Graves and Dr. Elizabeth Riddle Graves, important physicists. She noticed that "Mrs. Graves was one of many wives of great scientists . . . who were very brilliant scientists themselves." At first Frances was worried about working with physicists because she did not know anything about physics. She was quickly reassured as she discovered her calculations were correct according to "one of the mysterious machines in the basement." She had to lock up her work in the safe at night, and she often left the office worried that she might talk in her sleep.

The pressure was building. "The strain of getting up at the crack of dawn, living in a very high altitude, working under extreme tension all day and coming home to wash, iron, shine shoes, straighten lockers, drill, etc." caused Frances to break down. She was transferred back to Fort Sill, Oklahoma, where she spent weeks in the hospital. The four months she had been at Los Alamos seemed like a dream, everything from the jukebox in the trading post to the geniuses assigned to create one of the biggest innovations in history and even the secret visit by Albert Einstein.

While Frances was in the hospital, a woman from post intelligence was in the bed next to her with a fake nervous breakdown to ensure Frances did not reveal anything about her assignment while she was hospitalized. After seven weeks, Frances was able to leave the hospital and she was given a medical discharge from the army. After she spent time recuperating, she entered the University of California at Los Angeles in the veterans rehabilitation program. It was almost a year before Catherine Filippi released the announcement to the press, and Frances finally felt great relief to see "splattered across the front pages of all the daily papers, information that it had been necessary to keep locked inside . . . for over a year."

WASHINGTON—PRESIDENT TRUMAN ANNOUNCED TODAY THAT THE UNITED STATES ARMY AIR FORCES HAVE STARTED USING A REVOLUTIONARY NEW ATOMIC BOMB AGAINST THE JAPANESE. . . . THE NEW BOMB PRODUCES MORE POWER THAN TWENTY THOUSAND TONS OF T-N-T. AND IT PRODUCES A BLAST MORE THAN TWO THOUSAND TIMES AS GREAT AS THE LARGEST BOMB EVER USED BEFORE.

THE FIRST OF THE NEW REVOLUTIONARY TYPE BOMBS WAS DROPPED SIXTEEN HOURS AGO ON THE IMPORTANT JAPANESE ARMY BASE OF HIROSHIMA. THIS IS A CITY OF 318-THOUSAND POPULATION THAT HAS LARGE ORDNANCE, MACHINE TOOL AND AIRCRAFT PLANTS AS WELL AS A MAJOR QUARTERMASTER DEPOT. . . . SAID THE PRESIDENT: "IT IS AN ATOMIC BOMB. IT IS A HARNESSING OF THE BASIC POWER OF THE UNIVERSE. THE FORCE FROM WHICH THE SUN DRAWS ITS POWER HAS BEEN LOOSED AGAINST THOSE WHO BROUGHT WAR TO THE FAR EAST."

23

HIROSHIMA

On August 6, 1945, Anna Tanaka and her aunt were walking to the train station in Kure, twelve miles west of Hiroshima City. They intended to buy train tickets for a visit to the countryside, where other family members were living and growing food. At eight o'clock that morning, Anna looked up in the direction of Hiroshima City and saw a big sun flash, followed by a mushroom cloud.

At first Anna and her aunt thought poison gas had been dropped from the American planes. The next day, they got a ride into Hiroshima with a cousin who had a truck for his restaurant business. They wanted to check on Anna's older sister, a student nurse at the Red Cross hospital. The truck was only allowed to the edge of the city; they had to walk the rest of the way. Amid the chaos of incoming patients, Anna and her aunt were relieved to find the young nurse safe, but she was too busy to talk to them. Anna and her aunt walked past many rooms with people "packed in like a can of sardines. Dead." Many were badly burned and were suffering. Because of the summer heat, the smell of decaying bodies was intense. They set off again for the train station, but sirens went off. They could see another American B-29 bomber flying overhead. Anna's aunt was frightened and jumped into a ditch, imploring Anna to do the same, but Anna refused, saying, "They aren't going to do anything, because they just came to see what they did."

Anna had heard the sirens many times while at home in Kure, where she and her sister lived with their aunt and uncle. Set between a mountain range and Seto Inland Sea, which adjoins the Pacific Ocean, it was a beautiful harbor town. Kure began as a fishing village and grew over time into a shipyard and then became home to the Japanese naval arsenal. During the war when the sirens went off, Anna and her family ran to shelter, either the public one or a six-by-six-foot one dug in their yard five feet deep. Kure was bombed harshly by Allied forces several times in the weeks before the atomic bombs were dropped. American forces targeted the warships docked there, retaliating for the attack on Pearl Harbor. Anna and her family were "scared stiff" when they saw the B-29s fly over because they dropped incendiary bombs that "lit up the sky like day," igniting fires. Seventeen hundred people died in Kure from the attacks leading up to the atomic bombs. Anna hated the sound of the sirens.

· · · · ·

Anna and her sister were born in Minneapolis, Minnesota. In 1932, when the girls were only three and five years old, their father, a Japanese immigrant, sent them to Kure to live with his brother and sister-in-law. The economy was poor in Minnesota due to the Great Depression. Their uncle was a vice president of a bank in Japan; their father thought they might have a better life there. The girls' mother, a German immigrant, had left her husband and daughters and returned to Iowa. Their father found it difficult to run his restaurant and care for his daughters.

After young Anna moved to Japan, she began calling her aunt "Mother." Many people in their neighborhood and at school treated the girls well, but the newly formed family was often aware of people staring at them, noticing that the girls were "mixed blood." Some people called them bad names. After the war started, some accused the girls of being spies for the United States, and the Japanese government approached them, asking that they return to the United States and become spies for Japan. Their aunt encouraged the girls to ignore the discrimination and politics and try to do especially well in school to make up for being part Caucasian. Anna never felt totally comfortable in Japan because of the prejudice she experienced, but she loved her aunt.

After several years of war, life in Japan changed. Rationing intensified. The family was forced to eat potatoes because of a shortage of rice. For protein, they sometimes ate barbecued grasshoppers. Anna's grandmother took her up into the mountains and taught her how to find edible mushrooms. She taught the girls

Street in Kure, Hiroshima, before the atomic bomb was dropped. *Courtesy Postcard Museum in Hyogo Prefecture, Japan*

Anna Tanaka, wearing monpe school uniform during the war in Japan. *Courtesy Anna Tanaka (Murakami)*

to make a soup of rice, soybeans, onion, tofu, and miso. Many fishermen had joined the Japanese armed forces, and fish, normally a staple in their diets, was in short supply. Anna's family raised vegetables in the country to complement the food they could buy in town within the rationed allotments.

Because of their country garden, they had a little more food than other people. A black market for food emerged. Their uncle's position in the bank also gave them access to food, even bacon. Once Anna packed a second lunch for a friend at school who had many siblings and did not have enough to eat. Someone told the police about the food Anna was sharing, and their whole house was searched because they were accused of participating in the black market.

Anna's education was disrupted by the war when her school was converted into a metalworks factory. For two years, the schoolchildren manufactured oil valves for ships. They also made silk and cotton cushions for the pilots to sit on. Anna often had to show her ID to get into the school after it became a factory because the guards did not think she looked Japanese. Her hair was lighter in color. Her sister's hair was as dark as the other Japanese girls'. Anna was reluctant to work at the factory after Japan began fighting the United States; she wondered what might happen to her father living in Minnesota. The girls' education was affected as well; a generation of students were short two years of schooling because they were working to support the war instead of studying.

Years later, Anna recalled that no one in Japan thought that they would lose the war, but many Japanese people thought it was a big mistake to bomb Pearl Harbor and directly involve the United States. When it became clear that Japan might not win, many people wanted the government to talk with the Americans. They thought the United States was willing to negotiate. Anna heard that even Emperor Hirohito implored the politicians to refrain from fighting further, but nothing would stop Hideki Tojo, the war minister and then prime minister. Although Tojo was forced to resign in 1944, the momentum he had fueled was difficult to stop.

• • • • •

Days after the atomic bombs were dropped and Anna's aunt jumped into the ditch, her aunt became sick. She lost all of her hair and developed a high fever, but she survived. Anna did not get sick, perhaps because she did not jump into the ditch, where moisture may have conducted the radiation. More than 150,000 men, women, and children died in Hiroshima within weeks of the bombing. Another 75,000 people died days later when Nagasaki was bombed. The total toll, including premature deaths occurring months and years later due to miscarriages, cancer, and other causes, was estimated to be 450,000.

When the occupation forces, consisting of US and Australian soldiers, landed, the Japanese government warned all women to leave the cities and hide in the country, worried that the soldiers might assault them. Anna's uncle lost his job at the bank, and the family continued to grow food in the country to survive. Her father sent things from Minnesota to help support them, which increased animosity toward the sisters. People referred to her father as a Yankee, using a terrible word in Japanese. Some people told Anna "Go home!" and called her "Blue eyes," associating her with the Americans and Europeans even though her eyes were not blue.

When the war was over, Anna entered a dressmaking school, inspired by her aunt, who was a kimono seamstress and teacher. She turned fabric from some of her uncle's old suits inside out to make women's clothes. When her neighbors provided the fabric, Anna made clothes for their children for free. She was proud of her sewing abilities, which allowed her to fit into the Japanese culture and feel useful.

In 1951, Anna, at age twenty-two, returned to Minnesota with her sister to care for their aging father. Because their English was not very good, he found jobs for them as a nanny and housekeeper, which initially upset them. They felt they were qualified for better jobs, and they were terribly homesick. The girls wrote to their aunt, asking to return to Japan. Later Anna understood the importance of knowing English well and appreciated what her father had done for them. In 1952, she married James Murakami, a Japanese man born in California. He had been relocated to the Gila River internment camp with his parents and siblings until he began serving in the US Army. He became part of the occupation forces in Germany. He returned after the service to attend Dunwoody Institute in Minneapolis. Anna worked as a seamstress at a well-known department store until she became a mother. Caring for her three children became her career.

 . . . . .

Ruth Erickson, one of the navy corps nurses who was at Pearl Harbor on December 7, 1941, when the naval base was attacked, was subsequently assigned to hospital ships and hospitals on bases throughout the war. Coincidentally, on V-J Day, she was on the USS *Haven* at port in Honolulu, close to where she had been when the war began. Ruth and the other nurses were given secret orders out of Honolulu.

Once at sea, they learned they were headed to Japan. The harbors had to be swept for mines as they approached the Japanese shores. The USS *Haven* eventually tied up to a railroad pier in Nagasaki. They were there to evacuate Allied POWs. Hundreds of servicemen came off of the trains. Tears rolled down their cheeks—the nurses' and the servicemen's—as they were brought aboard. Many of the men experienced burns caused by the atomic bomb blast, as well as suffering from poor nutrition and living conditions during their incarceration. Before the USS *Haven* left shore, the nurses had an opportunity to ride through Nagasaki on a bus to witness the devastation caused by the "great white light." Little was known at the time about the lingering impact of radiation. The nurses returned to the USS *Haven* and headed back to the United States with their seven hundred fifty patients.

24
POSTWAR

In December 1944, Jay C. Hormel announced postwar plans for his meatpacking plant, anticipating reduced production and the eventual return of nearly two thousand employees from military service. The company sought to increase sales as the war wound down, so all current employees and returning veterans would have a job. One of the plans was an innovative idea for women veterans. Jay Hormel encouraged the establishment of an American Legion Post, SPAM Post 570, in Austin, Minnesota, which became one of the first all-women posts in June 1946 when it was chartered with thirty-five members. His plan was to "supplement the company's male sales organization with product demonstration teams of girls . . . for a long time he had felt an acute need for more direct contact between the company and the housewife, he thought girl demonstrators could do it."

By June 1947, the first team of veterans, now Hormel saleswomen, began demonstrating Hormel products at stores and providing musical entertainment at Lions and Kiwanis Clubs. They were reasonably well paid and had an opportunity to see the country. They were a hit, and an eight-year nationwide run began.

Later that summer, Hormel recruited fifty-eight women with musical talent. The company provided musical instruments and direction so that Post 570 could participate in the annual American Legion drum and bugle competition in New York. In early August, legionnaires gathered from all parts of the country at Eastern Military Academy, in Stamford, Connecticut, where they practiced marching and playing eleven hours a day, so long that the neighbors in the area began to complain. "This Is My Country," "Pennsylvania Polka," "Minnesota Rouser," and "Give My Regards to Broadway" were among the tunes the women of Post 570 perfected.

On August 28, 1947, the Hormel Girls, also called the Spamettes, hit the field, where they were the only all-women corps playing in the American Legion competition. They scored well with all of the judges except one, who might have been biased because they were women. He gave them a low score for "general effect." In contrast, another judge noted that their bugling was "music that no other Corps could match . . . they brought forth tones that practiced ears will not forget for a long time." But the one low score prevented them from becoming finalists. They had to settle for placing thirteenth out of the thirty-seven corps, which was not bad for a group that had just begun playing together less than a month before.

The next day, Post 570 participated in a parade, performing for two million people lined up along Fifth Avenue in New York City. The crowds loved them, and the members of Post 570 were proud to represent the hundreds of thousands of women who had served in World War II. One man, their drill instructor, marched behind them with a sign, "All-Girl Spam Post 570—Men's auxiliary."

After the drum and bugle corps competition, the Hormel Girls resumed demonstrating products and performing at local service clubs across the country. The caravan consisted of sixty women; thirty-five shiny, white Chevrolets; and five trucks carrying musical instruments and equipment. All of them rolled into a town together, making a noticeable impression. They broke into teams, visited grocers, and ended the day with a two-hour performance in auditoriums that held fifteen hundred grocers and their guests. They played Dixieland, Latin, and classical orchestral music with vocal pieces and comedy acts.

In early 1948, they began a radio broadcast, *Music with the Hormel Girls*, which debuted on a station in Los Angeles. They were soon heard coast to coast on two hundred twenty-seven radio stations. By 1953, the show was the fourth most popular radio show in the country.

Although the hours were long and the women had to watch their weight and appearance, the Hormel Girls received ten days off every three months with pay, and they were well compensated. They were paid fifty dollars per week as base pay and received bonuses for high sales. They were housed in upscale hotels and received thirty-three dollars a week for food and laundry. During the war, women working in privately owned factories would typically make fifty dollars a week, but after the war, women's wages in factories across the country dropped 26 percent, to thirty-seven dollars a week.

Hormel Girls. *Hormel Corporate Archive*

Despite the hard work and somewhat paternalistic atmosphere, the women appreciated the opportunity. Many left when they married, but most stayed. They saw a great deal of the country comfortably, as stars. They valued the independence and good compensation. As television became increasingly popular in the 1950s, after eight successful years, the Hormel Girls radio and road shows ended in 1953.

．．．．．

Most corporations had reduced opportunities at the end of the war due to declining demand for production compounded by the returning servicemen. Twin Cities Ordnance Plant (TCOP) in New Brighton closed in September 1945, after producing four and a half billion cartridges and employing thirty-seven thousand people. While the plant provided vital ammunition for the troops and the jobs were important, especially for women, there was a hidden cost to the environment. Environmental damage and exploitation does not happen only on battlefields. The devastating impact in war zones is obvious, but the environmental impact of production plants is less evident initially.

In the 1980s, pollutants were discovered on the TCOP site affecting the groundwater, soil, and health of New Brighton residents. Chlorinated solvents, explosives, metals, volatile organic compounds (VOCs), polychlorinated biphenyls (PCBs), polycyclic aromatic hydrocarbons (PAHs), and lead were the primary pollutants found in the water and soil. The state board of health determined that the chemical contamination "posed a long term chronic health problem." It directed the city of New Brighton to replace its water supply.

TCOP land qualified as a Superfund site, meaning the pollution was significant enough that the federal Environmental Protection Agency (EPA) would manage the cleanup and force the parties responsible, the army in this case, to either perform cleanups or reimburse the government for EPA-led work.

According to the EPA, seventy-five years after the plant closed, "more than 94,000 cubic yards of contaminated soil have been treated to meet Army industrial use standards. More than 200,000 pounds of VOCs [were] removed from deep soils. Approximately 1,500 cubic yards of PCB-contaminated soil [were] incinerated. Approximately 1.2 billion gallons of groundwater [were] treated each year. Approximately 226,445 pounds of VOCs [were] removed from the groundwater. Land use is still restricted to 'Army industrial.'" Groundwater treatment of the site is expected to continue until 2040, a century after the plant began operating. While women benefitted from jobs at TCOP and the ammunition was necessary for the war, the cost to the environment was significant.

．．．．．

In addition to reduced opportunities in the corporate sector, with the exception of the Army and Navy Nurse Corps, "there were no provisions for servicewomen in the postwar military." Some veterans qualified for educational opportunities under the GI Bill, but most colleges and universities struggled to accommodate the large numbers of returning servicemen. B. J. Hanson, one of the WASPs, contacted the university in Grand Forks after the war in hopes of resuming premed coursework. The school sent a letter notifying her that the only degree program open for her after the war was home economics. She gave up her dream of becoming a physician.

Some women in the military tried to transfer their skills to the private sector. Betty Wall, another one of the WASPs, brushed up her résumé, including her commercial pilot's license, four-engine rating, instrument instructor's certificate, and seaplane rating for a job as a pilot with Northwest Airlines. At her interview, she was told that women did not fly commercially, but she could have a job in the front office. Instead, Betty went to air traffic controller's school and found a position in North Platte, Nebraska, where she was given the worst shift and did not feel welcome. She gave up on that occupation and tried fifteen other jobs in the following years: office worker, archery instructor, cashier. Eventually, this experienced, competent pilot returned home to help care for her aging mother. Soon Betty Wall married another World War II veteran, and they had five children.

Many women, including Ruth Gage Colby, Alice Sickels, Ruth Tanbara, Grace Holmes Carlson, Louise Boie Saunders, and Emily Peake, continued their important work in communities and advocating for peace.

Kae Eisenreich was offered a job in St. Louis by Northwest Airlines after the affiliated Northwest Aeronautics finished its army contract, but she turned them down to get married. Her husband went into the insurance business and eventually opened his own office in Faribault. They adopted two children after fertility treatments were unsuccessful. Kae's husband's clients began to ask for financial planning advice. He suggested that Kae get a broker's license, which she did. She then opened an office in Faribault, as possibly the first outstate woman broker in Minnesota.

Ferne Chambers married a submarine sailor after she was discharged from the marines. He stayed in the navy for twenty years. They lived near San Francisco, Honolulu, and San Diego until he requested to become a recruiter. He was able to get assigned to Minnesota so they could return with their two sons. After the war, he developed a drinking problem. Ferne focused on raising her boys, working at a Ben Franklin in Coon Rapids, and creating art: dolls, purses, Christmas tree pins, and paintings.

· · · · ·

Women of Minnesota joined the military, worked outside the home in nontraditional fields, and became involved in their communities for varying reasons. They were motivated to do their part to help win the war. Some were looking for financial independence or hoping to escape poverty. Some were looking for adventure, an opportunity to grow and learn. Regardless of their motivation, when the war ended in 1945, a significant transition began for women and for men, those who would become known as the Greatest Generation.

ACKNOWLEDGMENTS

I am grateful for all public and academic libraries, historical societies, and archives, especially the Rochester Public Library, the University of Minnesota Libraries, and the Gale Family Library and archive at the Minnesota Historical Society. These repositories and gathering places are cornerstones of our democracy, providing free access to information and our stories.

Thank you to my colleagues at the University of Minnesota Rochester for sustaining a culture of creativity and innovation where I have thrived. A special thanks to those who covered classes and other responsibilities during my sabbatical so I could finish this book, including Jennifer Wacek, Aaron Bruenger, and Norman Clark. Jessie Barnett and Kristin Osiecki provided me with information on the impact that war can have on our environment. Our librarian, Mary Sancomb Moran, helped me track down articles and books, many of them through interlibrary loan. Thank you to our chancellor, Lori Carrell, for leading our bold vision, and to UMR's students, who teach and challenge us every day, and I mean *every day*.

I am grateful to my writing group, Yuko Taniguchi, Bronson Lerner, and Jeremy Anderson, who provided encouragement and candid feedback on early and late drafts of this manuscript. Catherine Watson and Patricia Francisco Weaver helped me hone my craft leading up to this project, and Sun Yung Shin provided insightful perspective in the eleventh hour. My longtime mentor, Sister Ingrid Peterson, has provided wise counsel, a witty sense of humor, and, as she puts it, "a foot in my back," inspiring me to keep writing one word at a time for more than thirty years.

I am especially grateful for those who told their stories and the family members, friends, and archivists who collected and preserved those stories, in particular, the Minnesota Historical Society's Greatest Generation Oral History Project, through which hundreds of people throughout the state were interviewed by dedicated interviewers and writers, including Brian Horrigan. Thomas Saylor's collection of stories published in *Remembering the Good War: Minnesota's Greatest Generation* and Dave Kenney's *Minnesota Goes to War: The Home Front During World War II* were both helpful guides for me. Staff and volunteers at historical societies and archives who were especially generous with their time include Krista Lewis, Pat Carlson, and the Women's History Circle of the History Center of Olmsted County; Sue Doocy of the Mower County Historical Society; Steve Nordrum of the Hormel Corporate Archive; Renee Zeimer of the W. Bruce Fye Center for the History of Medicine at Mayo Clinic; Virginia Wentzel, who shared the nursing school history of Rochester, Minnesota; Mary Peterson of the Virginia [Minnesota] Area Historical Society; Aimee Brown, curator of the Special Collections at the Kathryn A. Martin Library at University of Minnesota Duluth; and Eric Van Slander, who patiently assisted me at the National Archives at College Park, Maryland. Ruth Manchester generously shared her research on Dorothy Wahlstrom with me.

The World War II veterans and survivors I had the honor to personally meet provided special inspiration: Rose Polga Bayuk, Anna Tanaka Murakami, and Helen Friedline Chadwick. The families of Blanche Shoquist Peterson, Ellie Thiry Summers, and Julia F. Herrick were generous in sharing letters and memories. I was especially touched by the stories of hundreds of women of the Iron Range who, under difficult financial conditions in a rather remote part of the state, did more than their share in the military, nurse corps, mines, and factories.

Many friends supported me by listening to my stories and frustrations during the research and writing process. Marsha Hall, Claire Bender, Bethany Krom, Jill Caudill, Sue Ramthun, Stephanie Carlson, and Dawn Littleton have endured my storytelling for years. Gretchen McCoy read a rough draft and diplomatically suggested what needed to be "fixed." Carole Stiles encouraged me by emphasizing a commitment to the well-told story. Thank you to these and other friends who encourage and inspire me, especially those who tirelessly advocate for justice.

Writers sometimes complain that it is not possible in this century to have meaningful relationships with editors, but such a thing is possible at Minnesota Historical Society Press. Shannon Pennefeather has survived editing two books I have written. There should be an award for that. This book would not be what it is without her gifted touch. Ann Regan provided wise counsel and cheerleading during a couple of the most challenging steps in the process. Josh Leventhal encouraged me from the moment I suggested a book about the courageous women of Minnesota. I am also grateful to Anna Matthews for her detective work tracking down photos that add so much to the written word in this book.

My deepest gratitude goes to my family. To my mother, Marlys Peterson, for taking me to the public library, where I fell in love with stories and books before I could read. To my father, who supported my education. To my siblings—Ann Garritty, Sandy Kelm, Roger Peterson—their spouses, and my nieces and nephews—a small but mighty bunch—who have encouraged and supported me in various ways. To my husband, Ralph, who shared my love of books, writing, and ice cream. I miss him deeply. To my grandchildren, Harper and Heath, who inspire me with their many questions, their dreams, and their sense of wonder. To my daughter, Kris, whose commitment to her family and community is making this a better world, and she has just begun! Without her encouragement, close reading, and sense of humor, I could not have written this book. And last, but not least, a sincere thank-you goes to Beethoven, my canine companion, who relatively patiently sat next to me while every word of this book was written, rewritten, and revised again.

Because of all of these people and organizations, my life and work have been enriched beyond measure.

WORLD WAR II TIMELINE

1931   Japan invades Manchuria

1933–34 Adolf Hitler becomes chancellor and president of Germany; the first concentration camps are established

1935   Jewish people are no longer considered citizens of Germany

1938   Great Britain, France, and Italy endorse Germany's annexation of the German-speaking regions of Czechoslovakia

1939   Germany invades the remainder of Czechoslovakia and Poland
Great Britain, France, Australia, and New Zealand declare war
Soviet troops enter eastern Poland and Finland

1940   Germany invades Netherlands, Belgium, and France
French and British troops forced to flee French coast at Dunkirk
German troops enter Paris (June 14)
France surrenders (June 22)
Battle of Britain (begins July 10)
German bombing of London, the Blitz (begins September 22)
Germany, Italy, and Japan sign pact of cooperation (September 27)
Military draft begins in United States (November)

1941   United States begins Lend-Lease program supplying food and ammunition to Britain
Germany invades Soviet Union (August)
Mass murders and incarceration of Jews occur in German-occupied areas
Japan attacks US naval base at Pearl Harbor (December 7)

1942   First US troops arrive in Britain (January)
United States surrenders to Japan in the Philippines, Bataan (March)
Internment of Japanese people begins in United States (April)
Japanese invade Aleutian Islands, part of Alaska Territory (June)
Battle of Midway between Japan and United States (June 4–7)
Operation Torch under General Eisenhower in North Africa (November)

1943   US troops retake Aleutian Islands from Japan (May-June)
Italy under Mussolini surrenders to Allied troops (September 8)
Allies bomb and enter German-held areas

1944   Japan sends troops into China
General MacArthur recaptures New Guinea from Japanese
Allies enter France on Normandy Beach, D-Day (June 6)
Allies liberate Paris (August 25)
Battle of the Bulge (begins December 16)
Allies liberate concentration camps, including Dachau

1945   Allies intensify bombing and land attacks on Japan
President Roosevelt dies (April 15)
Hitler commits suicide (April 30)
Germany surrenders, Victory in Europe (V-E) Day (May 8)
United States liberates Philippines (July)
United States drops atomic bombs on Hiroshima and Nagasaki
(August 6 and 9)
Japan surrenders, Victory in Japan (V-J) Day (August 14)

Based on information from *A World War II Timeline* by Elizabeth Raum (Smithsonian; Mankato, MN: Capstone Press, 2014).

SOURCE NOTES

Notes to Chapter 1: A Long Way From Home

Ruth Erickson's experience is summarized from an oral history provided by the Historian, Bureau of Medicine and Surgery, U.S. Navy, found at https://www.history .navy.mil/research/library/oral-histories/wwii/pearl-harbor/pearl-harbor-attack -lt-erickson.html and from an interview conducted by Florence Schubert on May 14, 1991, on file at the W. Bruce Fye Center for the History of Medicine, Mayo Clinic, Rochester, Minnesota.

A History of Virginia, Minnesota by Marvin Skarud (typescript, 1941) and the 1931 *Roosevelt High School Yearbook* were consulted.

The lists of women from Virginia, Minnesota, who served in the military and in nonmilitary roles during World War II were compiled by Louise Grams and Betty Birnsthil and are on file at the Virginia Area Historical Society, Virginia, Minnesota.

Notes to Chapter 2: Internment, Resettlement, and Advocating for Peace

Information about Eleanor Roosevelt in this chapter came from *No Ordinary Time: Franklin and Eleanor Roosevelt: The Home Front in World War II* by Doris Kearns Goodwin (New York: Simon & Schuster, 1995). Mrs. Roosevelt's April 26, 1943, "My Day" column can be found at https://www2.gwu.edu/~erpapers/myday/displaydocedits .cfm?_y=1943&_f=md056480, and her related speech published in *Collier's* 112 (October 16, 1943): 21, 71 can be found at https://www2.gwu.edu/~erpapers/documents/ articles/challengetoamerican.cfm.

Information about the nurses came from *Nisei Cadet Nurse of World War II: Patriotism in Spite of Prejudice* by Thelma M. Robinson (Boulder, CO: Black Swan Mill Press, 2005), *Saint Marys School of Nursing Alumni Quarterly* (October 1943), "Saint Marys Hospital Annals" (1943), and interviews conducted by Virginia Wentzel. These materials can be found through the W. Bruce Fye Center for the History of Medicine, Mayo Clinic, Rochester, Minnesota. John Nobuya Tsuchia's *Reflections: Memoirs of Japanese American Women in Minnesota* (Covina, CA: Pacific Asia Press, 1994) was also used.

Information about the Japanese internment camps came from the US National Parks Service, https://www.nps.gov/subjects/internment/index.htm, and the Japanese American National Museum, http://www.janm.org/nrc/resources/internfs/.

Information on Japanese immigration to Minnesota can be found in Michael Albert's essay "The Japanese," published in *They Chose Minnesota: A Survey of the State's*

Ethnic Groups, edited by June Drenning Holmquist (St. Paul: Minnesota Historical Society Press, 1981), 558–71. Information about the Military Intelligence Service Language School can be found in this brochure published by the Twin Cities chapter of the Japanese American Citizens League: https://www.tcjacl.org/wp/wp-content/uploads/2014/04/MISGuide2013.pdf.

Information about Alice Sickels and the St. Paul Resettlement Committee came from her memoir, *Around the World in St. Paul* (Minneapolis: University of Minnesota Press, 1945), and St. Paul Resettlement Committee (St. Paul, Minn.) records, 1942–53, manuscript collection, Minnesota Historical Society.

Information about Ruth Numura Tanbara comes from her papers, 1906–2008, manuscript collection, Minnesota Historical Society.

Experiences of Japanese American Women During and After World War II: Living in Internment Camps and Rebuilding Life Afterwards by Precious Yamaguchi (New York: Lexington Books, 2014) provided helpful information about the internment camps and the pressure Japanese people felt to prove loyalty to the United States. "Reflections of Cultural Identities in Conflict: Japanese American Internment Camp Newspapers during World War II" by Catherine A. Luther, published in *Journalism History* 29, no. 2 (Summer 2003), was also consulted.

Information about Fanny Fligelman Brin can be found in her papers, 1896–1958, including Ruth F. Brin's essay "She Heard Another Drummer: The Life of Fanny Brin, and its Implications for the Sociology of Religion," manuscript collection, Minnesota Historical Society, and Barbara Stuhler's essay "Fanny Brin: Woman of Peace," in *Women of Minnesota: Selected Biographical Essays*, edited by Barbara Stuhler and Gretchen Kreuter (St. Paul: Minnesota Historical Society Press, 1977).

Information on anti-Semitism in Minnesota during the 1930s and 1940s can be found in *Minnesota Goes to War: The Home Front during World War II* by Dave Kenney (St. Paul: Minnesota Historical Society Press, 2005).

Information about Grace Holmes Carlson came from her papers (1929–86) and interviews of her by Carl Ross conducted in July 1987, manuscript collection, Minnesota Historical Society, and Elizabeth Raasch-Gilman's article "Sisterhood in the Revolution: The Holmes Sisters and the Socialist Workers' Party," *Minnesota History* 56, no. 7 (Fall 1999).

Notes to Chapter 3: Witnessing the War Emerge

Information about Mary Welsh Hemingway came from her memoir, *How It Was* (New York: Alfred A. Knopf, 1976); her papers at the John F. Kennedy Presidential Library and Museum, Boston, Massachusetts; and articles she wrote for *Life* magazine (April 28 and August 4, 1941).

A transcript of President Franklin Roosevelt's December 8, 1941, address to Congress, requesting declaration of war, can be found in the Library of Congress collection, https://www.loc.gov/item/afccal000483/. An audio file can be found at https://en.wikipedia.org/wiki/File:Roosevelt_Pearl_Harbor.ogg.

Information about the war included in Mary Welsh's memoir was confirmed in *The Library of Congress World War II Companion*, edited by David M. Kenney, Margaret E. Wagner, Linda Barrett Osborne, Susan Reyburn, and Staff of the Library of Congress (New York: Simon & Schuster, 2007).

Information about women journalists in the United States was found in Marion Marzolf's *Up from the Footnote: A History of Women Journalists* (New York: Putnam, 1977) and Nancy Caldwell Sorel's *The Women Who Wrote the War* (New York: Arcade Publishing, 1999).

Information about Minnesota women was found in "Minnesota Women Journalists During World War II" by Patricia Dooley, published in *Roots* 17, no. 2 (Winter 1989) and Margaret Towey Evan's column in *Gopher Tidings* (September 1944).

The article from the *Fairmont Daily Sentinel* was an undated newspaper clipping found in a scrapbook owned by Lydia M. Schaefer and provided by her daughter, Nina Schaefer Hesby.

Notes to Chapter 4: Within the German Resistance Movement

Information for this chapter came from *Rebellious Spirit: Gisela Konopka* by Janice Andrews-Schenk (Edina, MN: Beaver's Pond Press, 2005); Gisela Peiper Konopka's memoir, *Courage and Love* (Edina, MN: Burgess Printing, 1988); and Gisela Peiper Konopka's papers at the Archives and Special Collections, Elmer L. Andersen Library, University of Minnesota.

Notes to Chapter 5: Carol the Riveter, Millie the Miner, and the WOWs

Information about women working at Hormel was found in the corporate newsletter *Squeal* (November 1941 to November 1, 1945), on file at the Hormel Corporate Archives, Austin, Minnesota; *In Quest of Quality: Hormel's First 75 Years* by Richard Dougherty (North St. Paul, MN: Central Publications, 1966); and *The Hormel Legacy: 100 Years of Quality* by Doniver A. Lund (Austin, MN: Geo. A. Hormel & Co., 1991). Hormel archivist Steve Nordrum also provided information verbally. Information about the Walt Disney Corporation campaign to encourage women to collect grease is portrayed in this video: https://vimeo.com/49890741.

Information about Barbara Hadley, Reika Mary Drake Schwanke, and Elizabeth Dahlgren is on file at the Mower County Historical Society in Austin, Minnesota, and includes several articles published in the *Austin Daily Herald*. Additional information about Elizabeth Dahlgren comes from her book *We Were First! We Heard the Guns at Wewak: Elgin Field WWII WACs* (Brownsville, TX: Springman-King, 1977).

Information about the Twin Cities Ordnance Plant was obtained from company newsletters (August 1941 to October 1945) and other materials in the corporate files at the Minnesota Historical Society. Two articles published in the *Minneapolis Star Tribune* (August 7 and 28, 1941) were also used. Mark Haidet's presentation about the company given at the New Brighton Historical Society on April 26, 2018, can be found at http://www.newbrightonhistory.com/april-26-2018-annual-meetin.html. See also Patricia Dooley's article "Gopher Ordnance Works: Condemnation, Construction, and Community Response," *Minnesota History* 49, no. 6 (Summer 1985): 215–28.

Carol Johnson Fistler's memoir is on file at the Douglas County Historical Society in Superior, Wisconsin. Information on Globe Shipbuilders and other related businesses is available at the Kathryn A. Martin Library, University of Minnesota Duluth.

Mining information came from interviews and other information on file at the Iron Range Research Center at the Minnesota Discovery Center in Chisholm, Minnesota. Information also came from Stephanie Hemphill's article "Women in the Mines," published in *Minnesota History* 61, no. 3 (Fall 2008): 92–101. Thomas Saylor's *Remembering the Good War: Minnesota's Greatest Generation* (St. Paul: Minnesota Historical Society Press, 2005) was also consulted.

Notes to Chapter 6: Accompanying General Eisenhower and the Troops into Africa

Information on the American Red Cross comes from *The American Red Cross: A History* by Foster Rhea Dulles (New York: Harper, 1950) and *The Compact History of the American Red Cross* by Charles Hurd (New York: Hawthorne Books, 1959). The American Red Cross *Prisoner of War Bulletin* is on file at the University of Minnesota Wilson Library, Minneapolis. Information on the American Red Cross chapters and activities in Minnesota is available in the Minnesota Historical Society archives under "Red Cross Service Record," "Red Cross Bulletin," and "Record of the War Years" for the years 1942–45.

Information about Mildred Louise Boie Saunders came primarily from her letters and papers held by the Special Collections at Smith College Library in Northampton, Massachusetts, and her article "Red Cross in Cairo," published in the August 1944 edition of *Ladies' Home Journal*.

Information about Blanche Erickson Peterson was found in letters and diaries shared by her son and daughter-in-law, John and Berny Peterson.

Prudence Hathaway Burns Burrell's information, including a video interview, can be found on the History Makers online archive of African American Oral Histories, http://www.thehistorymakers.org/biography/prudence-burrell-41; in the Library of Congress "Experiencing War: Stories from Veterans Project" interview by Katie Cavanaugh, March 19, 2002; as well as in her memoir, *Hathaway* (Detroit: Harlo, 1997).

Notes to Chapter 7: Fighter Planes: Women Who Flew Them and Built Them

Information about the formation of the WASPs can be found in Sally Van Wagenen Keil's book, *Those Wonderful Women in Their Flying Machines: The Unknown Heroes of World War Two*, expanded edition (New York: Four Directions, 1994). Jacqueline Cochran's "Final Report on Women Pilot Program" is available in her papers held at the Eisenhower Library Archive, Abilene, Kansas, https://www.eisenhowerlibrary.gov/research/online-documents/jacqueline-cochran-and-womens-airforce-service-pilots-wasps.

Information about Betty Wall is available in *And Still Flying . . . The Life and Times of Elizabeth "Betty" Wall* by Patrick Roberts (Victoria, BC: Trafford, 2003) and in a film by Steve Cloutier: *Betty Wall: Girls Don't Fly,* https://www.youtube.com/watch?time_continue=355&v=K7KDubhzmYo.

An interview with Betty Jane (B. J.) Hanson Erenberg, conducted by David Riley on November 2, 1979, is included in the Minnesota Historical Society's Greatest Generation Oral History Project.

Kae Eisenreich's interview by Brian Horrigan (2007) and Millie Bowers Johnson's interview by Ben Petry and Andy Wilhide (2008) are part of the Minnesota's Greatest Generation Oral History Project, on file at the Minnesota Historical Society.

Information about Disney's creation of Fifinella can be found in Jennet Conant's book, *The Irregulars: Roald Dahl and the British Spy Ring in Wartime Washington* (New York: Simon & Schuster, 2008).

Virginia Mae Hope's papers and one of her flight jackets are in the Minnesota Historical Society collection.

Information about Char-Gale was obtained from the Stearns County Historical Society, St. Cloud, Minnesota. Information about the gliders and Northwest Aeronautics came from an article by Jim Johns published in the Fall 2008 issue of *Allies*, a newsletter for members and friends of the Military Historical Society of Minnesota in Little Falls, found at https://www.mnmilitarymuseum.org/files/7815/0186/6478/ALLIES_Vol-XVI-No-4_2008-Fall.pdf, and Angelo DePonti's papers (1929–91) in the Minnesota Historical Society manuscripts collection.

Articles from the *Austin Daily Herald* (August 24 and September 21, 1942) on file at the Mower County Historical Society provide descriptions of the training courses offered in Austin, Minnesota.

Information about Northwest Airlines Modification Center came from Johannes R. Allert's article "Northwest Airlines' Modification Center in World War II," *Minnesota History* 63, no. 8 (Winter 2013–14): 324–33, and the Northwest Airlines corporate records at the Minnesota Historical Society.

Information about the formation of the women's reserve in the marines is available in Mary V. Stremlow's essay "Marine Corps Women's Reserve," in *In Defense of a Nation: Servicewomen in World War II*, edited by Jeanne Holm and Judith Bellafaire (Arlington, VA: Women's Military Press, 1998).

Ferne Chambers Krans's interview by Ben Petry and Konrad Krans (2008) and her papers are held at the Minnesota Historical Society.

An image and description of the women marines' cricket mascot created by Disney can be seen in an undated El Centro, California, newspaper article found here: http://www .usmilitariaforum.com/forums/index.php?/topic/234796-disney-design-for-wwii -women-marines-aviation-squadron/.

Ruth Telander Johnson Ryder's story can be found in her obituary published in the *Minneapolis Star Tribune*, April 28, 2016.

Information about Patty Berg comes from articles in the *Guardian* (September 12, 2006) and in the *Minneapolis Star Tribune* (March 10 and June 27, 2015).

Notes to Chapter 8: *Semper Paratus*, Always Ready

Information about Emily Peake's life came from Jane Pejsa's book *The Life of Emily Peake: One Dedicated Ojibwe* (Minneapolis, MN: Nodin Press, 2003) and from Brenda J. Child and Karissa E. White, "'I've Done My Share': Ojibwe People and World War II," *Minnesota History* 61, no. 5 (Spring 2009): 196–207.

Information about the SPARS came from an essay by Mary E. McWilliams published in *In Defense of a Nation: Servicewomen in World War II*, edited by Jeanne M. Holm and Judith Bellafaire (Arlington, VA: Military Women's Press, 1998).

The following article reviews the potential dangers of zinc cadmium and the studies conducted in Minneapolis: National Research Council, Subcommittee on Zinc Cadmium Sulfide, "Toxicologic Assessment of the Army's Zinc Cadmium Sulfide Dispersion Tests" (Washington, DC: National Academies Press, 1997). Summary available at https://www.ncbi.nlm.nih.gov/books/NBK233502/.

Notes to Chapter 9: Lives Lost on US Soil: The Aleutian Islands

Information on the Aleutian Islands and related military installations was found in the 1980 report resulting from Congress's Commission on Wartime Relocation and Internment of Civilians, https://www.archives.gov/research/japanese-americans/justice -denied, and "Unalaska Historic Preservation Plan: 1994–95 Edition," prepared by Nancy Green for the Unalaska Historic Preservation Commission. Information on the islands can be found in "Alaska's Far-Out Islands: The Aleutians" by Lael Morgan, *National Geographic* (September 1983).

Brian Garfield's *The Thousand-Mile War: World War II in Alaska and the Aleutians* (New York: Doubleday, 1995) was referenced.

Information on the military presence in the Aleutian Islands during the war is found at "World War II National Historic Landmarks: The Aleutian Campaign," National Park Service, https://www.nps.gov/articles/wwii-nhl-aleu-campaign.htm.

Information on the service and deaths of Helen Roehler and Ruby Toquam was found in undated newspaper clippings from the *Fairmont Daily Sentinel* in Lydia Schaefer's scrapbooks, provided to the author by her granddaughter, Nina Hesby. Additional information on Helen Roehler is included in *Our Hallowed Ground: World War II Veterans of Fort Snelling National Cemetery* by Stephen E. Osman (Minneapolis: University of Minnesota Press, 2005).

Information about Etta Jones comes from *Last Letters from Attu: The True Story of Etta Jones, Alaska Pioneer and Japanese POW* by Mary Breu (N.p.: Alaska Northwest Books, 2013).

Notes to Chapter 10: Betty Crocker, Wives, and Mothers

Information about Betty Crocker and Marjorie Child Husted came from "Betty Crocker: Marketing the Modern Woman" by Susan Marks-Kerst, published in *Hennepin History* 58, no. 2 (Spring 1999): 4–19; *Finding Betty Crocker: The Secret Life of America's First Lady of Food* by Susan Marks (Minneapolis: University of Minnesota Press, 2005); "Marjorie Child Husted: Boardroom Pioneer," in *More Than Petticoats: Remarkable Minnesota Women* by Bonny E. Stuart (Helena, MT: Globe Pequot Press, 2004); *Business Without Boundary: The Story of General Mills* by James Gray Business (Minneapolis: University of Minnesota Press, 1954); and Betty Crocker, *Your Share: How to Prepare Appetizing, Healthful Meals with Foods Available Today* (Minneapolis: General Mills, 1943).

Information about Hilda Rachuy came from her article "Help, Housing 'Almost Impossible to Find': A Single Mother and World War II," *Ramsey County History Magazine* 26, no. 4 (Winter 1991): 12–17.

Information on Lavina Stone Murray was found in an interview with her conducted by Thomas Saylor in 2002, available in the Greatest Generation Collection, Part I, at the Minnesota Historical Society. Additional contextual information is available in David Vassar Taylor's chapter "The Blacks," in *They Chose Minnesota: A Survey of the State's Ethnic Groups*, edited by June Drenning Holmquist (St. Paul: Minnesota Historical Society Press, 1988).

Information on Marianne Hamilton was found in her papers and in an interview with her conducted by Brian Horrigan and Ben Petry on May 21, 2008, and on file at the Minnesota Historical Society.

Notes to Chapter 11: On the Farm

Information on Ruth Storlie Rosten came from an interview conducted by David Ripley in 1980, available in the Greatest Generation Oral History Project at the Minnesota Historical Society.

Information about Linda James Benitt came from the William A. Benitt and Family Papers at the Minnesota Historical Society and Heather Munford's blog entries on April 17 and May 15, 2013, found on the Center for the History of Medicine at Harvard Countway Library site, https://cms.www.countway.harvard.edu/wp/?p=7431.

Information on Josephine Skavanger Sletto came from her 1980 interview with Patrick Moore, on file with the Minnesota Historical Society.

Information on the World War II prisoner of war camps in Minnesota is found in *Behind Barbed Wire: German Prisoners of War in Minnesota During World War 2* by Anita Albrecht Buck (St. Cloud, MN: North Star Press, 1998).

Information about Mexicans is available in *Mexicans in Minnesota* by Dionicio Valdés in the People of Minnesota Series (St. Paul: Minnesota Historical Society Press, 2005); "A Report to Governor C. Elmer Anderson of Minnesota" by the Governor's Interracial Commission (1953); and *North for the Harvest: Mexican Workers, Growers, and the Sugar Beet Industry* by Jim Norris (St. Paul: Minnesota Historical Society Press, 2009).

Notes to Chapter 12: Between "Boogie Woogie Bugle Boy" and "Somewhere Over the Rainbow"

Information on the Andrews Sisters comes from *Swing It: The Andrews Sisters Story* by John Sforza (Lexington: University of Kentucky Press, 2000) and *Over Here, Over There: The Andrews Sisters and the USO Stars in World War II* by Maxene Andrews and Bill Gilbert (New York: Kensington Press, 1993).

Information on Judy Garland came from *Get Happy: The Life of Judy Garland* by Gerald Clark (New York: Random House, 2000).

Information on the USO was found at www.uso.org and in *Home Away From Home: The Story of the USO* by Julia M. H. Carson (New York: Harper Brothers, 1946).

Information on the St. Paul USO was found in Minnesota Historical Society collections.

Notes to Chapter 13: Radar Research and Navy Intelligence

Information on Julia Herrick came from her papers at the W. Bruce Fye Center for the History of Medicine, Mayo Clinic, Rochester, Minnesota; her personnel files obtained from the National Archives in St. Louis, Missouri; "Medium-Frequency Crossed-Loop Radio Direction Finder with Instantaneous Unidirectional Visual Presentation," by L. J. Giacoletto and S. Stiber, published in *Proceedings of the IRE* 37, no. 9 (September 1949), DOI: 10.1109/JRPROC.1949.230952; "Gustave Shapiro: An Interview Conducted by Robert Colburn," October 19, 1999, Interview #375 for the Institute of Electrical and Electronics Engineers (IEEE) History Center, available at https://ethw.org/Oral -History:Gustave_Shapiro; historical folders on the Army Signal Corps at Fort Monmouth on file at National Archives, College Park, Maryland; and personal email from family members. "Julia Herrick," *Proceedings of the IRE*, 50th anniversary issue (May 1962), found at https://ethw.org/Julia_F._Herrick.

Information about Veda Ponikvar was found in the following sources: her navy personnel file at the National Archives in St. Louis, Missouri; Thomas Saylor's *Remembering the Good War: Minnesota's Greatest Generation* (St. Paul: Minnesota Historical Society Press, 2005); her obituary in the *Minneapolis Star Tribune*, October 14, 2015; interview by Ross Carl (1988), on file at the Minnesota Historical Society; from Wanda Moeller based on interviews; and on file at the Iron Range Research Center at the Minnesota Discovery Center, Chisholm.

Information about Helen Friedline Chadwick is based on service records; information provided by her son, Philip G. Chadwick; and a brief interview conducted in her home near Peterson, Minnesota, on July 6, 2019. Other information about the WAVES doing code work was found in *Code Girls: The Untold Story of the American Women Code Breakers of World War II* by Liza Mundy (New York: Hachette, 2017) and *The Secret in Building 26: The Untold Story of How America Broke the Final U-Boat Enigma Code* by Jim DeBrouse and Colin Burke (New York: Random House, 2005).

Notes to Chapter 14: Life of a WAC Stateside

Information on Anne Bosanko Green came from her letters and the foreword by D'Ann Campbell published as *One Woman's War: Letters Home from the Women's Army Corps, 1944–1946* (St. Paul: Minnesota Historical Society Press, 1989).

Notes to Chapter 15: D-Day and the Liberation of Paris

Information for this chapter comes from articles written by Mary Welsh for *Life*, February 23, 1942, and September 11, 1944; her memoir *How It Was* (New York: Alfred A. Knopf, 1976); and her letters and papers at the John F. Kennedy Library and Museum, Boston, Massachusetts, including her interview with Wood Simpson.

Notes to Chapter 16: The 28th General Hospital During D-Day and the Battle of the Bulge

Information about Mabel Johnson is available in her papers collected at the Minnesota Historical Society.

Information about Rose Polga Bayuk was obtained from an interview with her and her son, Mark Bayuk, and a short biography they provided in October 2018.

Notes to Chapter 17: Liberation of Dachau

Information about Dachau concentration camp and Dorothy Wahlstrom came from the talk, "A Nurse's Perspective," she gave at the Twin Cities Holocaust Commemoration on April 18, 1985, at B'nai Emet Synagogue in St. Louis Park, Minnesota; Unit Histories of the 116th and 127th Evacuation Hospitals, Records of the Office of the Surgeon General (Army), WWII Administrative Records, 1940–1949, Unit Annual Reports, Record Group 112, box 408, National Archives, College Park, Maryland; "In the Wake of the War," an article written by Elisabeth May Craig and published in the *Portland (Maine) Press Herald*, May 28 and 29, 1945, is included in the unit histories listed above; *KL: A History of the Nazi Concentration Camp* by Nikolaus Wachsmann (New York: Farrar, Straus and Giroux, 2015); Dorothy Wahlstrom's papers in the Upper Midwest Jewish Archives, Elmer L. Andersen Library, University of Minnesota, Minneapolis; Dorothy Wahlstrom's memoir published in *Witnesses to the Holocaust: An Oral History*, edited by Rhoda G. Lewin (New York: Twayne Publishers, 1991); "From Minnesota to Dachau: Captain Dorothy Wahlstrom's Story" by Ruth Manchester, published in *The Connection: Army Nurse Corps Association* (June 2017); Dorothy Wahlstrom's military discharge record and yearbook listings provided by Ruth Manchester; Anthony Penrose's "Introduction" to Hilary Roberts, *Lee Miller: A Woman's War* (New York: Thames & Hudson, 2015).

Information about Vera Brown Peters was published by Al Zdon in *War Stories II: Further Accounts of Minnesotans Who Defended Their Nation* (Mounds View, MN: Moonlit Eagle Publications, 2010).

Notes to Chapter 18: War Bride

Information about Nelly Bettex Croes was derived from her unpublished memoir, "Nelly's Journey," on file at the Mower County Historical Society, Austin, Minnesota.

Information about Victor Croes and Hormel came from the June 1, 1951, issue of the corporate newsletter *Squeal* and *In Quest of Quality: Hormel's First 75 Years* by Richard Dougherty (North St. Paul, MN: Central Publications, 1966).

Notes to Chapter 19: Civilian Relief in Italy and Austria

Information about Mildred Louise Boie Saunders came primarily from her letters and Red Cross reports held by the Special Collections at Smith College Library in Northampton, Massachusetts.

Information about American Red Cross activity in Minnesota can be found in the "Record of War Years" in the American Red Cross collection at the Minnesota Historical Society.

The review and related information about *Better than Laughter* by Louise Boie Saunders came from the University of Minnesota Press website.

Notes to Chapter 20: Serving in the Pacific Theater

Information on the Mayo Clinic unit can be found in the W. Bruce Fye Center for the History of Medicine, Mayo Clinic, Rochester, Minnesota, and in the article "Mayo in the Pacific" by Teresa Opheim, *Mayo Alumnus* (Spring 1990).

Information about Gertrude Esteros came from Thomas Saylor's interview with her in 2003 as part of the Minnesota's Greatest Generation Oral History Project, on file at the Minnesota Historical Society.

Notes to Chapter 21: Cryptographers and Spies

Information about Josephine Downey comes from her papers at the Minnesota Historical Society.

Information on the OSS, Julia McWilliams Child, Eleanor "Ellie" Thiry Summers, Amy Elizabeth Thorpe Pack ("Cynthia"), and Jeanne Taylor came from *Sisterhood of Spies: The Women of the OSS* by Elizabeth McIntosh (Annapolis, MD: Naval Institute Press, 1998); *Cora DuBois: Anthropologist, Diplomat, Agent* by Susan C. Seymour (Lincoln: University of Nebraska Press, 2015); *The Last Goodnight: A World War II Story of Espionage, Adventure, and Betrayal* by Howard Blum (New York: Harper Collins, 2016); and

A Covert Affair: Julia Child and Paul Child in the O.S.S. by Jennet Conant (New York: Simon & Schuster, 2011).

Information about Jeanne Taylor also came from her papers at the Minnesota Historical Society and the personnel folder and other folders in the O.S.S. History collection at the National Archives in College Park, Maryland.

Additional information about Eleanor "Ellie" Thiry Summers was provided by her son Chris Summers by email.

Notes to Chapter 22: The Manhattan Project

Information about Catherine Filippi Piccolo was found in her papers on file at the Minnesota Historical Society.

Frances Jacobs's memoir "Nervous in the Service" is on file at the Minnesota Historical Society.

Notes to Chapter 23: Hiroshima

Information about Anna Tanaka Murakami was found in Thomas Saylor's 2003 interview on file at the Minnesota Historical Society and in an interview with her by the author in October 2018. Her daughter, Judy Nomura Murakami, also provided information, including a biographical sketch written by June Evers Benson in 2012 and 2013.

Information about Ruth Erickson came from an interview conducted by Florence Schubert on May 14, 1991, on file at the W. Bruce Fye Center for the History of Medicine, Mayo Clinic, Rochester, Minnesota.

Notes to Chapter 24: Postwar

Information on Hormel came from *In Quest of Quality: Hormel's First 75 Years* by Richard Dougherty (North St. Paul, MN: Central Publications, 1966) and *The Hormel Legacy: 100 Years of Quality* by Doniver A. Lund (Austin, MN: Geo. A. Hormel & Co., 1991). Information on the Hormel Girls came from Mary Mosley's memoir and other clippings on file at the Mower County Historical Society, Austin, Minnesota, and the article "The Hormel Girls" by Jill M. Sullivan and Danelle D. Keck in *American Music* 25, no. 3 (Fall 2007), DOI: 10.2307/40071663, found at https://www.jstor.org/stable/40071663.

Information about Betty Wall is available in *And Still Flying . . . The Life and Times of Elizabeth "Betty" Wall* by Patrick Roberts (Victoria, BC: Trafford, 2003).

Kae Eisenreich's interview by Brian Horrigan (2007) is part of the Minnesota's Greatest Generation Oral History Project, on file at the Minnesota Historical Society.

Information on the Environmental Protection Agency's Superfund project in New Brighton, Minnesota, is available at https://cumulis.epa.gov/supercpad/CurSites/ csitinfo.cfm?id=0504010&msspp=med, and further information on the site is available at the Minnesota Pollution Control Agency, https://www.pca.state.mn.us/waste/ new-brightonarden-hills-superfund-site-aka-twin-cities-army-ammunition-plant or-tcaap.

Information on the women's service branches can be found in *In Defense of a Nation: Servicewomen in World War II*, edited by Jeanne M. Holm and Judith Bellafaire (Annapolis, MD: Military Women's Press, 1998).

Ferne Chambers Krans's interview by Ben Petry and Konrad Krans (2008) and her papers are held at the Minnesota Historical Society.

An interview with Betty Jane (B. J.) Hanson Erenberg, conducted by David Riley on November 2, 1979, is included in the Minnesota Historical Society's Greatest Generation Oral History Project.

INDEX

Page numbers in *italic* type indicate illustrations.

IMAGE CREDITS

Front cover: Virginia Hope, *MNHS Collections*

Back cover: left, Mabel Johnson, *MNHS Collections*; right, top to bottom, Grace Obata, *W. Bruce Fye Center for the History of Medicine at Mayo Clinic*; Mayo Hospital unit nurses, *History Center of Olmsted County*; Catherine Filippi, *MNHS Collections*; ordnance plant workers, *Hennepin County Library*

The text of *A Woman's War, Too,* has been typeset in Karmina, a typeface designed by Veronika Burian & José Scaglione. Book design and layout by Wendy Holdman.